PRACTICAL GAME
DEVELOPMENT
WITH UNITY®
AND BLENDER™

ALAN THORN

Cengage Learning PTR

CENGAGE
Learning®

Professional • Technical • Reference

Australia • Brazil • Japan • Korea • Mexico • Singapore • Spain • United Kingdom • United States

Practical Game Development with Unity® and Blender™
Alan Thorn

Publisher and General Manager, Cengage Learning PTR: Stacy L. Hiquet

Associate Director of Marketing: Sarah Panella

Manager of Editorial Services: Heather Talbot

Senior Marketing Manager: Mark Hughes

Senior Product Manager: Emi Smith

Project Editor: Kate Shoup

Technical Reviewer: Michael Duggan

Copyeditor: Kate Shoup

Interior Layout Tech: MPS Limited

Cover Designer: Mike Tanamachi

Indexer: Kelly Talbot Editing Services

Proofreader: Kelly Talbot Editing Services

For product information and technology assistance, contact us at **Cengage Learning Customer & Sales Support, 1-800-354-9706**.

For permission to use material from this text or product, submit all requests online at **cengage.com/permissions**.

Further permissions questions can be emailed to **permissionrequest@cengage.com**.

Library of Congress Control Number: 2014937090

ISBN-13: 978-1-305-07470-5

ISBN-10: 1-305-07470-X

Cengage Learning PTR

20 Channel Center Street

Boston, MA 02210

USA

Cengage Learning is a leading provider of customized learning solutions with office locations around the globe, including Singapore, the United Kingdom, Australia, Mexico, Brazil, and Japan. Locate your local office at: **international.cengage.com/region**.

Cengage Learning products are represented in Canada by Nelson Education, Ltd.

For your lifelong learning solutions, visit **cengageptr.com**.

Visit our corporate website at **cengage.com**.

Printed in the United States of America
1 2 3 4 5 6 7 16 15 14

This book is dedicated to everybody that helps make so many wonderful tools and software programs freely available to so many game developers worldwide.

Acknowledgments

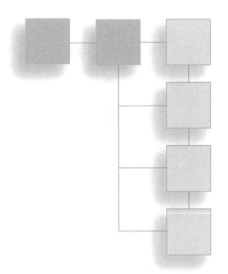

Many people, events, and scenarios conspired to make this book what it is, and to ensure its quality. Among those people, I'd like to thank Emi Smith for helping to arrange the book and managing the process generally; Kate Shoup for her editorial skills and recommendations; Michael Duggan for his technical reviewing; and all the other people who contributed in some way. There are simply too many to list here separately. Oh, and I'd also like to thank you, the reader, for taking an interest in game development and for choosing this book to help you along. I hope it proves useful to you.

Alan Thorn, 2014.

London.

ABOUT THE AUTHOR

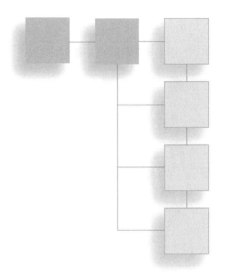

Alan Thorn is a freelance game developer and author with more than 12 years of industry experience. He is the founder of London-based game studio Wax Lyrical Games and is the creator of the award-winning adventure game *Baron Wittard: Nemesis of Ragnarok*. He has worked freelance on more than 500 projects worldwide including games, simulators, kiosks, and augmented reality software for game studios, museums, and theme parks.

He has spoken on game development at venues worldwide and is the author of more than 10 books on game development, including *Teach Yourself Games Programming*, *Unity 4 Fundamentals*, and *UDK Game Development*. Alan Thorn is currently working on an upcoming game, *Mega Bad Code*. For more information on Alan Thorn and Wax Lyrical Games, visit www.alanthorn.net and www.waxlyricalgames.com

CONTENTS

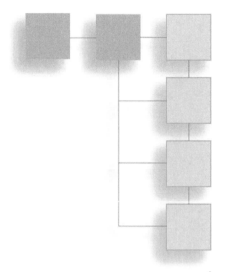

INTRODUCTION

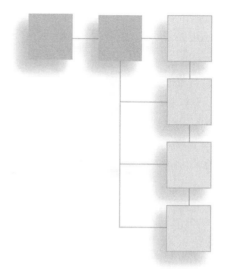

This is a book about making video games. It's a holistic and practical book. It's holistic in that it touches on almost every discipline directly related to games, from programming and level design to 3D modeling and image editing. It covers a range of software, too. It explores Unity and Blender primarily, but also other tools, including GIMP.

The book is practical in two senses:

- It expects you not just to read and absorb what's written here, but to follow along and get involved where required.

- It discusses issues, software, and ideas in ways that focus on their use-value in the real world of making games as opposed to their value and relevance in theory. We'll inevitably touch on theory, too, but only insofar as it helps you get tangible results in practice, at the level of working with real software and real tools.

We will not go beyond to consider abstract mathematical problems or unsolved issues or potentialities; these things will be left to other books and references. In short, the only type of knowledge presented here will be the kind that gets you concrete results with currently available software and tools. That's knowledge you can use right here and right now, as well as for the foreseeable future.

I should say here that, despite the book's practical and holistic focus, it's not a step-by-step tutorial on how to make a game from start to end. This book assumes you're already familiar with the basics of game development. It assumes you already know the kinds of tools and practices involved in a general and overall sense. It assumes you're ready to begin making a game, and what you're seeking now is some concrete and tangible examples of how all the different tools, workflows, and concepts come together in a real-world practical sense.

A tutorial on Unity teaches you Unity, and a tutorial on Blender teaches you Blender. This book, however, should be seen as a higher-order guide. It shows you multiple tools and focuses specifically on how you bring them together in a single workflow to get tangible results. There's a special kind of empowerment that comes from learning this. Specifically, it encourages you to see game development from a multi-disciplinary perspective. By seeing how the tools fit together and by developing proficiency in each, you bring a degree of balance to your work. This balance has special value if you plan to manage software teams and projects, and if you plan to work in small teams or on lone projects where you must put your hand to everything. So, in essence, this book is not just about showing you how software and tools come together, it's about making you a more powerful developer.

SOFTWARE AND TOOLS

For a practical and holistic book on game development, software plays an important role. The larger part of this book concentrates on software and its use. There are so many different applications in use in the contemporary industry that it's not feasible or useful to cover them all. So a choice must be made. Here I've chosen Unity and Blender. We'll also briefly explore GIMP and others. In case you're not familiar with these tools, I've included their website URLs here:

- **Unity.** This is a game engine. For more information, see https://unity3d.com/.
- **Blender.** This is 3D modeling and animation software. You can download it from www.blender.org.
- **GIMP.** This is image-editing software. You can download it from www.gimp.org.

So why have I selected these tools and not others? The answer comes in several parts:

- All the tools listed are downloadable and completely free. (Unity has a free version too!) This means you may download and use the tools right now, without paying anything. Of course, you need a computer and an Internet connection, and you also need to spend time learning and using the tools—a significant investment. But the tools themselves cost you nothing.
- The tools are powerful and rising. You don't need to take my word for that! Currently, all the tools listed are used in many indie studios and have contributed

toward hundreds of commercial, freemium, and free games. Examples of these games include *Yo Frankie!* and *Dead Cyborg*.

- The tools are continuously developed, maintained, and supported by a large community, and there's already a wealth of documentation and information about them and their use. This means you can use the tools while feeling a certain degree of comfort knowing that if you encounter a specific problem, it's likely a solution has already been found by others and is documented online.

- Because the tools are free to everybody, it gives the book the widest accessibility possible. These tools can be used by anybody, whatever their budget.

My choice of tools shouldn't be read as a negative judgment on the alternatives not discussed here. There are many alternative and commercial tools (such as Photoshop, Maya, 3DS Max, Strata, ZBrush, Mudbox, and others) that are not covered in this book. This isn't because there's something wrong or missing in these tools; there isn't. It's simply because some or all of them are cost-prohibitive to many smaller teams and indie developers who form the target audience of this book.

Hopefully, this book will reassure you (if you needed any reassuring) that what matters most when developing games is the developer's attitude, imagination, skill, and creativity— *not* the tool he or she uses. The tool can make a difference to your comfort and the speed at which you work, as well as how compatible your work is with others who may be using different software, but it's ultimately your skill and determination that gets the final results. That's why a skillful developer who uses nearly any tool with proficiency, commercial or not, can produce incredible work. For this reason, the free tools here can get you professional-grade results. By professional-grade, I mean results that are demonstrably good enough for a commercial game that appeals to a contemporary audience. Yes, they can help you make games that sell!

TARGET AUDIENCE

Nearly every book has a target audience, and this book is no different. In short, if you're thinking about making a game and you don't want to spend money on software and tools, and if you want to see practical and concrete examples of how a game might come together (as well as tips and tricks), then this is probably the book for you. Also, if you have a really great idea for a game, and you love the idea of working for yourself, and you're prepared to do whatever it takes to realize your vision but just need some guidance on how to approach it, then this is probably the book for you, too.

That's actually quite a broad audience. It includes game development students, hobbyists, indie developers, small to medium size studios, solo developers, and even seasoned game developers looking to broaden their skill set to work in new areas outside their comfort zone. Wherever you may be within that target audience spectrum, you may notice this book's multidisciplinary flavor. That's very much a reflection of the demands made on professionals within the contemporary industry—especially for small to medium sized studios.

Game development is a technical discipline that's evolved to encompass many sub-fields, including software development, physics, artificial intelligence, graphic design, 3D modeling, animation, music production, software testing, and others. Consequently, small studios on limited budgets quickly find that, to be successful and survive in business, their team members need to learn fast and become generalists to some extent, developing skills and know-how across the board. For very small teams especially (such as one- or two-person teams), a generalist skill set is essential. And so it's for this small-to-medium-sized studio audience that this book is primarily intended.

That inevitably means this book won't really teach you how to be "expert" in any one field, but rather how to be a capable generalist—the kind that's needed for commercially successful indie game development. It's about becoming an "expert generalist" or a "specialist generalist." You'll learn a bit of coding, level design, 3D modeling, animation, and more. It's undoubtedly a tough journey, but you'll probably need to make it if you and your teammates want to create games for a full-time living in the long term.

Of course, the learning won't end with this book. Learning is a never-ending process. This book is simply meant to give you enough of what you need to start making games. Now more than ever before, individuals and small teams are finding commercial success as game developers for all kinds of systems, especially desktop PCs and mobile devices. You could be among them. This book can help you get started.

I've spoken about whom this book is for. Is there anybody who *wouldn't* benefit from this book? Although it's not my purpose to dissuade anybody from learning, I do think there are two groups of readers who may not find this book useful. The first is someone who's never studied game development before in any sense—someone who's never programmed, created graphics, or even considered how games might work under the hood. Certainly, everybody must begin learning somewhere, but this book is probably not that place. The book assumes you already have a foundation of knowledge from which to begin. This foundation includes a general knowledge of what a game engine is and how content-creation tools like 3D modeling software relate to it. It also includes a basic knowledge of programming (preferably in C#, JavaScript, or C++), and a basic proficiency in the concepts underpinning 3D graphics such as vertices, edges, and polygons. If you don't have this knowledge, then you can get it by reading some of the books I list in the "Recommended Books" section in Appendix A, "Game Development Resources," at the end of this book.

The second group of readers that might not benefit from this book are established or aspiring developers seeking to become specialists—that is, those seeking specialized knowledge in only one field of development such as in programming or 3D graphics. For example, if you see yourself as a programmer exclusively or as an artist exclusively, and you are looking for a book dedicated to that field alone, then this book will probably not give you what you want. As I've said, this book is primarily for budding generalists, not specialists. Of course, I don't really believe there's any incompatibility between the two. They are not mutually exclusive. You can be a specialist and a generalist together. But even so, this book is for developing your generalist side.

WHY IS THIS BOOK NECESSARY?

This book has a special and unique value in the industry right now, primarily because of its holistic focus. With growing numbers of studios and individuals starting game development each year, there's an increasing demand for generalists—people who can adapt and change gears to fulfill different roles, contributing toward the final game. To complete competitive and market-ready game projects, on time and within budget, more and more indie studios and individuals need to develop a well-rounded arsenal of game development skills. This arsenal must span multiple disciplines.

You can, of course, learn it by piecing it together through experience and by consulting multiple books and videos specializing on the subjects you need. Indeed, some of your arsenal must be assembled that way. But this book can you give an advantage as a generalist. Why? Because it's specifically written with the generalist in mind. It shares valuable insights into specific problems encountered during development, which require a generalist outlook to solve in the absence of an expensive team of specialists.

If you want to create fully working games and don't have access to a large team of specialists, then you'll need to become a generalist yourself—a kind of "Swiss Army knife." In this book, you'll find plenty to help to guide you in being a generalist—in being able to change modes when needed to get things done. This can help save you lots of money and resources, because you won't need to hire others to do what you can already do yourself. This can also help you become more employable, because it increases the range of disciplines where you can genuinely be of service, especially in the world of indie games. And finally, this can help you run your own business as an indie studio, because it gives you informed and detailed insight, at practically every stage of development, as to what's needed to push your game forward as well as how it can best be managed in the long term.

DOES THIS BOOK TEACH EVERYTHING ABOUT GAME DEVELOPMENT?

If you pick nearly any computer book at random and scan the reader reviews for it online, you'll see one type complaint that surfaces again and again. It goes something like this:

> *This book doesn't teach everything there is to know about the subject. It leaves some things unsaid. Additionally, what it does teach can be learned for free online.*

I want to tackle that complaint right here, in the context of this book. First, this book does *not* teach everything there is to know about game development. Neither does it teach everything there is to know about how Unity and Blender can work together. That's because no book, or video, or course could teach such a thing as that. There's practically no limit to how these tools and technologies may be applied, just as there's no limit to what an artist can make with paint brushes or clay.

What this book seeks to offer is not an all-encompassing guide to game development. Rather, it offers a set of practical tips and workflows that I've developed from 12 years of industry experience, working with Blender, Unity, and other tools. These tips and workflows have proven valuable in producing successful and complete games, both for my own companies as well as for my clients.

Yes, *almost* everything in this book (but perhaps *not quite* everything) can be learned online for free. This, however, should not be entirely surprising, nor should it be seen as a criticism. Game development is a discipline that bridges both the arts and sciences. It's not an arcane or mysterious body of knowledge to which only a few have access. Nearly everything I say here has, in some form, been said before. The value of this book is not so much in the newness of what I say, but in the originality and structure of its presentation. You could learn nearly everything here for free by spending days, weeks, and perhaps even months researching online independently. Or you could read this book.

This book's main value comes from the fact that I've done lots of the hard work for you. I've brought together the knowledge in one convenient volume, and I've arranged and presented it in an optimized order to make it more digestible and memorable. So, this book doesn't teach you everything about game development and it doesn't reveal esoteric wisdom. But it can make your work and learning a lot simpler and smoother.

HOW SHOULD THIS BOOK BE READ?

This book has been written to work well for two types of reader: the tutorial reader and the reference reader. Tutorial readers want to learn like they're in a classroom, tackling subjects in order one at a time. This reader will read the book in sequence, chapter by chapter, from start to finish. The reference reader, in contrast, will make frequent use of the index and speed-reading techniques to identify specific areas of interest in the book, and then visit them for more details.

This book is amenable to both reader types, but I think the most can be gotten from it if you approach it as a tutorial reader. Reading the book in this way means you may encounter subjects you either don't find interesting or already know, but it may also lead to surprises and unexpected turns, revealing new gems of information that can prove valuable for you. Since I want you to get the most from the book, I recommend approaching it as a course or complete tutorial.

IS THIS BOOK OUT OF DATE ALREADY?

Nearly every technical book (like this book, for example) has a lifetime. When readers approach a book like this, they typically want to get the most from it. They want to know not only that the knowledge within works *here and now*, but that it stands a strong chance of remaining valid for the foreseeable future. By the time you read this, time will have moved on since its writing, and knowledge in the games industry moves very fast. So the question arises as to how current this book can possibly be *for you, right now*.

To answer this, it's important to recognize that this book is about practice and software—software that changes and is updated frequently by the developers. The developers are constantly adding new features and improving existing ones. So the chances are high that, if you download the latest versions of the software, you'll be using more a recent version than what I'm using here.

The critical issue, however, is whether this really affects the validity of the knowledge presented in the book. The answer, based on how these tools have changed and adjusted in the past, is no. After all, if every change invalidated all previous knowledge, then nobody could ever begin to learn the software. Although the software does change, the changes are designed to integrate with the existing GUI and toolset so the software remains accessible to its established user base.

It might be that (due to changes) more options, settings, and controls are available to you than were available to me. But that alone does nothing to prevent you from following along with my steps and instructions, and even going beyond them by taking advantage of the new and additional features that I didn't have.

10-STAGE WORKFLOW

Throughout the 10 chapters in this book, different software and techniques are considered in depth. The chapters vary greatly in content. However, there's a single theme that runs through and unites them all, regardless of their differences. This theme I'll call the "10-stage workflow." It's outlined further in Chapter 1. In fact, Chapter 1 is called the "The 10-Stage Workflow." It describes the 10 steps that all games go through to move from concept to completion. These steps are by no means industry standard or agreed upon. Rather, they represent 10 steps I've identified while working on many different games over many years. Of course, there will always be exceptional projects and circumstances that don't fit nicely into the 10-stage pattern. That's to be expected when games differ so widely. But I've found that thinking in terms of these 10 stages for most projects can really help you and your team make quick and efficient progress when making games. I'll detail the 10 stages in Chapter 1, but I wanted to introduce the concept here to make you especially alert to it.

COMPANION FILES

Because this book covers software and its use, and because you're expected to follow along, it comes with companion files. These files include all the projects and assets for the work we'll be covering. In short, the files include everything you need to follow along with me in the tutorial sections and reproduce the results you'll see in the screen shots. These files span all the software we'll be considering, including Unity, Blender, GIMP, Inkscape, and Audacity. Consequently, you'll need this software to open and edit the files. The companion files themselves can be downloaded from the following URL: www.cengageptr.com/downloads.

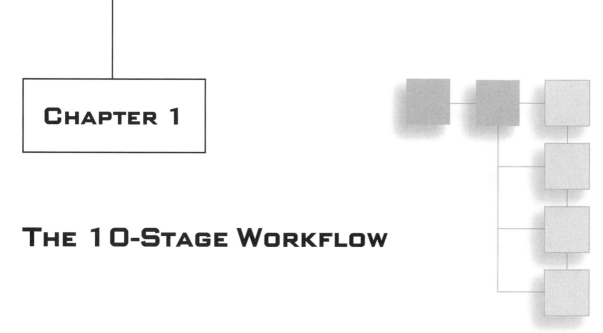

CHAPTER 1

THE 10-STAGE WORKFLOW

The art of programming is the art of organizing complexity....

—Edsger W. Dijkstra

By the end of this chapter, you should:

- Understand the 10-stage workflow
- Be able to apply the 10-stage workflow to your own projects
- Appreciate the practical importance of planning and design
- Be able to create a game design document for your projects
- Be able to manage your game projects

Creating a game is no small matter. It doesn't matter how simple or complex you may think a game is based on how it looks or plays; creating a game is a significant project of engineering. You should recognize this before you start making a game. This can help protect you from underestimating the work involved. Underestimation must rank as one of the primary causes for abortive projects, because over-ambitious designs are quickly abandoned.

Certainly, jumping in at the deep end, without planning, to work hours or even days on a game with friends or alone can be a fun learning exercise, even if the game never reaches the finish line. But if you're serious about making money from games, then your projects need to get finished. Gamers don't pay for incomplete games. Well...sometimes they do, but you can ignore these exceptional cases here. (Sometimes gamers pay for alpha versions, development versions, and work-in-progress games, but even in these cases there's an expectation that the game will get finished at some point soon.) So finishing your games is important in all cases.

If you include all "student" and "hobbyist" projects (and I see no reason why you shouldn't), then it's probably true that a majority of games are never completed. Development gets frozen, put on hold, or canceled. So it's important for you to take the matter of game completion seriously. How can you do this? First, by recognizing the distinct phases or stages that a game goes through during development. This can help give you a clearer picture of the work involved, from beginning to end.

Doing this might sound like an academic or theoretical matter. Perhaps it is. Even so, it has significant practical implications. These implications can make the difference between a project that runs smoothly and one that doesn't. Consequently, this chapter considers the main phases of development and their implications. In short, game development can be broken into 10 distinct stages, which I call the 10-stage workflow. This is not a standardized or "industry agreed" workflow, nor is it a concept or pattern that's discussed in any textbook, as far as I'm aware. Rather, it's a workflow that I've identified while working on more than 500 projects during the past 12 years. Of course, there will always be some exceptional cases and projects that don't fit this pattern—perhaps your game is among them. But these stages are, nonetheless, general and abstract enough to apply to most games on a practical level.

Note

Throughout this book, I'll offer tips and guidance on making games. In presenting these, it may sound like I'm promoting my workflow and ideas as the best or only solutions. This isn't true, of course. There's no single "best" workflow, and many roads lead to the same destination. I don't deny this. But, for this book to keep a practical and hands-on focus, I'll concentrate on just one workflow and approach as though it were the best one.

INTRODUCING THE 10-STAGE WORKFLOW

Imagine the game-development process as a timeline, from left to right, top to bottom, or beginning to end. The 10-stage workflow, which I'll discuss here, requires you to break down that line into 10 divisions. The divisions are not usually equal in size because time is distributed differently between the stages. In other words, some things take longer than others to do.

Figure 1.1 illustrates a common 10-stage breakdown, with design stages accounting for a sizable chunk of development time. In total, the workflow consists of the following:

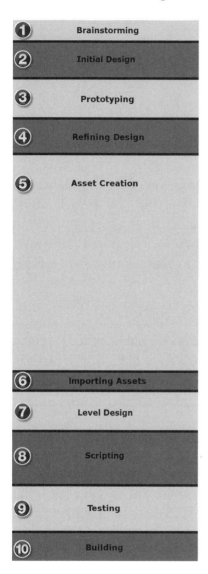

Figure 1.1
The 10-stage workflow breaks down time in game development into 10 separate stages, typically of unequal length.

- Brainstorming
- Initial design

- Prototyping
- Refining design
- Asset creation
- Importing assets
- Level design
- Scripting
- Testing
- Building

The workflow begins at game conception and ends with game completion. Usually, the steps are performed in order, each step being completed before the next begins. Some may call this development pattern the *waterfall* method, because development unfolds in discrete and sequential stages like water cascading downward in a waterfall. However, despite its similarities to the waterfall method, the 10-stage workflow is focused specifically on game creation and its unique development stages.

Note

> Readers familiar with Agile, the software development method, may feel a tension exists with the 10-stage workflow due to its linear nature (refer to Figure 1.1). Agile encourages developers to see workflow in bursts or cycles rather than lines. But no tension need exist. Each iteration or cycle in Agile may be seen as the initiation of a new 10-stage workflow.

In the 10-stage workflow, each stage in the sequence may be thought of as a module of activity. It has an input and an output. Its input comes from all the outputs of all previous stages. Its output is the completed work produced in that stage. What goes on between input and output varies from game to game and studio to studio. For this reason, what matters most is not what goes on between the inputs and outputs, but that the output from each module matches what you intended. Let's see these stages in more detail.

STAGE 1: BRAINSTORMING

When you're ready to make a game, you need to begin with brainstorming. Everybody who makes a game goes through this stage, and it must always be the first one. Brainstorming is primarily about ideas, but there's more to it than that. You need to develop connections between ideas. The point of this stage is to generate a picture, mental or physical, of the game you want to make.

Note

> With brainstorming—and in fact, with all the stages in the 10-stage workflow—there's no right way to do it. What matters is what you get out of it. Results need to be in line with your intentions. If they're not, then you may need to repeat and fine-tune your work in the stage until it matches your expectations.

Take care not to rush this stage. It's easy to misjudge your own ideas, thinking they're clearer than they really are. There's an ancient Indian proverb: "You don't know yourself as well as you think you do." This proverb has relevance to brainstorming, which is one reason why it's important to write down your ideas as you do it. The act of writing them down in a clear, intelligible way can help you clarify them for yourself as well as to others.

For example, say you're making a role-playing game (RPG). You have an idea about how the game will look, some characters, some monsters, and maybe even some towns. You're not yet sure exactly how those towns will be laid out or which stats the monsters will have (and that's fine). But you likely don't yet know which systems your game will be released for, how much you will sell it for, or whether it be multi-player or single-player.

It's critical to answer these and other similar questions early because they'll influence how the game is implemented and the schedule you'll follow. Mobile games have specific resolution and performance requirements that PC and console games don't. Unlike single-player games, multi-player games introduce restrictions on the number of objects and characters that may interact simultaneously due to bandwidth issues. These technical limitations create boundaries within which you must work, and you'll need to identify them before designing your game. The brainstorming stage is an ideal time to do that.

Following are some critical issues that your brainstorming should address. Note that some games will not have these issues due to their specific nature. For example, sports games typically don't need a background story or a list of main characters. But if these issues are relevant to your game, and if you don't yet have concrete answers to the questions they raise, then it probably means you're not finished with the brainstorming stage. So try to address these issues before moving to the next stage.

- **Full or working title.** This is the full title of your game (if you know it) or at least a working title for use during development until a full title is decided. Having a full or working title is also useful for referring to your game in development blogs and social media, as well as for purchasing a Web domain and preparing marketing materials, if appropriate.

■ **Genre.** This is the type of game you'll make. It could be part of an existing genre, a hybrid genre, or even a completely new genre. Some existing and famous genres include (but are not limited to) the following: RPG, strategy, simulator, sports, adventure, first person shooter (FPS), platform game, MMORPG, and casual.

Note

In video games, genres are only very loosely defined (if at all). Typically, in RPG games, such as *Skyrim* and *Diablo*, players must control a party of fantasy-like characters as they explore a world filled with goblins and dragons, solving mysteries and completing battle-oriented quests. In action games, such as first-person shooters like *Quake*, *Doom*, or *Duke Nukem*, the player controls action heroes who blaze around battlefields, alien compounds, or enemy bases, shooting nearly everything in sight. In contrast, adventure games, like *Myst* and *Monkey Island*, are often story-heavy, featuring lots of conversations, mystery, and puzzle solving. There's plenty of variety in the world of games; the number of different genres increases each year as new innovations are made.

■ **Setting, characters, and background story.** Outline the story, the general setting, and the characters for your game. You don't need comprehensive details such as the background for each character or a map of every location; these details are refined and developed in the next stage, initial design.

■ **Platforms.** These are the systems on which you're game will run for the gamer. They may include any of the following: Windows, Mac, Linux, Android, iOS, Windows Phone OS, BlackBerry, Web, Flash, and consoles. This is no small decision. Different systems have different standards about acceptable levels of resource demands and performance.

■ **Supported resolutions.** These are the pixel dimensions of your game when run, in terms of width and height on the screen. Knowing this is especially important for designing scalable 2D and GUI graphical assets. Make resolution an early consideration for your game to ensure it'll look good at all your target resolutions.

■ **Commercial model.** This defines how you plan to sell your game. This could be a single, upfront fee; a free-to-play model that offers additional virtual goods and add-ons in-game at a cost; an ad-sponsored model in which revenue-generating ads are shown to users; or another model altogether. There are plenty of models to choose from, and the effectiveness of each is hotly debated (although this is neither the time nor place to weigh in on that issue). The bottom line? You'll need to choose one or more models—and the sooner you make an informed choice, the better.

Note

Those interested more in game business models may find the following link helpful: www.adobe.com/devnet/flashplayer/articles/right-business-model.html.

- **Target audience.** Is your game suitable for all audiences, ages, and interests? Or is it targeted toward a specific group of gamers, such as action-gamers, mature audiences, or young audiences? This is another question that must be answered early. It affects not only the type of content you'll include (and exclude) from the game, but also the kind of publishers and gaming outlets that will accept your product for their catalogs.

The preceding list is not necessarily exhaustive. There are likely to be many more questions for you to answer regarding your game, but these will typically be game specific. In answering them, you begin to define limits and parameters, marking the space inside which you work. These limits are instructive for designing your game in later stages. They tell you how far you may go with your imagination in any direction before you have to stop.

Indeed, the creation of new restrictions is ultimately what each stage of the 10-stage workflow does. The further along you progress, the more restricted you become until you reach the final step of completion, where you move no further. These restrictions might initially seem a bad thing, but there's another way to see them, too: They are strong guides and markers, keeping you on the right track and path toward your destination. It can be easy to get lost in any engineering project, but the restrictions can help protect you from this danger. Well…they can help protect you only as long as you honor them! So, when you complete the brainstorming stage, make sure you take your own answers seriously.

STAGE 2: INITIAL DESIGN

After the brainstorming stage it's time to create the first revision of your game design document (GDD), keeping in mind the restrictions from brainstorming. This document will be the output of the initial design stage. It may include (but is not limited to) the following:

- Text
- Diagrams

- Sketches
- Artwork
- Photos
- Charts
- Tables
- Lists

Think of the GDD as a read-only PDF file that tells the reader what your game will be as comprehensively as possible, leaving out nothing. It should be possible for someone who reads the GDD in its entirety to develop an accurate understanding of what your game will be. If your GDD does its job properly, you shouldn't need to add or explain anything further to the reader. If you *do* need to do this, then take that as feedback on how you can further refine and improve the GDD. Measure the quality of your GDD by how clearly you express your design to the reader. If your reader forms a clear and complete understanding of the game solely on the basis of the GDD, then you've written it correctly. If the reader doesn't, the document is lacking something. You'll need to find out what it is and then add it.

The initial design stage typically takes much longer than the brainstorming stage because it requires you to be very precise and specific about your game. Note, however that, the GDD, when completed in this stage, doesn't need to be considered final. It's a first revision. Later stages will expand on and refine the document through further revisions. That being said, at every stage, you should write the GDD *as though it were* a final revision. This ensures it is written with the completeness it deserves.

In practice, the GDD is typically refined in subsequent revisions. That's not because you are planning ahead of time to refine it later. It's only because later considerations (particularly from the prototyping stage) will shed new light and information on old plans that will lead you to go back and change your plan. You don't know in advance which, if any, plans will change, so write them all as though they're final.

What will the GDD say about your game? In short, it should say everything there is to say. If someone asked you in conversation on a rainy afternoon, "So, tell me about your game then, leaving out nothing!" your answer would be the GDD, which could run into hundreds of pages. That means the GDD varies for each game, because no two games are identical.

Following are the critical details that most GDDs will include. These are provided to give you guidance about structuring your document. I've divided the "ideal" GDD into three main sections:

- Game overview
- Game details
- References

Game Overview

It doesn't matter what kind of game you make, there will always be someone who won't like it without even playing it. That's because your game simply won't be "their kind of game." These "dislikers" will listen to the initial details of your game—such as system requirements, genre, title, storyline summary, and others—and ignore the rest because they're no longer interested.

I recommend using the "game overview" portion of the GDD to list all the general details for your game in such a way that practically anyone will tolerate listening to it. This means this part will be the shortest. By writing the GDD in this way, you begin to organize your game details.

This part should list the initial details I just mentioned (system requirements, genre, etc.) as well as almost all other information from the brainstorming stage. But it shouldn't elaborate on these details—that's for the next part. So if you're making an RPG, the game overview should list the game title, platform, genre, summary, and similar details, but it shouldn't list all locations, weapons, enemies, character, and class types, nor should it list the different quests or sub-quests. Similarly, if you're making a sports game, the game overview won't list all the different players, match rules, stadium venues, or uniforms. Naturally, this pattern of elimination applies to all genre types, whatever game you're making.

Game Details

This part, the "game details," is where you go into more depth on your game. Based on the information in the game overview, the reader should have a solid overview of your game and what to expect. This part refines and elaborates on what came before. In the game details, you should list all game modes, weapons, characters, styles, objects, and more. You can present this information in a chatty, novel-like way (some people do), stretching the information across many pages and paragraphs of descriptions. But I strongly recommend structuring your content with lists and using a numbering system to tag each game element with a unique number so it can be identified among all the other elements. Each weapon, location, character, and object should have its own name and number. Be systematic in your approach.

References

By reading the game overview and game details, your reader should learn almost everything about your game. Even so, they'll likely have some questions. For RPG games, these might be, "What does the town map look like for town X?" or "What does the statistics sheet look like for character X?" For sports games, they might be, "What does the uniform for team X look like?" or "What does the league table look like for League X?" All of these questions link to maps, statistics, graphs, charts, and other kinds of reference data. These belong in the last part of the GDD. Together, they might be called the "*Appendices.*"

Note

If you're a one-person team, don't think you haven't any need for a GDD. The GDD can not only help you communicate your design and its details, it can help you clarify and remember your own thoughts. For this reason, every game needs a GDD.

STAGE 3: PROTOTYPING

Prototyping is essentially a feasibility study. It's where you hand over the first revision of your GDD to your team of programmers, who will use it to create a draft, miniature version of the game. This is known as the *prototype*. The prototype is to games what the initial sketch is to a painting.

The prototype isn't in theory or on paper. It really is a tangible, playable game. It doesn't look glamorous, however. It doesn't have sounds, animations, or any special effects. Gray boxes stand in for characters and weapons, and other similar primitive objects (spheres, rectangles, pyramids, and cones) represent other objects. Typically, no art assets are created for the prototype except for blank images, matchstick men, or sketch-like creations. The prototype won't be a complete or fully featured version of the game; it will support only the core or main functionality.

Upon completion of the prototyping stage, you will have achieved the following:

- **Appraisal of workload.** In the prototyping stage, programmers get a glimpse of the future. During implementation, you can see how much of the design (in the GDD) translates smoothly into a game on the computer. That means you can finally make educated projections about how long the full game will take to implement as well as how much it might cost. From that, you will be able to determine whether you need to hire extra staff or purchase third-party tools.

- **Troubleshooting.** Did you encounter any technical hurdles or problems during prototyping? If so, what do these problems tell us? Did the problems arise because of design specifics, or were they simply because we failed to see them in the best way? Questions like these allow you to see the game as an engineering project and to foresee potential problems before they arise in the finished product. This means you'll get to devise solutions ahead of time. Sometimes, these solutions simply require us to see development from a new perspective. And other times, they lead you back to moderate or adapt the design.

- **Visualization.** The prototype can help others see how the final game should look and work. In theory, the GDD should be enough to convey this knowledge—but theory doesn't always translate into practice. Some people don't like reading design documents. Others are too busy to read, while still others find they simply don't retain information from reading. The prototype will give these people a hands-on, interactive look at how the game should play. This can spur both unexpected inspiration and new insights—new ideas and thought experiments for the design that weren't obvious or clear when the design was only on paper. These are the insights that lead people to say, "Hey, now that I see this up and running in a prototype, I think we could improve the game by adding this new feature."

STAGE 4: REFINING DESIGN

Prototyping takes the GDD for a test run. The output of the prototyping stage is a set of suggestions, amendments, ideas, corrections, and improvements. The purpose of the refining design stage is to integrate these suggestions, amendments, ideas, corrections, and improvements into the GDD. This is achieved through an iterative process that involves the following steps:

1. You think about changes.

2. You make them in the document.

3. You judge them.

If you don't like the changes, you repeat the process until you get something you're satisfied with. This process keeps going until you produce a complete GDD representing the final design.

In theory, the output of this stage should be an immutable GDD—one that you cannot and must not change. It should be the ultimate authority on what your game will be and how it will work—a constant that guides development and that cannot be altered in later stages. In practice, however, I've found this immutability difficult to honor in all circumstances. In real-life situations, there's always something that leads me to change the GDD at some point. Sometimes this happens when a team falls behind schedule and decides to cut back on features to reduce its workload. Other times, it's because the developers find new ideas that they want to include in the game. All these scenarios—and more, frequently—tempt us to make design changes further along the line.

Doing this can be innocuous, but it can also be dangerous because new designs can invalidate or break existing work based on old designs. Consequently, if you find yourself wanting to make design changes after the refining design stage, be alert to the practical implications of those changes. Don't dismiss any and all changes entirely, but be cautious and reluctant to accept changes. For example, changing an adventure game into an action game is typically not a good move if the decision is made late in development after most assets are created. But extending the length of an adventure game by adding new characters and locations, if you feel it's too short as is, may be a smart move when the proposed changes can be integrated into the game with minimal disruption.

Project Management

So far, the 10 stages have been covered in sequence, as though game development were entirely linear and the same for everybody involved. However, particularly after stage 4, development could proceed differently depending on the structure of your team. If you're a one-person team, for example, then it's likely you'll proceed with the 10-stage workflow in sequence as given here. But if your team consists of multiple people, each with different skills and experience, it's likely that multiple stages will happen in parallel as each person concentrates on his or her tasks. The programmers will do programming, the artists will do "art stuff," and so on. Whatever the case, the implementation stages encompass a lot of work. That work must be managed and coordinated. This process is called "project management."

You can, of course, proceed without any coherent project management in place. If you do, however, you'll likely wind up wasting time and resources. If work is not managed carefully, people could end up sitting around with nothing to do but wait for others to complete their work. This is not a productive use of resources.

So how do you manage the project successfully? Unfortunately, the answer to that question could fill a whole book. Instead, I'll list some abbreviated tips and tricks that are practical and can get you up and running quickly. That being said, I do recommend finding out more about project management. Some recommended reading can be found in Appendix A, "Game Development Resources."

Identify Resources

Start by understanding all the resources you have to manage in the project. Here's what you'll need to know:

- All the members of the team and their role
- Where those people will be when they're working (in the same room or on the other side of the world)
- The time differences between each location
- All the tools and software you have to work with and who should be using them (in this book, the software will be Unity, Blender, GIMP, Inkscape, and Audacity)
- How much time you have in total and until the final deadline
- How much money you have to work with (the complete budget)

Make sure you know all these things because they'll influence how you build a workable schedule.

Compress Space

Distance is time. If two members of your team are on opposite sides of the globe, there will be an inevitable delay in communication between them due to time-zone differences. As some people wake up, others go to bed. This delay in time translates to a social distance because team members won't be able to communicate with each other in real-time.

Be creative in reducing the impact of this time delay. By doing so, you can compress space, bringing those people closer together. One way to do this is to create a virtual office—an online place where members can log in to post messages, view tasks, view deadlines, see the progress of their work, and generally feel integrated into the team. There are software tools available to do this, including BaseCamp (www.basecamp.com), Active-Collab (www.activecollab.com), Unfuddle (www.unfuddle.com), and others.

Schedule Work

There's no such thing as a complex problem. A complex is an aggregation of smaller, constituent pieces. Complex problems are therefore merely collections of smaller problems.

Sometimes it can be tricky to identify all the constituent pieces of a complex, but project management requires you to do so. Thus, you must break down game development into small, manageable chunks, such as "Build a werewolf character," "Program enemy intelligence," and "Compose soundtrack for level 1."

Most project-management software programs call these chunks "tickets." Each ticket represents a discrete task. The total work for developing a game can run into hundreds or thousands of tickets. Identify them all and then map them into a project calendar, giving each ticket a unique deadline that's consistent with your project's needs. Finally, assign each ticket to an appropriate team member. If you apply this process consistently and intelligently throughout the project, you'll find that your work runs more smoothly and easily.

Project management is covered here, before the remaining stages of the 10-stage workflow, because it has special relevance to them. The remaining stages involve lots of diverse work—from 3D modeling and animation to level design and coding. This work needs to be managed. Let's now visit the remaining stages to see what's in store.

STAGE 5: ASSET CREATION

Stage 5 is about making assets. Here, "assets" refers to all game graphics and animations. These include GUI graphics (like cursors and windows), 2D graphics (such as loading screens and backgrounds), audio, and 3D graphics (like meshes). If it's part of the game and the gamer will see it onscreen during game play, then it's a graphical asset.

Creating these assets is typically one of the longest and most expensive parts of development (unless you already have plenty of pre-made assets ready to use). If you want quality results, this stage really has no shortcuts. It requires time and dedication from artists. It's here, at this stage, that you'll use software like GIMP, Blender, and Inkscape. You'll see such software at work in the next chapter. There are, however, some points to keep in mind:

- ■ **Recycle assets.** If your game features many different environments (say, office environments), then it'll need objects like chairs. If that's the case, you can make only one or two chairs and then simply duplicate them throughout the environments where needed. You don't need to make each and every chair separately. Don't worry unduly about repetition, as the same object can look very different in other contexts and under specific lighting conditions. Sometimes, the repetition will be noticeable; you can fix it by adding new objects or changing existing ones. But don't assume all repetition will be noticeable from the outset. It can save you a lot of work.

- **Use photo references.** Most artwork tries to convey real-world believability. Even mythical creatures like dragons, goblins, and elves have a degree of realism about them because they resemble other animals or creatures that do exist. Practically all video game artwork is like this, and is based on photographic reference materials. That means artists took photographs and used them as reference materials for the artwork they created. This reference material is important. Don't assume all artwork is simply conjured out of the imagination without appropriate reference material. If you want your artwork to look good, then you'll need suitable references. Thus, set time aside to collect these references. You can either take photographs or use photos that you have available. Reserving time to do this is an investment that pays off in the long term. It'll make your asset creation smoother and simpler.

- **Outsource.** When you outsource asset creation, you turn to third parties and outside companies to make your assets. Outsourcing is especially common when a studio falls significantly behind schedule and requires help from additional artists to get back on track but they don't want to recruit new permanent staff. Doing this comes at a price, however—and that price may not be within the budget of every team. You'll need to make informed judgments about your own project and work and whether outsourcing is right for you.

STAGE 6: IMPORTING ASSETS

After you create game assets, you must import them into your game engine. For this book, graphical assets will be created in Blender, GIMP, and Inkscape, and these will be imported into the Unity game engine.

Importing assets from one package to another may seem a trivial process not worthy of its own stage in the 10-stage workflow. However, transferring assets from content-creation software to a game engine often requires lots of tweaking and setup. This setup can take time, and this time can be significant enough to affect development overall. For this reason, I've devoted a stage to asset importing. This issue is considered further in the next chapter. Following are some considerations that apply generally to importing assets.

■ **File formats and compatibility.** Be aware of which file formats are supported for import by your game engine. Each game engine supports its own range of file formats for meshes, animations, movies, and images. Know what these formats are and make sure your content-creation software supports them directly or that reliable converters exist to convert your assets into the supported formats. For this book, Unity, Blender, GIMP, and Audacity are compatible. That means you can make assets in Blender, GIMP, and Audacity, and then import them successfully into Unity.

Unity Supported Formats

For images, Unity supports the following file formats:

- PSD
- TIFF
- JPEG
- PNG
- GIF
- BMP
- TGA
- IFF
- PICT

For audio, Unity supports the following file formats:

- MP3
- OGG
- AIFF
- WAV
- MOD
- IT
- S3M
- XM

For meshes, Unity supports the following file formats:

- MA
- MB
- MAX
- JAS
- C4D
- BLEND
- LXO
- FBX
- 3DS
- OBJ

For movies, Unity supports the following file formats:

- AVI
- MOV
- ASF
- MPG
- MPEG
- MP4VIDEO
- Ogg Theora

More information on supported file types and import workflows can be found at the following URLs:

- http://unity3d.com/unity/workflow/asset-workflow/
- http://docs.unity3d.com/Documentation/Manual/AssetWorkflow.html

■ **Asset requirements.** Even if Unity officially supports your assets, it doesn't mean they're guaranteed to look good or perform well during game play. Before creating your first asset, understand the limitations and requirements of the engine. Pay attention to polygon counts, mesh structure, material counts, UV mapping, and other specifics. It's likely your engine will have stringent requirements regarding the structure and configuration of your assets, especially meshes. You'll look at the requirements for Unity later in this book, specifically in Chapter 2, "Blender-to-Unity Workflow," and Chapter 3, "Modular Environments and Static Meshes." For now, visit the following URL for more information: http://docs.unity3d.com/Documentation/Manual/ImportingAssets.html.

STAGE 7: LEVEL DESIGN

After you successfully imported your assets into the engine, you can use them to start building levels and environments for your game. The level-building process varies depending on your game. It may involve connecting mesh pieces, like building blocks, to form a complete environment for a 3D game. Or it may involve painting pixel-based tiles onto a background for 2D games.

The ultimate purpose of level design is to create a world for the user to exist in. To achieve this, the world must be engaging and interactive. For this reason, level design often works hand in hand with scripting and coding, which is the focus for the next stage.

There are at least three critical tips that apply to level design, although much more could be said:

■ **Use the modular method.** It's tempting to view levels and environments from the perspective of the gamer. From there, they seem like complete and unified entities. Avoid this temptation. When searching through maze-like dungeons or navigating vast expanses of desert or jungle terrain, it can seem as though the world is a single, complete unit manufactured *in-situ* by artists. Instead, think of levels in terms of Lego or building blocks. Levels are typically made from discrete and interlocking pieces, or tiles. This way of making levels is called the modular method. The level variation and size comes simply from larger and more complex arrangements of pieces. There are corner pieces, straight sections, cross sections, dead ends, and all kinds of other pieces. Each piece may connect to any other, allowing for a potentially infinite number of configurations and arrangements. I really love the modular method. It can make level design a joyful and fun exercise!

Note

Chapter 3 considers these techniques of level design when working with Blender. There, I'll show you how to make useful modular pieces that fit together seamlessly.

- **Design levels with a plan in mind.** If you create your environment assets in a modular way, it's easy to get carried away, with your imagination and creativity running wild. Using the Unity editor, for example, it's easy to start throwing your level pieces into the environment, connecting them any which way, and spontaneously creating all kinds of crazy, fun worlds. This is a great and blissful state to be in—but it can be dangerous, too. It can tempt you into building free-form levels and environments that lose all resemblance to your original plan. The more you do this, the further you move from your design. If it's not kept in check, it's possible to end up with levels and environments that have no connection whatsoever to your original purpose. The result is that time gets wasted. Make sure you only build levels that respect your designs, maps and blueprints. Improvisation can be a good thing, but only when it's consistent with your design and is done consciously.

- **Test your level on others.** So you've made some really splendid levels for your game. But are they *really* as excellent as you think they are? Now, it's my view that there are no matters of fact about level design and aesthetics. For me, there cannot be "good" or "bad" levels, or even "good" or "bad" games—at least, not in any objective sense. Maybe you agree with that view, or maybe you don't. Either way, if you plan to sell your game, then it matters what *other people* think. For this reason, you should let at least three other people test your levels in context at the earliest opportunity. Let them play your game and its levels and measure their reactions. See what they think of them and learn from their comments. Whether their comments are positive or negative, view them as opportunities for improvement. Don't take criticism personally or as a reason to get angry or sad. Don't let emotion cloud your judgment.

STAGE 8: SCRIPTING

Scripting, or coding, typically works hand in hand with level design. You not only want environments and worlds that look good for gamers, you want worlds that do things and behave in specific ways. Maybe you have elevators that should rise to upper floors whenever the player steps into them. Maybe you have monsters that should crash through walls and attack players whenever they enter a specific area. This sort of behavior must be coded (or programmed) in Unity using a scripting language. Unity supports three languages: C#, JavaScript, and Boo. All three of these languages are powerful, so choose whichever one you feel most comfortable with and which suits your needs.

Note

This book uses the C# language for scripting. That shouldn't be taken as any kind of negative judgment or commentary on the alternatives. It simply represents my preference and programming background.

Coding can take a long time and involve a lot of work. Be sure to consider the following issues when coding:

- **Plan your code.** Never code blind. Before you write even your first line of code, have a clear understanding of what you want to do. After all, the first step to solving a problem is clearly understanding what the problem is. In addition, don't just think about your specific problem here and now; think about whether your problem is only a specific case of a more general kind and whether similar problems might arise elsewhere. If so, try solving the general problem so it applies to all specific cases. For example, maybe you want to code a monster that searches for health-restore potions whenever it is injured during battle. This sounds like a general problem. Certainly, you want to program a specific monster with this behavior. But perhaps you'll also want other monsters to share the same behavior, too. If so, then consider programming this behavior in a general way so it can be reused among all creatures. You'll see this design in action in the latter half of this book.

- **Be consistent.** Unity offers you the luxury of using different scripting languages. You can use C#, JavaScript, or Boo. You can, in fact, use a combination of all three across your project. However, I strongly advise against this. Pick one language and apply it consistently across your project. This ensures you never have to jump between different mindsets and thought patterns while coding. It adds a certain degree of comfort and ease to your development. If you're downloading and reusing code that someone else has written in a different language, then I recommend recoding it into your chosen language unless you have a really good reason not to, such as budgetary or deadline constraints.

- **Use code comments.** Code comments are human-readable statements that programmers attach to lines of source code to improve its readability. Be sure to use comments even if you're the only programmer on the team and nobody else will be reading the code. Sure, it's easy for you to understand your code while you're writing it, but after weeks or months have passed, your code will begin to look very different to you. Code comments can help both you and others. They can help you remember what your code is doing years after you've written it, and it can help other programmers pick up and adapt your code quickly if required. The idea is to write code that's easy to maintain, and comments help make that possible.

Tip

I recommend consulting the article "How to Write Unmaintainable Code" by Roedy Green (http://thc.org/root/ phun/unmaintain.html). It's a tongue-and-cheek tutorial on how to write "unmaintainable code," but can be instructive on how *not* to do it, too. It's written with the Java language in mind, but its principles apply more generally to all languages.

STAGE 9: TESTING

The testing stage covers a range of sub-phases that are determined by your game and its state of completion. Testing is ultimately about the play-testing done by you as well as others to make sure your game behaves according to its design and cannot be broken by legitimate methods.

When you or others test your game, play it with the intention of breaking it. If the player has the option of two doors, X and Y, and if it's clear the game wants and expects you to pick door X, then choose door Y instead. This stage involves playing and replaying the game as far as is reasonable and within your schedule.

There are several tips and considerations that apply to testing.

- **Test early.** Don't think of testing as something that happens only when the game is complete. Testing should be a constant process. Test specific features and changes as you code them. Then schedule regular slots throughout development to perform more general and rigorous tests, ensuring all features hang together as intended. Avoid wishful thinking and be ruthless in testing. Don't ignore or be afraid of encountering bugs that could involve lots of work to repair. If you encounter a bug or problem and the cause is not obvious to you, then use Unity's debugging features. Be systematic. This involves testing the relevant features, one at a time and in isolation, to follow a process-of-elimination approach.

- **Don't test alone.** Just as an author is likely a poor proofreader of his own work, a developer may be one of the worst testers of her own software. Sure, the compiler will catch syntax errors, and you may catch obvious and glaring errors, but the subtle errors will frequently pass you by. This is a common phenomenon in all fields of software development, not only games. For this reason, welcome and encourage others whose opinions you value to test your game throughout its development. You may be surprised at the errors they find. When errors *are* found, view it as a cause for celebration, not disappointment. No developer wants errors in their software, and finding them is the first step toward their elimination.

- **Use version numbers.** Be serious and systematic about giving your software meaningful version numbers for major and minor releases that are easily viewable by the user. When errors are detected and corrected, increment the version number so each version can be uniquely identified. This allows users—and you—to know whether they're playing the latest version. Further, if new errors arise during development, these numbers enable you to identify the version where errors were introduced. This can help you identify the code changes that may be the cause.

- **Track bugs.** Keep a list of all the reported bugs and their circumstances, even if they've been repaired. Don't remove any reported bug from the list. Doing this lets you not only itemize all outstanding bugs, but search through past bugs to check for relevant similarities and relationships that could shed new insight on solving the outstanding ones. Testing and bug-fixing is a mystery-solving process, so be the best detective that you can be.

STAGE 10: BUILDING

The final stage of the 10-stage workflow is building. It can take months or maybe even years for a game to reach this stage. In this stage, a game has been created and tested, and must now be finalized to run as a self-sufficient and stand-alone application on other people's computers.

If you expect your game to be an app available from the Apple App Store, Google Play, or the Windows Store, then you'll need to build your game. Additionally, if you want your game to run as a Windows, Linux, or Mac desktop program, or as a console application, then you'll also need to build your game.

In many respects, building is made simple in Unity. It still requires careful consideration, however. This is addressed further throughout the book. Some critical issues, however, are discussed here:

- **Tailor builds to platforms.** One appeal of using Unity is its ability to build and deploy games to many systems, including Windows, Linux, Mac, Android, iOS, Windows Phone, BlackBerry, Web, and consoles. There's a relevant slogan that's often repeated: "Build once, deploy anywhere." This concept conjures up a picture of simplicity in which you create your game and then simply press a button that will make it work for all supported systems. Indeed, building really can be that simple with Unity if it's configured correctly, but that doesn't mean your game will work well when it runs. Making sure your game is truly playable on all target systems requires careful management. Unity offers settings and techniques to help with this; it's important to use them. The process of tailoring your game to work well across devices is known as "optimization." Nearly every subsequent chapter in this book will have something to say on the issue.

■ **Know your target hardware.** Nearly every OS-specific game, like a PC game or mobile game, has minimum system requirements—the minimum kind of hardware and software a gamer will need to play the game successfully. Sometimes, games also include a recommended system specification, which is the minimum hardware and software needed to play the game with optimal performance, as intended by the developers. You can consider both the minimum and recommended specifications as your "target hardware"—the kind of device you intend your game to run on. Make sure you have access to this type of system when building and testing your games. Not only that, decide what your target hardware will be *before* you create your game, not after. This will let you decide on acceptable levels of performance and whether your game needs further tweaking and refinement to improve its performance. Having an established target hardware lets you benchmark your game to make measured judgments about how well it performs.

■ **Know app store requirements.** If you want your game to be listed in app stores, such as the Apple App Store or Google Play, then know their requirements and acceptance policies regarding game submissions. Each of these stores, and others, have rules and requirements about what your game may or may not contain in terms of language, violence, and content. In addition, they have requirements about file size and the general structure of your application, such as icon sizes and supplementary files and data. Invest time from the outset to know these requirements and integrate them into your game to create acceptable builds. If you're unsure about an issue, contact their support channels to find answers.

RECOMMENDATIONS FOR WORKING PRACTICE

The 10-stage workflow outlined here is intended as a general guide for developing most types of games, from casual brick-matching games to expansive MMORPGs. Even when the workflow doesn't apply to you in its entirety, it's still likely to offer you much that is valuable. Be sure to get the most out of it by applying all that's relevant for you.

If this is your first time making a video game, I have some additional recommendations:

- **Have realistic ambitions.** Set achievable goals and then pursue them with energy. Nearly everybody feels excited and energized about a game they're intending to make. It's easy to add on new features and expand the design to make the game even grander and more fantastic in scope. But it's also easy to take on more than you can really manage in practice. If you have a small team and a small budget, take care to set realistic limits to avoid disappointment. If you cannot realistically estimate a final deadline and budget from the outset, take that as a warning that your design is lacking and may need changing. If, after deep consideration, you still cannot settle on a budget and deadline, your design may need scaling back to be made more manageable.

- **Don't multi-task.** If you feel overwhelmed, stressed, or simply daunted by the extent of work outstanding, be sure you're not multi-tasking, or trying to do too much at once. Instead, focus on one task and dedicate yourself to that. Move forward only when that task is completed. Games are multidisciplinary projects. They require work that spans many fields. But that doesn't mean you have to work in all those fields at the same time, jumping from coding to graphics and music and design without any clear direction or division of labor. Be organized and focused. Complete tasks one at a time.

- **Play less and make more.** A group of game-development students once asked me how they could be more productive on their game project. They had an original idea and skillful team members, but they were frustrated by how long their game was taking. I visited their studio in Chicago to see if I could help them. I soon discovered that they played multi-player death match games during working hours—a lot. In fact, it turned out that game-playing accounted for around 65 percent of their working day. It's true that valuable inspiration can be found in playing games. But it's also possible for this line of thinking to become a dangerous rationalization that prevents you from making important progress with your work. Be honest with yourself about how you balance time during development.

- **Don't blame the tools.** It commonly happens during development that you encounter obstacles and problems. This often happens regardless of the tools you use, be they Unity, Blender, GIMP, or any other tool. In such cases, it's easy to feel limited or restricted by the software, as though it's not good enough or it's holding you back.

But blaming the software can be destructive to both your work and the game. Instead of blaming, try seeing the tool with new eyes and viewing the problem from a new perspective. Take a break and come back to it later. Search online and on the forums for more information and help. There's usually more than one road to the same destination, and tools designed for a specific purpose can often be used inventively to complete tasks for which they weren't intended. Once you condition yourself to stop blaming the tools and recognize their versatility, you gain a new level of power with them. Don't ask, "Who is to blame?" Instead, say, "I know the software can do it. But how?"

Summary

This chapter marks the starting point on a practical journey to using Unity and Blender together, along with other content-creation software. Its ultimate purpose is to establish a mindset and consciousness toward working with games and game development.

The 10-stage workflow breaks down development work into 10 discrete steps. The exact order and execution of these steps will differ by game and team. Regardless, the steps arc across game-development work and mark out specific stages and regions of time. The remaining chapters of this book concentrate specifically on stages 5 onward. That is, they concentrate more on asset creation, coding, and building than on design aspects, such as creating a game design document. This is intentional; it's simply because software, such as Unity and Blender, is typically used only after a game design is already in place. Its purpose is to create assets and create levels, and that's what we'll use it for here. For this reason, stages 5–10 will be the most relevant for us. I will not, however, cover the software in order of the 10-stage workflow throughout subsequent chapters. Rather, the topics are arranged by subject matter and their relationship to each other in terms of how the software interoperates with the Unity engine.

This chapter also offered tips and guidance targeted at people who are making their first video game, although others may find value in the advice, too. That advice may be summarized as having realistic ambitions, not working on too much at the same time, making games instead of playing them, and not blaming the tools if you feel stuck or unsure about how to proceed with your work. If you can follow those four rules while working through the remaining chapters in this book and beyond, I think you'll find game development to be a beautiful experience. And yes, that includes game development with Unity and Blender.

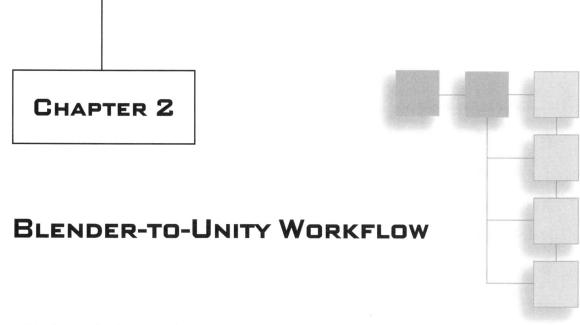

CHAPTER 2

BLENDER-TO-UNITY WORKFLOW

Simplicity is the ultimate sophistication.

—Leonardo da Vinci

By the end of this chapter, you should:

- Be able to configure Blender for use with Unity
- Understand the basics of a Blender-to-Unity workflow
- Appreciate the issues involved with importing and exporting meshes
- Understand sharp edges and the Edge Split modifier
- Be able to export models in the FBX format

Almost every video game makes use of real-time polygonal models, known as "meshes." They're called "polygonal models" because their form and substance is defined geometrically through vertices, edges, and faces. Meshes are used to represent practically every tangible in-game object—from guns and buildings to people and monsters. There is a wide variety of applications available to video-game artists for making meshes, but the software considered in this book is Blender. It's a free, cross-platform 3D modeling software, available from www.blender.org/.

Note

If you're looking for some concrete examples of what Blender can do, take a look at the Sintel short movie project, available at www.youtube.com/watch?v=eRsGyueVLvQ.

This chapter doesn't discuss Blender as though you've never used it before. There are already plenty of free and commercial tutorials available that focus on Blender and its basic use. These tutorials expand on the fundamentals, such as the Blender GUI, keyboard shortcuts, modeling and texturing basics, and more.

Tip

If you've never used Blender before or you require a refresher, please consult the "Recommended Reading" section in Appendix A, "Game Development Resources," before proceeding with this chapter. The appendix lists several books and video training materials that can help you get started quickly.

Although this chapter does cover some issues like modeling and texturing, its main focus is on using Blender and Unity together. Consequently, the primary concern here will be for interoperability between the two—practical projects that span both applications. Specifically, in this chapter, you'll see proven tips and techniques for configuring the Blender GUI to support a speedier workflow. Then you'll look at how game-ready meshes are optimally exported for Unity, with appropriate shading, size, and structure. And if you're not sure what any of that means yet, don't worry. More is explained throughout the chapter.

CONFIGURING THE BLENDER GUI

When you start Blender for the first time and you continue using Blender at its default settings, your interface will look something like Figure 2.1. I say "something like" as opposed to "exactly like" because Blender updates are released regularly. That means you'll probably be using a newer version of Blender than mine, so your interface may be slightly different.

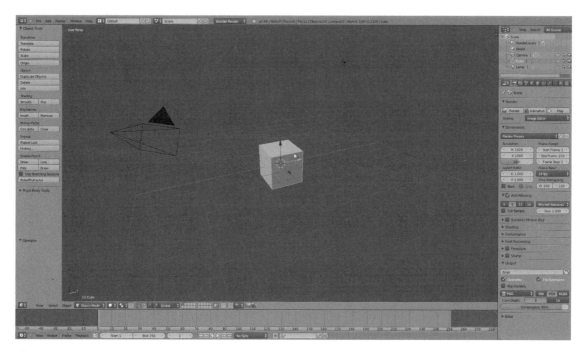

Figure 2.1
Blender (version 2.68a) in its default configuration. Your configuration or version (if different) may vary slightly.
Source: Blender.

Many users are happy with the default GUI settings and continue using Blender without ever changing any of them. However, I'm not among those people. I do change the default settings—quite significantly. I want to share with you the choices I make as well as the rationale behind them so you can follow my workflow if you think it'll be helpful for your own projects. I list my choices over the following subsections.

Dark Themes

The Blender GUI colors are defined in an external file or set, called a "theme." The default theme sets the GUI colors to a mid-tone gray, as shown in Figure 2.1. I find this tone too distracting for long-term use, however. The human eye is naturally attracted to brightness, lightness, and highlights. Consequently, when working with 3D models in the viewport using the default layout, the interface often calls out for attention, distracting us from our work. I solve this problem by darkening the interface with the Elysiun theme, shown in Figure 2.2.

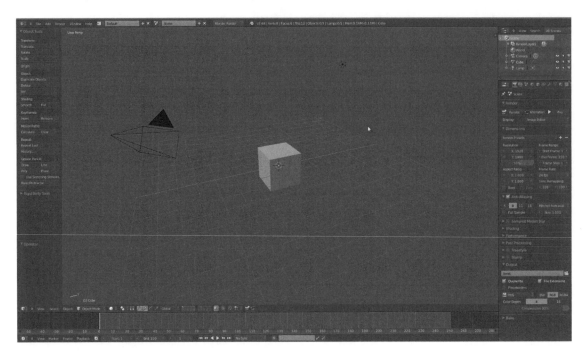

Figure 2.2
Darkening the Blender interface using the Elysiun theme.
Source: Blender.

To activate the Elysiun theme from the main Blender interface, follow these steps:

1. Select File > User Preferences or press Ctrl+Alt+U on the keyboard.

2. The Blender User Preferences dialog box opens. Click the Themes tab.

3. Open the Presets drop-down list and choose Elysiun, as shown in Figure 2.3. The GUI colors will change automatically.

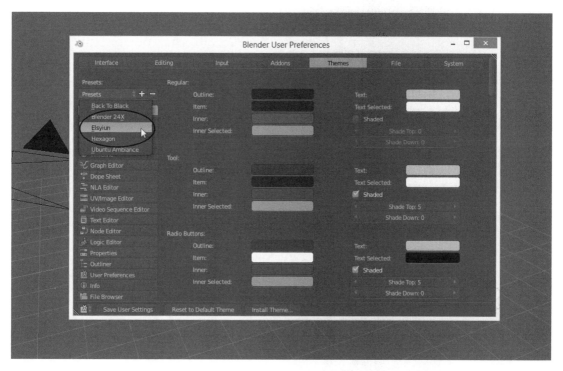

Figure 2.3
Selecting the Elysiun theme in the Blender User Preferences dialog box.
Source: Blender.

4. To apply these settings, click the Save User Settings button at the bottom of the User Preferences dialog box. Then close the dialog box to return to the main workspace.

If you later decide against using the Elysiun theme, you can restore the default by clicking the Reset to Default Theme button in the User Preferences dialog box.

Disable Python Tooltips

Blender is used by both artists, who make models, and developers, who extend the functionality of the software. Consequently, its default settings try to accommodate both types of users. However, when making games and real-time models, you're primarily acting as artists, and you want the interface behavior to be consistent with this.

One way Blender tries to accommodate developers is by displaying information about Python (a programming language used by developers) in tooltips whenever you hover the mouse cursor over a button or feature in the interface, as shown in Figure 2.4. Because you are using Blender as an artist rather than a developer, you don't need to see this information. You can safely hide it, meaning you have less to read and concentrate on.

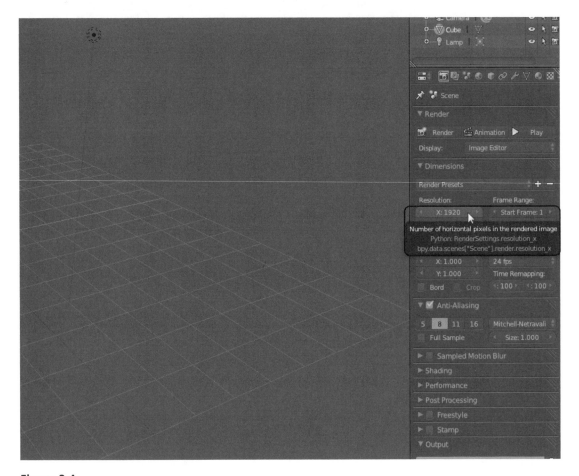

Figure 2.4
A context-sensitive tooltip in Blender. By default, this tooltip shows artist-relevant *and* developer-relevant information.
Source: Blender.

To disable Python tooltips, do the following:

1. Open the Blender User Preferences dialog box by choosing File > User Preferences.

2. Click the Interface tab.

3. Deselect the Show Python Tooltips checkbox.

4. Click the Save User Settings button. (Otherwise, the previous settings will be restored when the application is restarted.) See Figure 2.5.

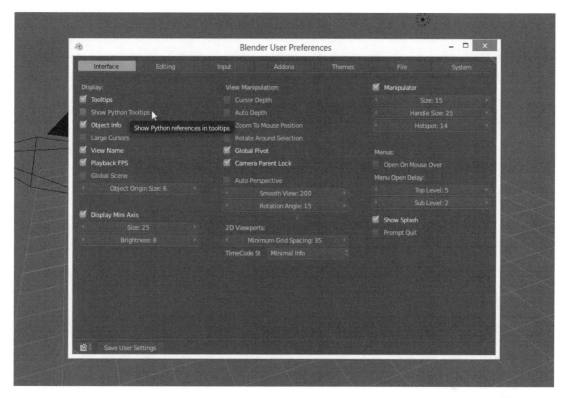

Figure 2.5
Disabling Python tooltips from the Blender User Preferences dialog box.
Source: Blender.

Maya Controls

For me, perhaps the biggest productivity enhancer when working with Blender and Unity is to use the Maya controls preset inside Blender. By default, Blender has its own unique set of keyboard shortcuts and controls for navigating 3D viewports. These keyboard controls differ from the Unity keyboard controls, which are based on the Maya keyboard controls.

Both Unity and Blender require you to work similarly in 3D, but having this asymmetry between the controls can be a productivity hurdle. It requires you to jump from one mindset to another when moving between the programs. As a result, I frequently find myself mistakenly using the Unity controls in Blender and the Blender controls in Unity—and that's no good at all. I overcome this obstacle by using the Maya control preset in Blender to make Blender work like Unity. That way, I use one consistent control scheme across both programs.

Note

Some might wonder why, when configuring the control scheme, I opted to make Blender act like Unity rather than making Unity act like Blender. The reason: Blender offers more flexibility and options for defining a control scheme. It comes with control-scheme presets built in, making it easy for me to activate and deactivate specified control schemes.

There are two ways to set the control scheme for Blender. The first is via the Blender Welcome screen and the second is via the Blender User Preferences Dialog box. To use the first method, do the following:

1. Start Blender.

2. In the Blender Welcome screen that appears, select Maya from the Interaction drop-down list (see Figure 2.6).

Figure 2.6
Selecting the Maya control scheme from the Blender Welcome Screen.
Source: Blender.

Tip

You can also display the Blender Welcome screen after Blender has started. To do so, click the Blender icon on the application toolbar, at the top of the interface by default. (This icon is circled in Figure 2.6.)

To use the second method, follow these steps:

1. Select File > User Preferences.

2. The Blender User Preferences dialog box opens. Click the Input tab.

3. Open the Presets drop-down list and choose Maya. (See Figure 2.7.)

4. Click the Save User Settings button to confirm the changes.

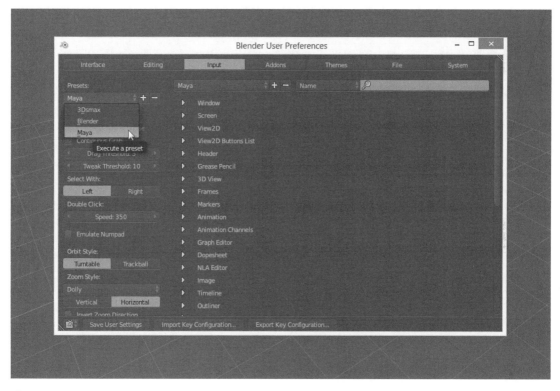

Figure 2.7
Selecting the Maya control scheme from the Blender User Preferences dialog box.
Source: Blender.

The Close-Without-Saving "Bug"

Before moving on, I want to briefly discuss an issue that's now become famous in the Blender community and to show you a solution that's not so commonly known. There's an unspoken law among almost all productivity software, from Microsoft Office and LibreOffice to game-development software like Unity and GIMP: Whenever users try to close a program but haven't saved their changes, the program must show a pop-up dialog box prompting the user to save their work to avoid losing their changes. Interestingly, however, Blender doesn't do this! If you close Blender, it'll simply exit without any pop-up warning whatsoever, regardless of whether you've saved your work or not. Then, when you restart Blender, it displays a fresh, new scene, and there's no obvious sign that any of your previously unsaved work has been retained. This leads many to angrily conclude that all their changes have been irretrievably lost. This conclusion is often reached "angrily" because there's an underlying conviction that the data loss could have been entirely avoided if only Blender had a conventional warning prompt at application exit.

Note

Some have tried to defend this "missing feature" on the grounds that Blender users should be professionals and should be careful with their work. I find this response deeply unsatisfying, however, because it ignores that all people (experienced or not) can easily make a mistake in closing an application with an unsaved file open. Thankfully, however, there's a solution to this problem! Read on....

The belief that Blender loses all unsaved changes is, in fact, mistaken. There's actually a method to easily retrieve all your unsaved work from the previous session. You simply select File > Recover Last Session (see Figure 2.8). This works because, on application exit, Blender automatically saves the open scene to a quit.blend file in the application directory. Selecting the Recover Last Session option simply opens that file. This tip for restoring data might seem simple (and it is—you just click an option from the menu). But due to the prevalent belief that Blender loses unsaved data, this option often goes unnoticed.

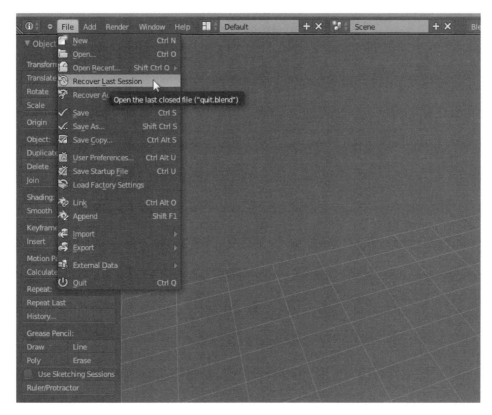

Figure 2.8
Recovering previous sessions to retrieve unsaved data.
Source: Blender.

You may still come away feeling uneasy about this. Perhaps you cannot shake off the feeling that, despite Blender's auto-save solution, it should just follow the convention of almost all other software in showing a warning prompt for unsaved changes. I recommend leaving aside this concern here, however. This book is not concerned with "shoulds" or "should nots." Rather, it's focused on the software as it is now. I think it's important to adopt this mindset as early as possible to get the most from the tools.

EXPORTING BLENDER MODELS TO UNITY

The most commonly discussed subject with regard to a Blender-to-Unity workflow is how to transfer models from Blender into Unity. A common method is to simply save your scene as a .blend file in Blender by choosing File > Save (the native Blender format) and then dragging and dropping that file into Unity. Unity will do the rest—at least, that's the theory! Sometimes this method gives you exactly the results you need, depending on your circumstances, and thus nothing more need be done. But often, the results are less than satisfactory—or things may not work at all. Here, I'll say a little about why this process can go wrong and then propose a solution in the form of a tutorial.

Note

> This section focuses on exporting Blender models to Unity in a general sense. It omits an in-depth discussion of animated models, such as rigged character meshes and other animated rigs. These are discussed later in the book.

.Blend Files

Blender's native file format is the .blend file. Thus, whenever you click File > Save to save your active project, Blender will save the data to a file with the .blend extension. Thankfully, Unity supports .blend files—meaning you can transfer your meshes into Unity straight from a .blend file. Just drag and drop the file from Explorer or the Finder into the Unity interface.

Although using this method might initially seem like a good idea, there are compelling reasons to avoid it:

■ **.Blend file imports depend on Blender.** Although Unity supports .blend files, it does so only indirectly. Unity really accepts only 3D files in the following formats: FBX, DAE, 3DS, DXF, and OBJ. Thus, when importing all other files, including .blend files, Unity actually launches the native program (Blender) behind the scenes to run its internal FBX converter. This converts the .blend file to an FBX file. As a result, anybody wanting to import .blend files into Unity must have Blender installed on their computer, even if they won't ever use it themselves. Unity needs it to perform the conversion. Now, although Blender is free and easy to get, the requirement can be annoying—especially since it can be avoided (as you'll see).

■ **.Blend files reduce export options and increase compatibility risks.** When Unity converts .blend files to FBX files behind the scenes using Blender, it doesn't give you any input or control over how the conversion works. It simply performs the conversion for you, using default settings, and then gives you the resulting mesh, whether it's how you like it or not. Of course, it might turn out fine, but it's only by coincidence that it will do so. Further, an additional risk is introduced from the Blender software itself. Specifically, Blender is frequently updated and edited by its developers. That means when Unity calls upon Blender to perform the conversion, the latest version (if it's used) may convert the file differently from earlier versions.

- **.Blend files are bloated.** This is not a derogatory statement about the .blend file format. It simply means that, by default, when Unity uses the Blender FBX converter, it tries to convert everything in your scenes from the .blend file. This includes objects you probably won't want to import such as cameras, lamps, empties, non-visible meshes, and more. These objects are perfectly serviceable in Blender but they don't translate meaningfully into Unity.

Note

More information on 3D formats and their technical implications can be found in the online Unity documentation at http://docs.unity3d.com/Documentation/Manual/3D-formats.html.

Tutorial: Exporting Manually to FBX

The upshot of the previous section is that, generally, you probably don't want to import your meshes into Unity via Blender's native .blend format. It might work successfully in the interim—perhaps during development, while testing meshes. But for importing final assets, it's usually preferable to use the FBX format, especially if you're shipping your projects to other developers or people on a team.

I've said already that Unity uses the FBX format internally when importing .blend files. But if you export your meshes manually as an FBX from Blender as opposed to relying on Unity's automation to do this implicitly, then you get far more control over export options. Plus, you remove Unity's dependency on external software, because Unity can import FBX files without requiring any help from external software.

In this section I'll show you how to export a simple cone primitive from Blender into Unity through the FBX format. Naturally, your production meshes will likely be more complex and refined than a cone primitive, but practically everything discussed here applies to all meshes in Blender, simple or complex. So let's go!

Creating Models

For this tutorial, let's start with a completely new Blender scene (refer to Figure 2.1 or Figure 2.2). For your own projects, you'll typically have a scene already created with your own models. Here, though, we'll delete everything except the camera. Then add a new cone object to the scene by selecting Add > Mesh > Cone. This will represent the mesh you want to export into Unity. (See Figure 2.9.)

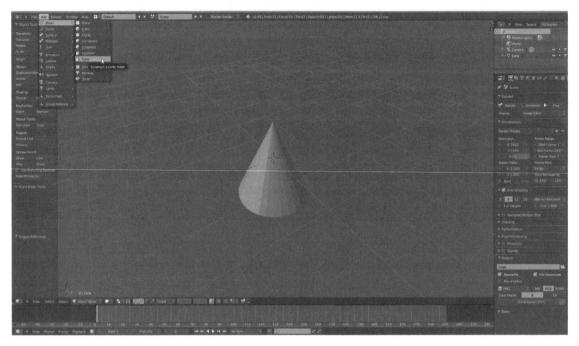

Figure 2.9
Adding a cone object to a new scene in Blender.
Source: Blender.

Dealing with Corrupted Shading

Note

This section and the next apply only if you're using Blender versions earlier than 2.69. From 2.69 onward, an FBX split-normals feature was added that corrects the issue discussed in these sections. For more information, see http://wiki.blender.org/index.php/Dev:Ref/Release_Notes/2.69. If you're using 2.69 or above, you can skip to the section titled "Understanding Object Origins" later in this chapter.

Let's jump the gun. If you were to export the cone mesh right now from Blender into Unity, whether via a .blend file or an FBX file (discussed later), you'd probably get a shading problem across the mesh surface when rendered in Unity. This would be apparent whenever you looked at the mesh in the Unity viewport or in the preview panel of the Object Inspector. The mesh would be smoothed and would look weird. This problem is due to a misunderstanding between the programs as to how the object normals should work. Figure 2.10 shows the discrepancy between how the cone is shaded in Blender and Unity.

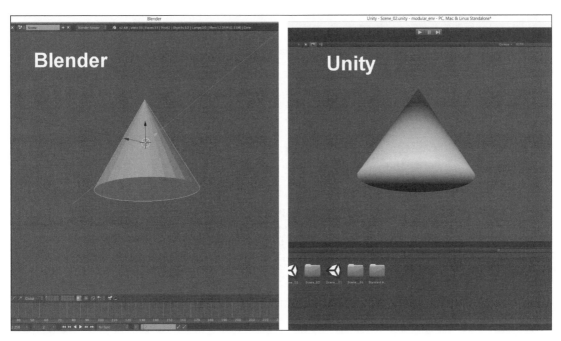

Figure 2.10
Shading problems on the mesh surface. In this mesh, the shading differences between Blender and Unity are especially noticeable where the cone edges meet the base.
Source: Blender.

Note

You don't need to follow along with this section. It discusses a hypothetical case. It's simply to show you a problem you'd encounter if you did follow along. Another unrelated issue you'd also encounter is that your mesh would import into Unity at a really small size. This is because Unity sets the mesh scale factor to 0.01 by default. You can see this in the Object Inspector panel when the mesh is selected (look ahead to Figure 2.11). You can fix this by changing the Scale Factor setting to 1. (More on this later.)

There's a quick fix for this shading issue that you can apply directly in Unity to primitive-like models, such as cubes, cones, and spheres. It involves selecting your mesh asset in the Unity Project panel and then choosing the Calculate option from the Normals drop-down list in the Object Inspector. (Be sure to click the Apply button afterward to confirm the changes.) Unity attempts to guess which parts of the mesh should appear smooth and which should appear sharp based on the angles between polygons. The result is a cone mesh that matches the shading featured in Blender, as shown in Figure 2.11. That means you've achieved a 1:1 likeness between both applications.

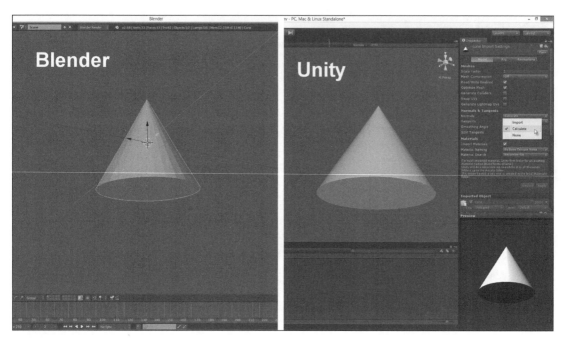

Figure 2.11
Using the Calculate Normals option in Unity to apply quick fixes to mesh shading issues.
Source: Blender.

This method of "fixing" mesh shading is generally restrictive, however, because you don't get fine control over which regions should be smoothly or sharply shaded. It works well for this cone mesh, but chances are your meshes will be different. That's why you'll generally resort to a more powerful technique in Blender. For now, just delete the cone mesh asset from Unity and return to Blender to refine the model (assuming you've been following along with me using a .blend file import).

Using Sharp Edges and Edge Split

The previous section showed you one possible way to fix corrupted shading. In this section, you'll see a generally preferred method.

Before exporting any model from Blender to Unity, you need to explicitly mark all sharp edges in the model if you want it to look as intended and don't want to rely on Unity's Calculate Normals option. A "sharp edge" is any place in the mesh where the surface shading should not be smoothed or blended across multiple faces. Typically, these will be edges that define corners, such as the edges of a cube or where a wall turns 90 degrees. Typically, however, you don't want to sharpen edges defining a human face or organic surfaces, because these should appear smooth.

For the cone mesh, you'll sharpen all edges around the circumference of the base because the underside of the cone defines a completely separate surface. To mark these edges as sharp, select the edges and choose Mesh > Edges > Mark Sharp from the 3D View menu, as shown in Figure 2.12.

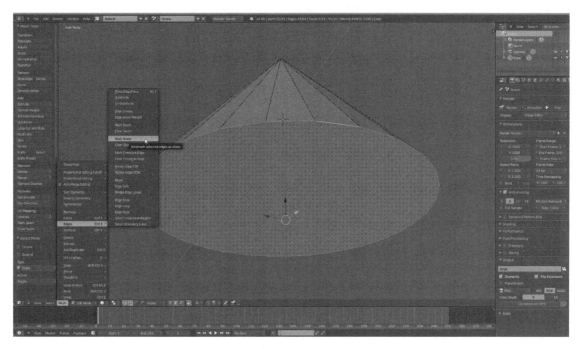

Figure 2.12
Marking sharp edges at the base of a cone mesh.
Source: Blender.

Marking all sharp edges in a model is only the first step in a two-step process. The next step is to apply an Edge Split modifier to the mesh. This separates all sharp faces in the model, disconnecting them at the vertices. The modifier will actually cut apart your mesh to force Unity into using sharp shading. But because it's a modifier in Blender, you still work non-destructively, as you can disable a modifier to retrieve your previous mesh (before the edit was made). So don't worry about losing any data or splitting apart your mesh—it can be undone.

To apply the Edge Split modifier in Blender, do the following:

1. Select your cone mesh in the scene.

2. Open the Object Modifiers tab in the Properties panel. (See Figure 2.13.)

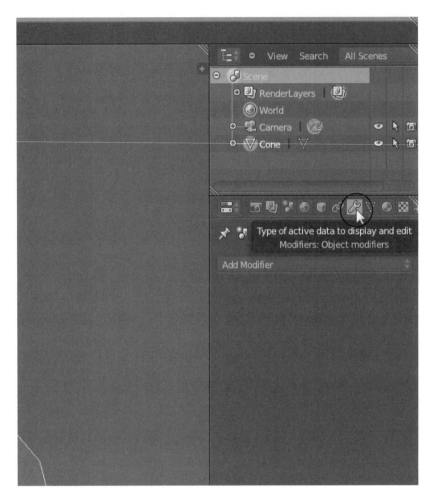

Figure 2.13
The Edge Split modifier is located in the Object Modifiers tab.
Source: Blender.

3. In the Object Modifiers tab, click the Add Modifier drop-down list and select
   Edge Split to add the modifier to the selected cone object.

4. In the modifier properties, deselect the Edge Angle checkbox, leaving only the Sharp Edges checkbox selected (see Figure 2.14). This forces Blender to cut the mesh edges based only on your Sharp Edge markings, not on edge angles regardless of whether the edges are sharp.

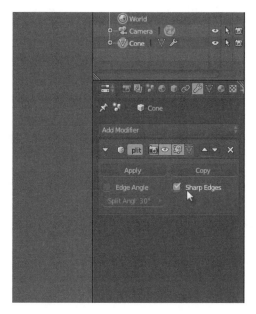

Figure 2.14
Adding the Edge Split modifier to the cone mesh to sharpen marked edges.
Source: Blender.

Caution

Do *not* click the Apply button in the modifier properties (refer to Figure 2.14). Clicking Apply will collapse the modifier history on the model, meaning that the changes will become permanent and irreversible in the mesh. Just leave the modifier as it is. You will return to it later when exporting to an FBX file.

Note

Applying the Edge Split modifier to a mesh makes its changes "permanent" and "irreversible" in a relative sense. You cannot remove a modifier and its effects from a mesh once applied. The only way to undo an applied modifier is through manual modification of the mesh—by remodeling the vertices, edges, and faces back to how you want them.

Understanding Object Origins

In both Unity and Blender, every unique object has a pivot, as it's called in Unity, or an origin, as it's called in Blender. (I'll call them origins.) An origin represents the center of a mesh. If you move the mesh to an absolute position in the scene, the mesh origin will be centered at that point. If you rotate the mesh, the mesh will turn around that point. In short, the origin of a mesh marks the center of its local coordinate system. When you export a mesh from Blender, you'll likely want its origin to be retained in Unity. This section shows you how to do that. Figure 2.15 illustrates how you can view the world space position of your objects in Blender from the Object tab. (The transform gizmo in the viewport is centered at the mesh's origin.)

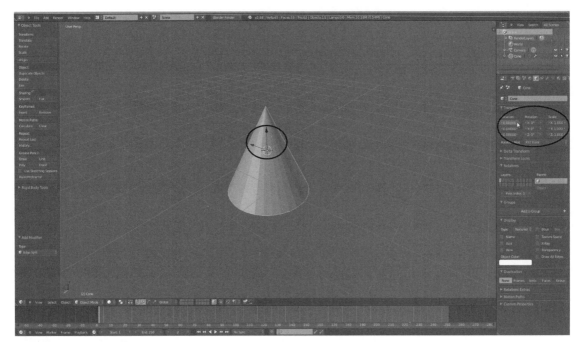

Figure 2.15
Viewing an object's world space position from the Object Properties tab in Blender. The gizmo in the viewport indicates the mesh's origin, centered at the world space position.
Source: Blender.

When modeling an object in Blender, it's likely its origin will not be where you want it. In some cases, you'll need the origin to be at a very specific position. For example, a character's origin will often need to be at its feet so it aligns with the world floor when imported into Unity.

For the cone object in Figure 2.15, the origin is aligned by default at the cone's center of mass. (The transform gizmo in the viewport reflects this.) The center of the cone passes through the world origin instead. However, suppose you want to set the origin at the base of the cone so the cone will rest on the floor when its world space position is (0,0,0). To change this, do the following:

1. Select the cone in the Blender viewport.

2. Then turn on Snapping (Incremental Snapping), as shown in Figure 2.16. That way, when you move the cone, it'll move in discrete increments aligned with the Blender grid as opposed to free and continuous stages that are aligned to nothing at all.

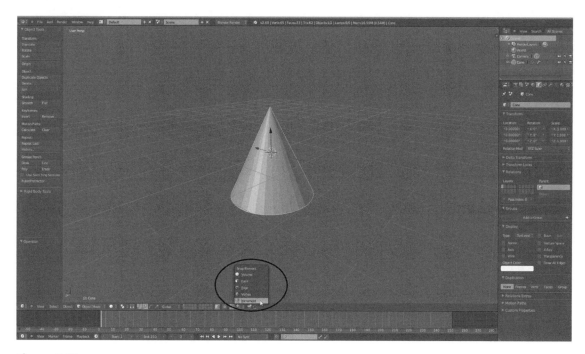

Figure 2.16
Enable snapping to move an object in discrete increments aligned to the Blender grid.
Source: Blender.

3. Use the transform gizmo to move the cone mesh upward until its base rests on the grid floor. Notice that the Blender 3D coordinate system names the up (vertical) axis "Z." As you move the object upward, its world space position changes; it should be (0,0,1). However, the mesh origin moves, too, because the origin is relative to the mesh. See Figure 2.17. Here, the cone base is aligned with the grid floor as intended, but the object origin (marked by the transform gizmo in the viewport) is still positioned at the cone's center of mass and not on the floor. You'll need to correct this to align the origin with the world space position of (0,0,0).

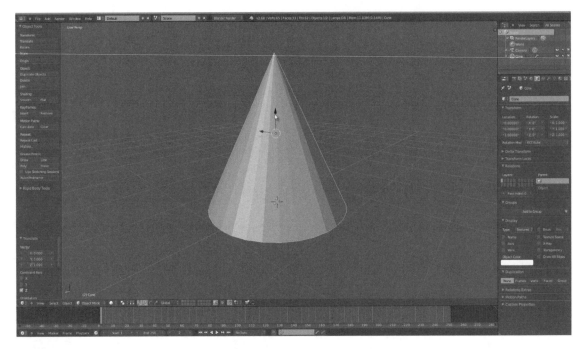

Figure 2.17
Moving the cone upward in the scene misaligns the object origin with the world center.
Source: Blender.

4. To change the mesh origin to match the world origin, use Blender's 3D cursor (the cross-hair icon in the viewport). Position the 3D cursor at the world origin if it's not there already. To do so, select Object > Snap > Cursor to Center, as shown in Figure 2.18.

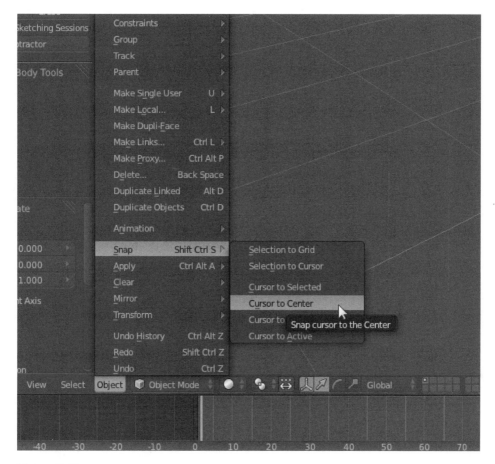

Figure 2.18
Snapping the 3D cursor to the world origin in preparation for relocating the cone mesh origin.
Source: Blender.

5. With the 3D cursor at the world origin, snap the mesh origin to match the 3D cursor. This creates a correspondence between the world and mesh origins. To do so, select the cone mesh in the viewport (if it's not selected already). Then choose Object > Transform > Origin to 3D Cursor. The transform gizmo on the mesh object will change location to the 3D cursor at the world origin, reflecting a change in the mesh's origin. In addition, the object's Z position in the Object panel will now be shown as 0 instead of 1 as it was before. In doing this, you've successfully aligned the mesh and world origins. See Figure 2.19 for the result.

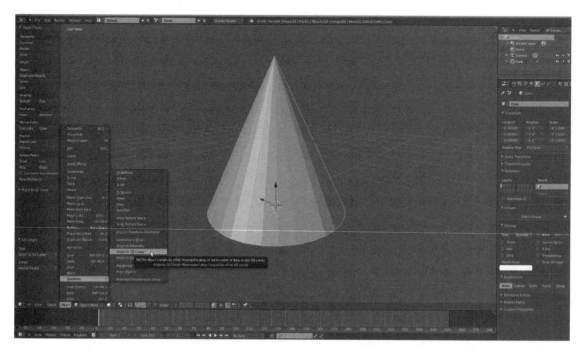

Figure 2.19
Aligning the mesh and world origins. This helps for importing meshes predictably into Unity.
Source: Blender.

Rotating Objects

Unfortunately, you're not done yet. There's more to do if you want to export your meshes predictably and cleanly from Blender into Unity.

To illustrate one task that still remains, let's engage in yet another hypothetical scenario. If you save and import your cone mesh into Unity now—either via a .blend file or an FBX file—it should initially look good from the Unity Project panel. But closer inspection will reveal a strange alignment problem. The mesh looks like it's been rotated 90 degrees or 270 degrees. In fact, it has been (see Figure 2.20). Selecting the mesh asset in the Project panel and viewing the transformation properties in the Object Inspector will confirm this. The cone mesh has been rotated 270 degrees on the X axis in Unity even though its orientation in Blender is 0 degrees on every axis. (If you're following along, your axis of rotation may be different.) There's a mismatch with regard to orientation. In other words, the orientation of the object in Blender doesn't match the default orientation of the object in Unity.

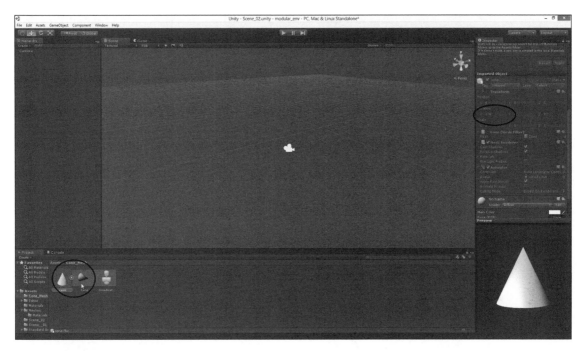

Figure 2.20
A mesh imported from Blender into Unity is rotated 90 or 270 degrees on at least one axis.
Source: Unity Technologies.

Note

As it stands now, if you drag and drop the cone mesh from the Unity Project panel into the scene, the mesh will probably orient itself correctly. Even if it doesn't, you can always rotate it manually with the Unity transform gizmo until the mesh looks correct. Some people are happy to do this, but I am not. I always prefer for my meshes to import with identity settings—that is, with a position of (0,0,0), a rotation of (0,0,0), and a scale of (1,1,1). By doing this, you can always know the starting orientation, position, and scale of your meshes.

You have this rotation problem because of a fundamental discrepancy between the Blender and Unity 3D coordinate systems. In Unity, Y is the up axis, but in Blender, Z is the up axis. Because of this, a compensatory rotation of 90 or 270 degrees is applied when importing from Blender to Unity to keep the mesh oriented the correct way as it enters a differently orientated coordinate space. The solution—as you'll see—is to apply this rotation offset at source (in Blender). Getting this to work right is actually a two-step process. You'll perform the first step here; the second will be performed later, when you use Blender's FBX Exporter tool.

Let's remove the cone mesh from Unity and return to Blender (if you've been following along in this part) and select the cone mesh in the viewport. With the cone mesh selected, use the Object Properties panel to rotate the mesh –90 degrees on the X axis. For some meshes, you may also need to rotate 180 degrees on the Y axis to ensure the model faces forward rather than backward when imported into Unity. See Figure 2.21.

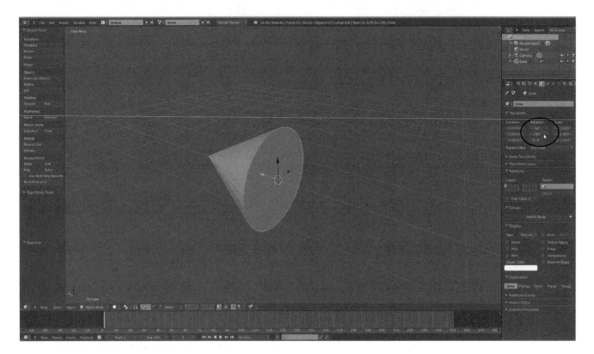

Figure 2.21
Rotating a mesh in Blender, in preparation for FBX export.
Source: Blender.

After you've rotated the mesh to the compensatory orientation, you need to apply the transformation. That means "baking" or "hard coding" the transformation into the topology of the mesh, leading Blender to think the mesh orientation is still 0 on every axis. To do that, ensure the mesh is selected, and then choose Object > Apply > Rotation & Scale (see Figure 2.22). And that's it for now! You'll return to this issue again when you export the model to an FBX file.

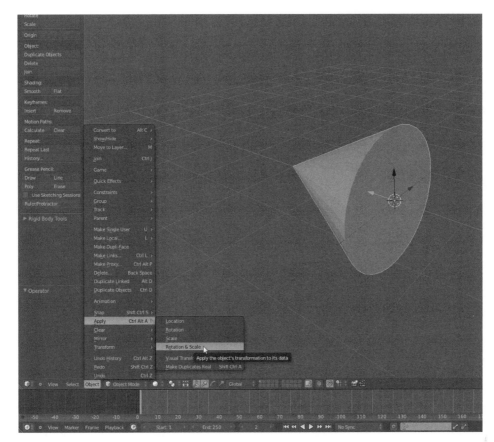

Figure 2.22
Applying transformations to an object.
Source: Blender.

Naming Your Object

This step in the export workflow is optional. At least, you can skip it and still have your model import successfully into Unity without the gamer ever noticing the difference. But if you're working with lots of different meshes in your game, it makes sense to invest time meaningfully naming each mesh so you can easily find what you're looking for and improve your organization. Don't underestimate the importance and usefulness of this step. It's easy for meshes to become muddled due to improper or unclear names. So let's give the mesh a name in Blender.

For the cone, Blender automatically assigns it the name "Cone." Typically, however, your meshes will need different names. So I'll change the cone name here to "MyCone" for illustration purposes. To do this, select the cone in the viewport, double-click the cone name in the Outliner view, and type a new name (see Figure 2.23). And that's it! You're now ready to export this mesh to an FBX file.

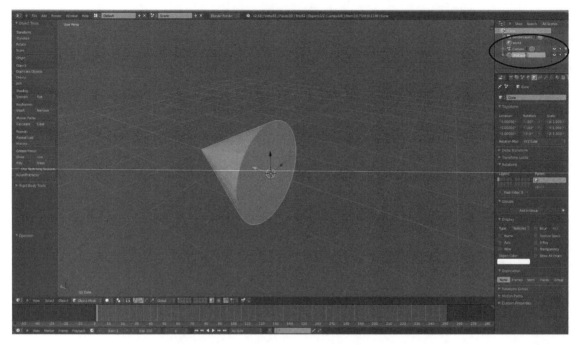

Figure 2.23
Naming your objects meaningfully before export can improve your efficiency overall.
Source: Blender.

Exporting to an FBX File

Every step in the export workflow so far has been preparation for this point. Here, you'll use the Blender FBX Exporter tool to save your cone mesh to an FBX file that imports cleanly into Unity.

Earlier in this chapter, I discussed the reasons in favor of importing meshes into Unity from FBX files as opposed to .blend files. Now, while this advice holds true, it's important not to disregard .blend files entirely within your workflow. Be sure to save your Blender scenes and meshes to a native .blend file for your reference in case you ever want to change or edit the meshes later. If you decide to change a mesh, don't load it back into Blender from an FBX. Instead, load it back from a .blend file. The FBX file is simply the vehicle for importing a mesh into Unity. So, before exporting your meshes to an FBX, be sure to save them also as a .blend file with the standard save command File > Save.

To export a selected mesh to an FBX file using Blender, do the following:

1. Select your mesh in the scene and choose File > Export > Autodesk FBX (.fbx).
   See Figure 2.24. The FBX Exporter window opens, with many export options. For a
   non-animated mesh, like the cone object and other kinds of props, your export
   options should look like Figure 2.25.

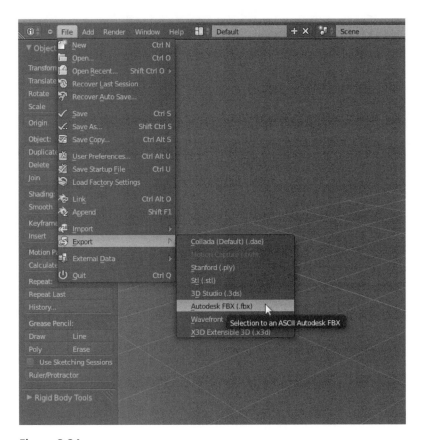

Figure 2.24
Starting the FBX export process for the selected mesh.
Source: Blender.

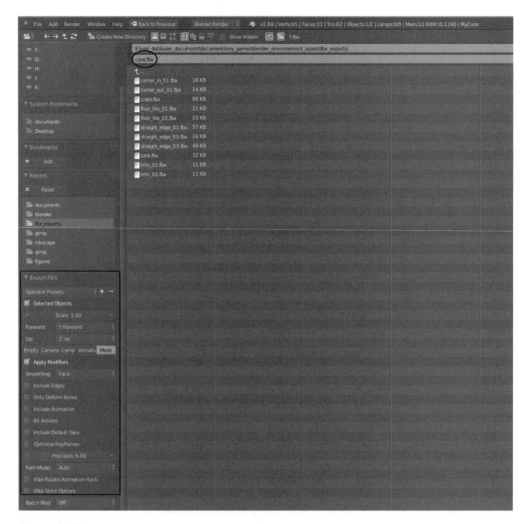

Figure 2.25
Exporting static meshes from Blender to Unity with the FBX Exporter.
Source: Blender.

2. Give your file a meaningful name. In Figure 2.25, the file is named cone.fbx. Each separate mesh you export should have its own unique, descriptive name.

3. Select the Selected Objects checkbox in the FBX Options panel. This exports only the selected mesh in the scene. If this checkbox is not selected, then all meshes and objects will be exported together as a single mesh group.

Note

The Scale setting is set to 1.00 by default to apply a normalized scale to your mesh. Generally, this value should always be 1.00. However, as you'll see, Unity appears to ignore this value, whatever it is. Instead, it uses a value of 0.01, whether that's what you want or not. You'll see a way around this problem later.

4. Specify the Forward and Up directions for the mesh. These settings form step 2 of the two-step process you began in the "Rotating Objects" section. These settings, combined with the object's orientation in the scene, ensure the mesh will be properly aligned when imported into Unity. Generally, these values will match Blender's coordinate space. That means Forward should be set to Y Forward and Up to Z Up. In some cases, you may need to play around with these values until your mesh is imported with an identity transformation—that is, a transformation with all values at their defaults: position (0,0,0), rotation (0,0,0) and scale (1,1,1).

5. Make sure the Apply Modifiers checkbox is selected. This ensures that all modifiers, including the Edge Split modifier (applied in the section "Using Sharp Edges and Edge Split"), will be baked and embedded into the exported FBX mesh. (Note that this will not affect your mesh in the original Blender scene; it affects only the mesh that results from the export.)

6. Make sure the Include Animation and Optimize Keyframes checkboxes are unchecked for non-animated meshes (static meshes). You'll learn more about exporting animated meshes later in the book.

Note

An alternative to using the FBX format is to use Collada (.dae). You can export meshes to this format via the File > Export > Collada command. Collada files support both static and animated meshes. More information on Collada can be found here: https://collada.org/.

Exploring FBX Files

The Blender FBX Exporter will produce a Unity-ready FBX file for your mesh. It's worth taking a quick diversion here to examine the file further. The FBX file is a human-readable ASCII file. It contains editable properties, if you wish to tweak them. You can open and read the file in any standard text editor, such as Notepad, Notepad++, or even MonoDevelop. See Figure 2.26.

Figure 2.26
FBX files encode human-readable ASCII text that can be edited in a text editor or integrated development environment (IDE).
Source: MonoDevelop.

Note

In theory, there shouldn't be any need to manually edit an FBX file exported correctly from Blender. But it's nonetheless helpful to know that FBX files are human-readable ASCII data that can be parsed and batch-processed, should you later need to adjust them in volume.

TUTORIAL: IMPORTING FBX FILES INTO UNITY

After you export your FBX mesh from Blender, you'll want to import it into Unity for inclusion in your games. To do this, you begin by simply dragging and dropping your mesh file, from Windows Explorer or Mac Finder, into the Unity Project panel, just as you'd import any other asset (see Figure 2.27). But it doesn't end there. There are additional settings you'll probably need to tweak. This tutorial considers those issues.

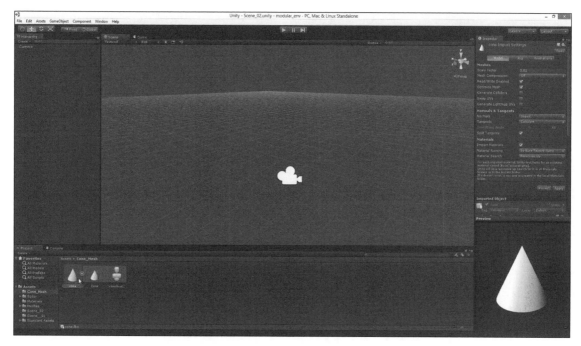

Figure 2.27
Importing FBX files into the Unity Project panel.
Source: Unity Technologies.

Lightmap UVs

If you're importing a static mesh for terrain, architectural, or other environmental props in your game, then you'll probably want to lightmap those meshes. Lightmapping is achieved through the Unity Beast Lightmapper, which you access by choosing Window > Lightmapping. "Lightmapping" is the process of determining how a mesh structurally responds to environment lighting—the shadows it casts and the highlights it receives—and then recording that data as pixels to a texture file. This texture file, known as a "lightmap," is then blended by Unity onto the mesh surface during gameplay to make the mesh appear illuminated by lights.

The point of this is to save the CPU or GPU from having to calculate the effects of lighting in real time. However, if you're to use this method successfully, your imported meshes will need to have lightmap UVs. That is, they'll need mathematical data built into them, defining how the lightmap texture should be mapped across their surface. If you don't have these, then lightmapping will appear corrupted. You can define lightmap UVs manually in Blender, but you can also have Unity generate them automatically from your meshes.

To generate lightmap UVs for an imported mesh in Unity, start by selecting the mesh in the Project panel to show its properties in the Object Inspector. Then simply select the Generate Lightmap UVs checkbox and click Apply (see Figure 2.28). Most of the time, this option works fine, but on organic and spherical meshes, the mapping may not be as you want it. In these cases, you'll need to manually create lightmap UVs in Blender. The next chapter discusses how to create UV maps and channels for your meshes.

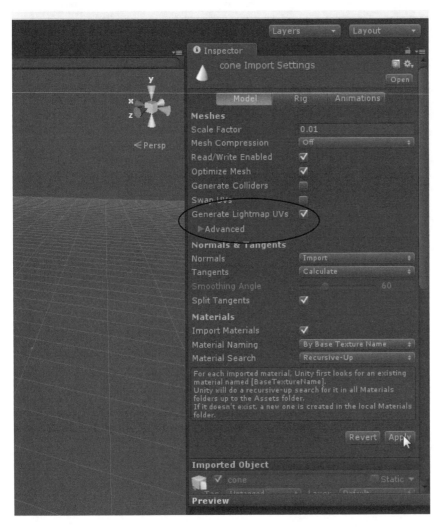

Figure 2.28
Generating lightmap UVs for imported meshes.
Source: Unity Technologies.

Scale Factor

Every time you import an FBX mesh into Unity, Unity will automatically set its scale factor to 0.01, regardless of what the scale factor may be in the FBX file itself. As a result, your mesh will look much smaller than it should when added to your levels. In fact, it may be so small you won't even see it in the viewport unless you zoom in. You can fix this by manually changing the mesh's Scale Factor setting in the Object Inspector to 1 (see Figure 2.29). However, this solution will quickly become tedious if you import many meshes, and especially if you frequently import and re-import meshes throughout the lifetime of the project.

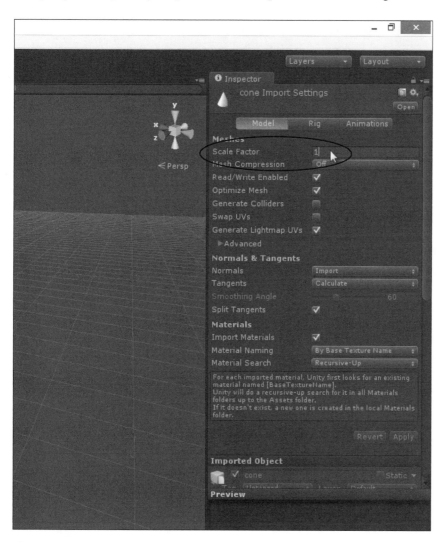

Figure 2.29
Changing the mesh's Scale Factor setting to 1 (as opposed to 0.01).
Source: Unity Technologies.

An alternative method is to write an editor script to customize how Unity behaves when importing meshes. That is, you can write a script file that forces Unity to automatically apply a scale factor of 1 to every mesh that is imported to the project. This technique will save you from having to specify the scale factor manually. To achieve this, create a new C# script file in the Project panel and name the file FBXFix.cs. Then add the following code to the file:

```
using UnityEditor;

public class FBXFix : AssetPostprocessor
{
    public void OnPreprocessModel()
    {
        ModelImporter modelImporter = (ModelImporter) assetImporter;
        modelImporter.globalScale = 1;
    }
}
```

Next, save or move this script file to the Editor folder inside the project. (If this folder doesn't exist, create it. Otherwise, just use any existing Editor folder.) The script file must be inside this folder; otherwise, it will have no effect. (See Figure 2.30.) To test this script file, simply import a new FBX file; the scale factor should be 1!

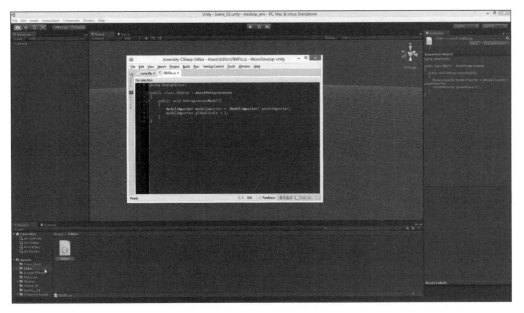

Figure 2.30
Importing meshes with a scale factor of 1 via an Editor script file.
Source: Unity Technologies.

Thus far, you've successfully exported a model from Blender and imported it into Unity with almost total fidelity.

Summary

This chapter is about import/export workflows between Blender and Unity. In short, whenever two programs of differing purposes and features exchange data, there's typically something lost in the translation. With Blender and Unity, you can transfer mesh data either through .blend files or through FBX files. This chapter generally recommends FBX for efficiency and compatibility. However, as you've seen, this is not all that can be said on the issue. Even if you export meshes from Blender through FBX files, there are still additional steps to perform if you want the mesh to perform as well as it can in Unity. This includes marking sharp edges in the mesh, rotating it, resetting pivots, and more. Further, even though everything said here applies to all meshes, there's even more to be said for animated meshes. For this reason, a later chapter considers animated meshes in more detail. The next chapter, however, considers a specific type of static mesh: namely, modular environment meshes.

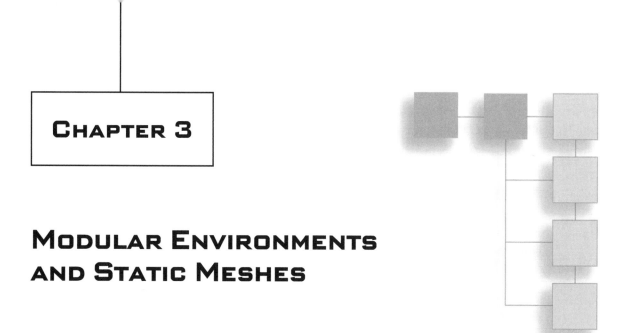

CHAPTER 3

MODULAR ENVIRONMENTS AND STATIC MESHES

Creativity is just connecting things.

—Steve Jobs

By the end of this chapter, you should:

- Understand static meshes and modular environments
- Be able to work with the modular building method
- Understand modeling to the grid and UV mapping
- Be comfortable with concepts such as mirroring, doubles, *n*-gons, and more
- Be able to build Unity scenes from modular prefabs

Many games, such as RPGs and first-person shooters, feature extensive environments such as forests, caves, space stations, office buildings, hospitals, secret laboratories, and more. Like all tangible things in a 3D game, these environments are made from meshes—that is, intricate arrangements of polygons, edges, and vertices, assembled together in a 3D modeling application. For the developer, building such complex environments presents some interesting technical challenges.

To the player, the game world appears seamless, connected and completely integrated. Interior lobbies and rooms fit nicely with neighboring corridors, and mountain landscapes change seamlessly into urban or desert terrain. It looks as though the whole environment is simply one huge mesh asset that's been imported into the engine. But this appearance is typically deceptive. Normally, the environment is made up from many smaller pieces or blocks, known as "modules." These are merely fitted together like LEGO bricks to look like a larger and complete whole, without really being so. This method of fitting together environments from pieces is known as the "modular building method," or just the "modular method." It is, essentially, the 3D–level design equivalent to 2D tile sets (if you're familiar with making tile-based 2D games).

Figure 3.1 shows a modular environment set for an interior science fiction environment. It might not look like much on its own, but by using and reusing these environment pieces, you can build larger and more integrated environments, as featured in Figure 3.2.

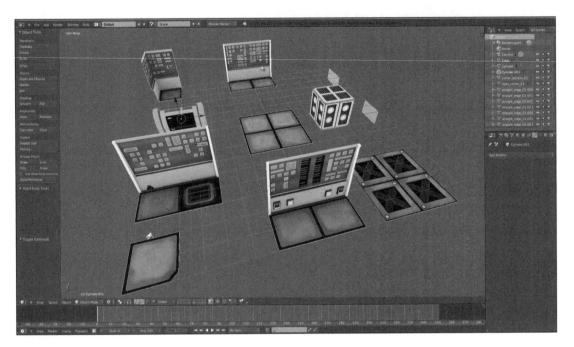

Figure 3.1
A complete sci-fi modular environment set made in Blender. By combining these pieces like building blocks, you can assemble larger environments.

Source: Blender.

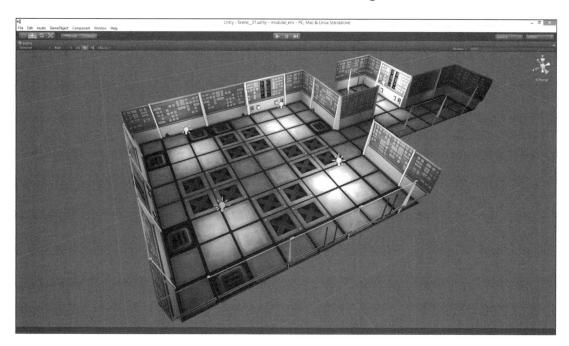

Figure 3.2
A sample environment composed from the modular environment set.
Source: Unity Technologies.

Advantages of the Modular Method

There are several distinct advantages to the modular method. These are as follows:

- **Reusability.** By breaking down an environment into modular pieces as opposed to handling it as a complete whole, you create the potential for reusability. That is, you can use and reuse the same pieces in different combinations to produce different environments—assuming you plan and size your modular pieces sensibly! (You'll see how to do that later in this chapter.) This reusability saves you from having to model similar-looking environments more than once, as you can just reuse the modular pieces.

- **Performance.** Reusability is almost always associated with performance efficiency, and especially with render performance efficiency. If Unity can interpret and understand a mesh environment in discrete and manageable modules as opposed to a larger single mesh, then you can improve run-time performance in your games. These benefits come largely from frustum culling, occlusion culling, and memory management.

Note

For more information on frustum and occlusion culling, consult the Unity online documentation at http://docs .unity3d.com/Documentation/Manual/UnderstandingFrustum.html and http://docs.unity3d.com/Documentation/ Manual/OcclusionCulling.html.

■ **Texture optimization.** Modular environments are texture-optimized because their texture-able surface area is far less than it appears to be. If an environment was modeled as a single complete mesh, then its associated diffuse-texture potentially would span the environment's entire surface area. But with modularity comes texture reuse, as each module reuses its own same texture-coordinates and texture space. That means a complete modular environment, no matter how large or small, requires no more texels (texture pixels) than its modular pieces.

GETTING STARTED WITH MODULAR ENVIRONMENTS IN BLENDER

The first step in making a modular environment, after planning it and deciding on the kind of environment you want to make, is to model it using 3D software, like Blender. From the outset, take special care regarding the size and proportion of your modules. This is critical to making pieces that fit together seamlessly and nicely.

It's important to remember while modeling that you're not building an environment. Rather, you're creating pieces and building blocks from which an environment could be made (after they are imported into Unity). One of the simplest and most effective ways to build interlocking modules is to imagine your final environment sliced up into a grid of equally sized cubes. Then your task becomes a process of building the environment geometry inside the imaginary cubes in such a way that they'd still fit together even if they were rearranged into a different grid. It's not essential that every module be able to fit together seamlessly alongside every other module; the idea is simply to keep all your modules as tile-able as you can to increase their reusability.

I like to start creating modular environments by sizing a cube in Blender. This represents the total volume of a base tile or base unit. (See Figure 3.3.) When created in Blender, the default cube has its center point at the world origin of (0,0,0), which typically isn't helpful. Normally, the cube center-bottom point should rest on the origin, marking the level of the floor plane. To achieve that, enable the Increment Grid Snapping option and constrain-translate the cube upward on the Z axis to rest exactly on the ground plane (see Figure 3.4).

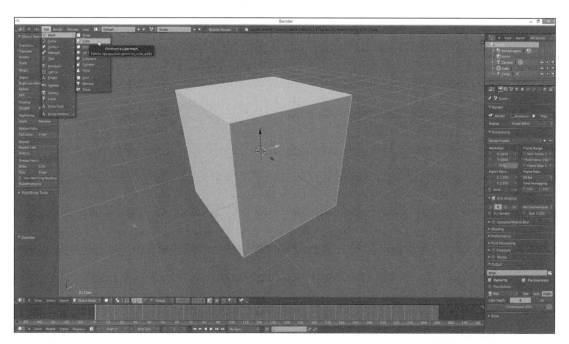

Figure 3.3
Creating a base tile cube in Blender for a modular environment set.
Source: Blender.

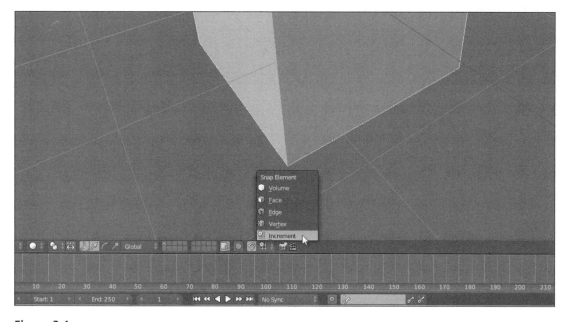

Figure 3.4
Enable Increment Grid Snapping to move the cube upward, resting its bottom-center point on the ground plane.
Source: Blender.

Snapping the cube in line with the ground, however, doesn't actually change the true mesh center, or its pivot. Typically, it's a good idea for the mesh origin to align with the world origin, which is also on the floor plane. By default, the 3D cursor is centered at the world origin; you can align the pivot for any selected object to the world origin by way of the 3D cursor. To do so, select Object > Transform > Origin to 3D Cursor. See Figure 3.5. If the 3D cursor is not aligned to the world origin, you can align it by selecting Object > Snap > Cursor to Center.

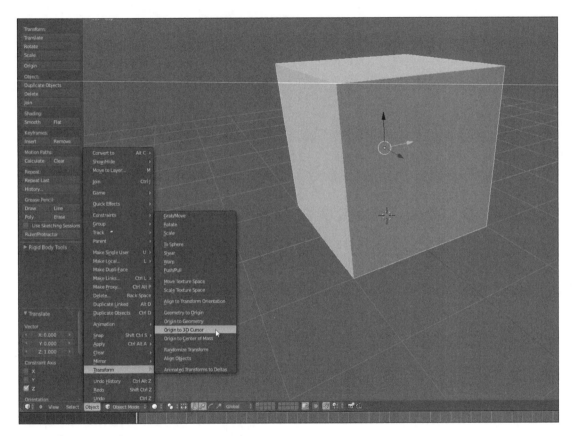

Figure 3.5
Aligning the mesh origin to the world origin via the 3D cursor.
Source: Blender.

The cube created so far represents the smallest block or module in the environment set, hence my calling it a "base tile." There's no right or wrong size for the base tile, as sizing depends a lot on your game and workflow preferences. However, I typically size the cube relative to the player character in Unity. So, for first-person and RPG games, I usually import and export my cube back and forth between Blender and Unity, sizing it against a first-person controller in a Unity scene until I get a base tile that entirely encompasses the player character while leaving some margin of space. Although you can use the Blender Scale tool (keyboard shortcut R) to size the cube, when sizing the base tile, I prefer to work in discrete numbers. Consequently, I use the Transform section of the N panel, as shown in Figure 3.6, to type size values for the X, Y, and Z dimensions using neat, round numbers with no fractional part. In Figure 3.6, the cube has been sized to $2 \times 2 \times 3$ world units (the larger dimension being height). Remember: In Blender, the Z axis refers to the vertical (up and down) axis.

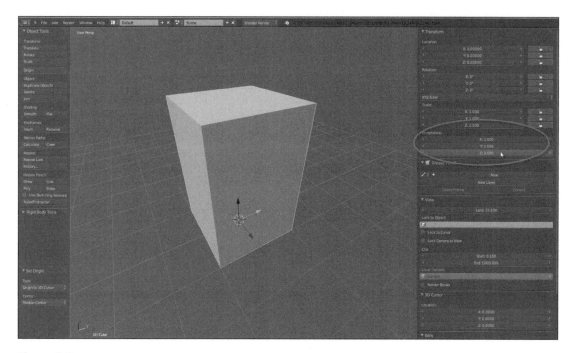

Figure 3.6
Establishing the base tile size using the N panel and round numbers.
Source: Blender.

Note

Remember to establish a 1:1 unit scale between Blender and Unity coordinates. (This was discussed in detail in Chapter 2, "Blender-to-Unity Workflow.")

EXTENDING FROM THE BASE TILE

Establishing the base tile is perhaps the most critical and important step in building modular environments. The base tile represents your raw unit of measure against which all other modules are sized. Here are some general dos and don'ts that pertain to a base tile once you've positioned and sized it in a Blender scene:

- **Keep a backup copy.** Never model, edit, or delete your original base tile. Always keep a backup copy of it in the scene. It will come in handy for sizing and measuring other modules you make in the environment set. After you establish your base tile, make a duplicate of it and keep the original on a separate, independent layer.

- **Use it as a reference.** Don't model with your base tile. Also, don't tweak it or change its vertices. Its purpose is to be a reference or guide for creating modular pieces for the environment set. The base tile represents the total volume and limits for the smallest module possible. Use the base tile as a wire-frame guide when modeling your pieces.

- **Use the base tile to size larger pieces.** Just because you've established a base tile as a reference for making environment pieces, it doesn't mean all pieces must be the same size as the base. The base tile may represent, for example, only the volume of a doorway section, including the door and floor and ceiling. If you need to make larger pieces, such as longer corridor sections, don't be afraid to do so. When making larger pieces, however, ensure that their size is a multiple of the base tile in every dimension (2×, 3×, 4×, etc.). Don't resort to fractional values, and don't choose round numbers that aren't equally divisible by the base-tile dimensions. This ensures that all tiles—both the base tile and larger tiles—can fit and stack inside a single, neat coordinate space of modular blocks. If you make your modules at any and every size, then tiling won't work. If you want your pieces to be truly modular, then they'll need to tile. See Figure 3.7.

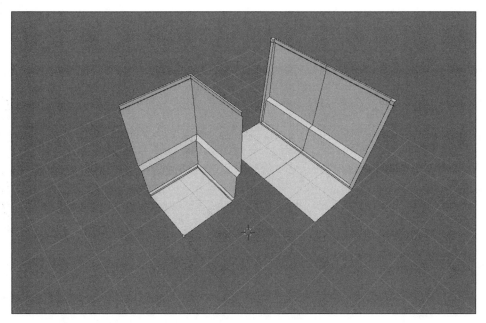

Figure 3.7
Use the base tile to establish the sizes of larger tiles and sections. Every large tile should be a multiple of the base. Here, the corridor section is twice the length of the corner section.
Source: Blender.

MODULAR ENVIRONMENT BLENDER WORKFLOW

Getting into the habit of modeling in terms of grids, cubes, and base tiles is not all you need to know about environment creation in Blender. There are many features and settings of the application that you can tweak or use creatively to make your workflow even simpler. The following sections cover some of these.

Flipping Normals

Indoor environments, such as rooms, caverns, and hollows, are typically seen by the player from the inside rather than from the outside. Thus, if you create a new cube or mesh in Blender with the intention of modeling an interior environment, you'll typically want to see the mesh from the inside. That is, you'll want the mesh polygons to be facing inward instead of outward to approximate floors, walls, and ceilings. That means that for many indoor objects, you'll want to flip their face normals. To achieve that, do the following:

1. View the object in Edit Face mode.

2. Press Ctrl+A or choose Select > Select All to select all the faces on the object.

3. Choose Mesh > Normals > Flip Normals. Blender flips the normals, as shown in Figure 3.8.

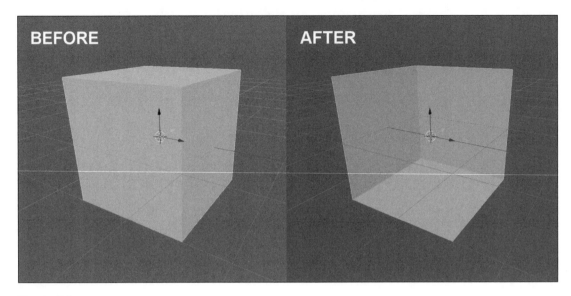

Figure 3.8
Before and after flipping a cube's normals. Flipping normals turns the polygon alignment inside out.
Source: Blender.

Note

If you're using the default Blender settings and your viewport is in Shaded mode, then flipping the normals may appear to have no effect. If this is the case, read the next section!

Backface Culling

By default, Blender renders every polygon as double-sided even though video-game polygons are single-sided. In video games, and in Unity, you can view only one side of a polygon at a time. If you attempt to view the back face, it will simply be invisible. In Blender, however, both sides of a polygon are drawn, which means that even if your faces and normals are flipped, they won't appear to have changed because the reverse side of a polygon is also rendered. This can make modular environment modeling difficult because you'll often want to see the interior of an object, such as the interior of a room, without the back faces getting in your way in the viewport.

Thankfully, Blender offers the Backface Culling option. You can access it in the Shading section of the N panel. To force one-side rendering, select the Backface Culling checkbox, as shown in Figure 3.9.

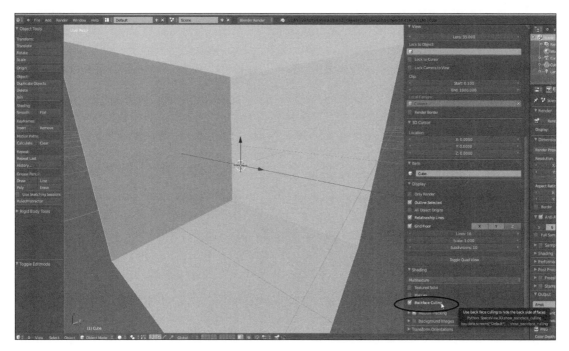

Figure 3.9
Select the Backface Culling checkbox to force one-side rendering in Blender.
Source: Blender.

Vertex and Incremental Snapping

If you're seeking to create seamless, tile-able environment pieces, then the importance of vertex and incremental snapping cannot be understated. It's crucial that snapping becomes second nature to you when working in Blender. In essence, snapping enables you to precisely align your vertices and models to specific world positions or to other vertices in the scene.

Vertex snapping enables alignment with vertices, and incremental snapping allows alignment with a grid. This snapping ability is critical for modeling pieces that will neatly and cleanly align at the edges when positioned in a grid formation inside Unity during the level-design stage. If so much as one of your modular pieces is out of alignment, even by only a few units at the edges, it could cause a noticeable mismatch in your environment when assembled in Unity. When the troublesome piece is aligned with a neighboring piece, holes or gaps can appear because the vertices between the two don't match up. Sometimes these holes can even be large enough for the player to fall through!

You could of course patch up the mistake in Unity by inserting box collider primitives wherever there are holes. This would prevent players from falling through. But this solution has the odor of shoddiness, running only skin deep. It doesn't truly get to the source of the problem, which is structural and at the mesh level. So be sure to use snapping to model your meshes with precision.

To use incremental snapping in Blender, activate the snapping tools (make sure the Magnet button is activated for snapping to take effect) and set the mode to Increment (refer to Figure 3.4). When snapping is active and in Increment mode, all object transformations are constrained to discrete increments on a grid, meaning that objects can move only in measured, rounded steps. This mode is especially useful for object-level transformations (as opposed to vertex-, edge-, or polygon-level transformations), and can bring objects into precise alignment. As you also saw earlier in this chapter in the section "Getting Started with Modular Environments in Blender," when creating a base tile cube, incremental snapping can be used to center an object's pivot to the world origin.

In contrast to incremental snapping, which allows for discrete transformations, vertex snapping enables you to precisely align one or more vertices in a mesh with another vertex elsewhere. If you need vertices to line up exactly on any or all axes, then vertex snapping is for you! For example, consider Figure 3.10. While modeling the wall section for an environment piece, I accidentally offset the top set of wall vertices over to the right side so they no longer align horizontally to form a straight edge with the vertices below.

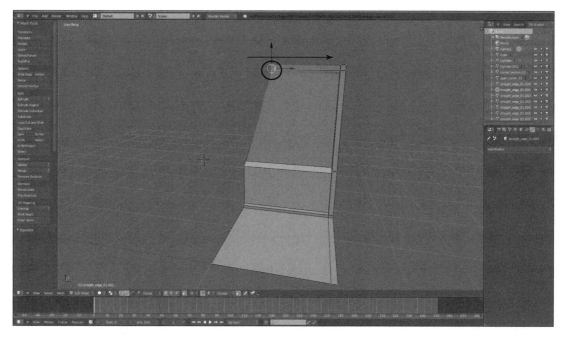

Figure 3.10
Misalignment of wall vertices in a mesh.
Source: Blender.

To realign those top vertices so they're in line with the ones below to form a straight wall, you could simply use the Transform tool and move the vertices until they look roughly right. But with snapping, you can be *exactly* right. To achieve that, do the following:

1. Select all the top vertices you want to move.

2. Activate vertex snapping in the toolbar. (Refer to Figure 3.4 for the snapping options menu.)

3. Constrain translation to the X axis via the transformation gizmo or the keyboard (press W, then X).

4. While holding down the mouse button, drag to move the selected vertices to any of the correctly aligned wall vertices below. The selected vertices will snap to the target vertices below, on the constrained axis. The result will be perfect alignment between the source and target vertices, with the source vertices snapping to the target. See Figure 3.11.

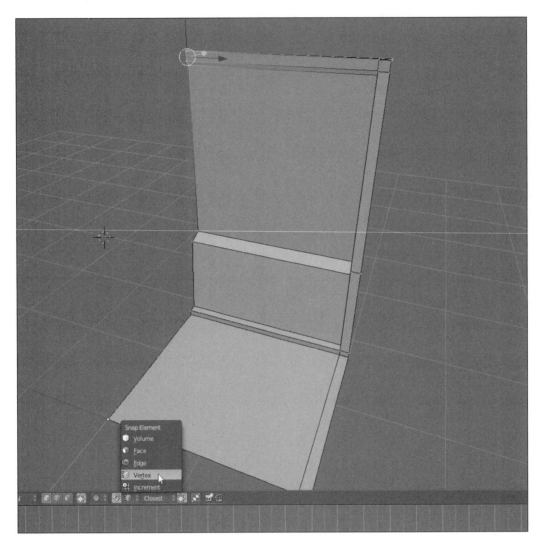

Figure 3.11
Snapping source vertices to the target using vertex snapping.
Source: Blender.

Note

More information on snapping options can be found in the Blender online documentation: http://wiki.blender
.org/index.php/Doc:2.6/Manual/3D_interaction/Transform_Control/Snap_to_Mesh.

N-gons

Meshes are composed of polygons—hence they're also referred to as "polygonal meshes." The simplest kind of polygon is a triangle, which has three sides. After that, you have quads, which have four sides. There is a potentially infinite number of polygons, including octagons, pentagons, decagons, enneadecagons, and others. These shapes are all classified by the total number of sides along their perimeter. Interestingly, by using multiple triangles in juxtaposition, you can form every other kind of polygon.

In 3D modeling and video games, all polygons with more than four sides are known as *n*-gons. In short, *n*-gons are to be considered your enemy. They should never appear in your geometry. For this reason, you should take steps in Blender to remove them. That is, if any *n*-gons are found in your mesh, be sure to divide and cut them up to form either quads or triangles instead. Sometimes, quads cannot be formed (depending on the nature of the shape). Triangles, however, can *always* be formed. See Figure 3.12.

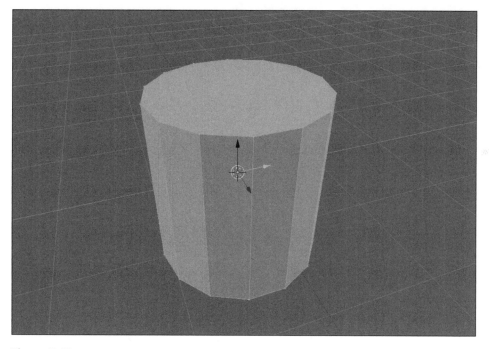

Figure 3.12
A cylinder object with an *n*-gon cap, made from a 14 sided polygon, or tetradecagon. This is bad. It performs poorly with real-time 3D games.
Source: Blender.

Blender offers several tools for re-topologizing your model—that is, rebuilding or editing it to feature only triangles and quads. One tool is Triangulate Faces, which you can access by choosing Mesh > Faces > Triangulate Faces when in Edit mode for an object (see Figure 3.13). This method, which applies to only the selected faces, quickly converts all selected polygons into triangles. It can be a quick way to get your model ready for importing into Unity, but can be clumsy because it offers you no control over exactly how the polygons are triangulated.

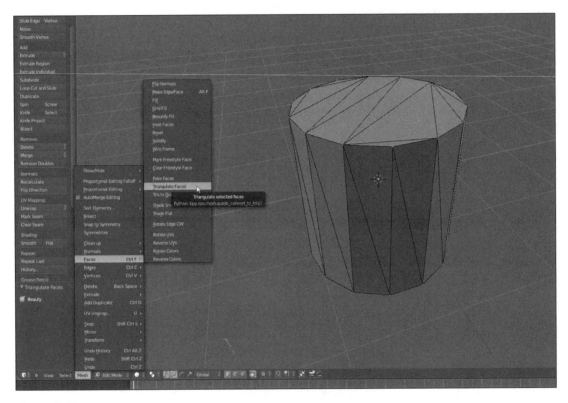

Figure 3.13
Use Triangulate Faces to convert the selected polygons, whether quads or *n*-gons, into triangles.
Source: Blender.

A second, more customizable, method for re-topologizing your model to eliminate *n*-gons is the Knife tool, accessible via Edit mode. With the Knife tool, you can interactively divide and reorganize mesh polygons by simply drawing and cutting into the mesh from the viewport in real time (see Figure 3.14). In essence, this is the "manual" method for correcting topology. It can take much longer to use than Triangulate Faces, but it offers potentially unlimited power and flexibility.

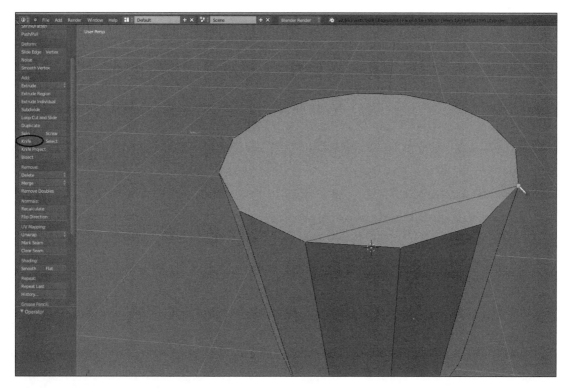

Figure 3.14
Using the Knife tool to dissect a model into quads and triangles.
Source: Blender.

Searching for *N*-gons

It might initially seem that identifying an *n*-gon is an obvious matter. After all, for any shape, you only have to count its sides to know whether it qualifies. But in practice, when looking at meshes with potentially hundreds or even thousands of polygons, spotting the *n*-gons among them (if there are any) is not always so easy. Thankfully, Blender can help you select every *n*-gon in a mesh with the click of a button (well...a few buttons). To do so, follow these steps:

1. Enter Edit Face mode for an object.

2. Deselect all faces.

3. Choose Select > Select Faces by Sides, as shown Figure 3.15.

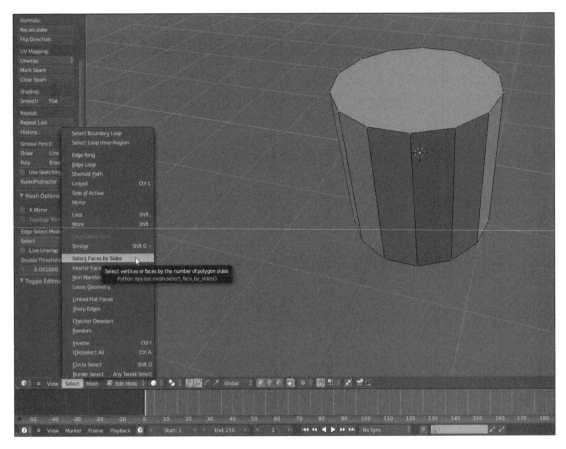

Figure 3.15
Select Faces by Sides enables you to select all faces in a mesh using the number of sides as your criterion.
Source: Blender.

4. To find all *n*-gons in a mesh, set a value of 4 for the Number of Vertices setting in the Select Faces by Sides group, which now appears in the toolbox on the left.

5. For the Type setting, choose Greater Than, because *n*-gons are faces with more than four vertices.

6. Deselect the Extend checkbox. This combination of settings will select all faces in the mesh with more than four vertices, and hence all *n*-gons (if there are any). You can use the Blender info panel in the upper-right to see the total number of selected faces in case it's not immediately obvious whether faces are selected or not. (See Figure 3.16.)

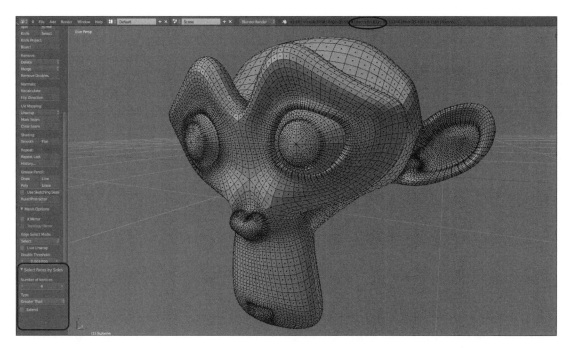

Figure 3.16
Selecting all *n*-gons in a mesh.
Source: Blender.

Undoing and Removing Doubles

Take care when using the Undo command in Blender. Some operations (in some versions), such as Extrude, are really multistep operations even though you perform them with just one click. For this reason they actually require multiple undoes to be fully undone. This is, perhaps, unintuitive. Because of this (and other reasons, too), your mesh can end up with doubled-up vertices (known as "doubles"). These are vertices that sneak their way into your meshes during the modeling phase and that exist in exactly the same spot as other vertices. In other words, you end up with at least two vertices on top of each other, making the duplication difficult to spot in the viewport. The best way to remove doubles is, after modeling, to select all vertices in the mesh (press Ctrl+A) and then select Mesh > Vertices > Remove Doubles. See Figure 3.17.

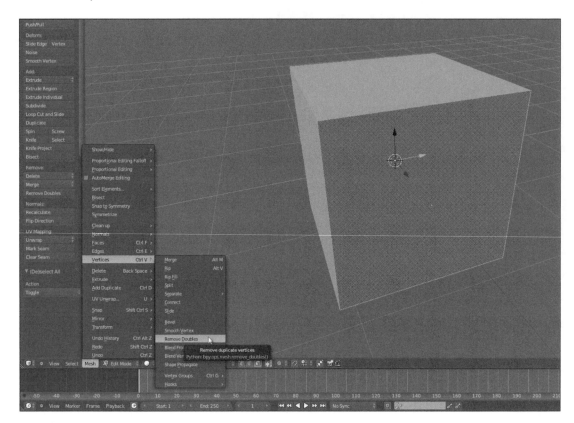

Figure 3.17
Choose Remove Doubles to eliminate problematic vertex duplicates from the mesh.
Source: Blender.

Mirroring

When modeling interior pieces for environment sets such as corridors and tunnels or other symmetrical pieces, it's often convenient to model only one side or half of the model (see Figure 3.18) and to create the remaining side by way of duplication. This practice is known as "mirroring."

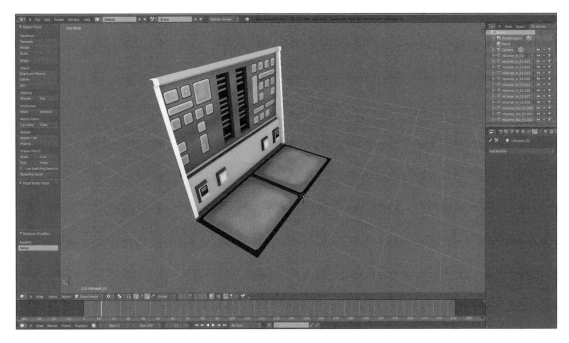

Figure 3.18
Modeling half a tunnel section in preparation for mirroring.
Source: Blender.

After you model a half section, you can generate a symmetrical duplicate using the Mirror modifier. This modifier is applied to a model via the Modifiers tab. Simply click in the Modifiers list and add the Mirror modifier (see Figure 3.19). The Mirror modifier can be a great time saver, but don't overuse it. It's easy for the eye to spot tiling, repetition, and patterns throughout an environment.

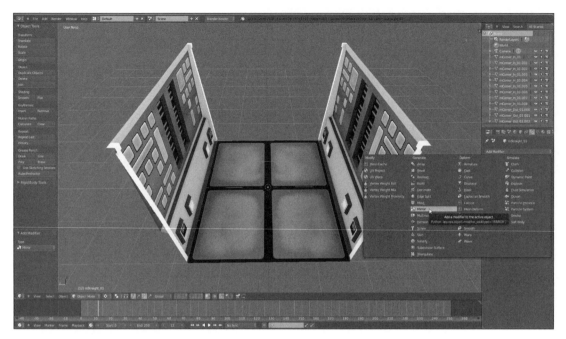

Figure 3.19
Applying the Mirror modifier to generate the opposite half of a corridor section.
Source: Blender.

Note

The Mirror modifier automatically centers the plane or axis of mirroring at an object's pivot or origin. Take care, then, to set an object's pivot before applying the Mirror modifier to ensure the mirror is as you'd expect. Refer to the discussion of setting an object's pivot in the section "Getting Started with Modular Environments in Blender" earlier in this chapter.

Remember: The mirrored geometry is procedurally generated and remains separate from the original mesh until the modifier is applied. In other words, the mirrored geometry will become an integral and baked part of the mesh only after you click the modifier's Apply button.

Using Vertex Groups

When creating meshes in 3D software, it's almost inevitable that you'll come into contact with lots of vertices, edges, and faces, which are the raw materials of modeling. In particular, vertices are numerous. You'll regularly select vertices to mark out regions and perform modeling operations. However, identifying and selecting all the vertices you'll need takes time, making vertex selection tedious. It can be particularly frustrating if you end up having to select the same vertices multiple times. (Maybe you'll need to run one operation on some vertices and then run a different one later on the same vertices.)

Fortunately, Blender offers a convenient feature, known as vertex groups, that lets you save your vertex selections. You can then reselect that group at any time, with the click of a button. To access vertex groups, click the Data tab in the Properties panel for an object. See Figure 3.20.

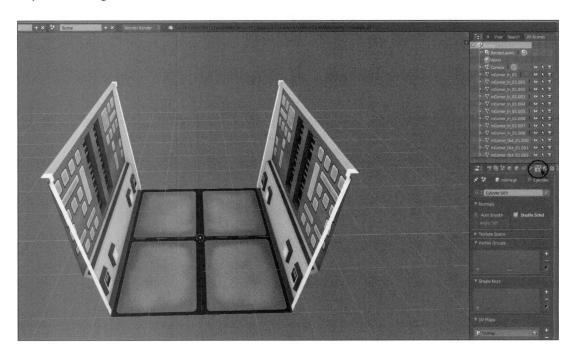

Figure 3.20
You can access vertex groups via the Data tab in an object's Properties panel.
Source: Blender.

To create a new vertex group, click the plus (+) icon in the Vertex Groups list. Assign the group a unique and meaningful name, describing the selection to be recorded. (See Figure 3.21.)

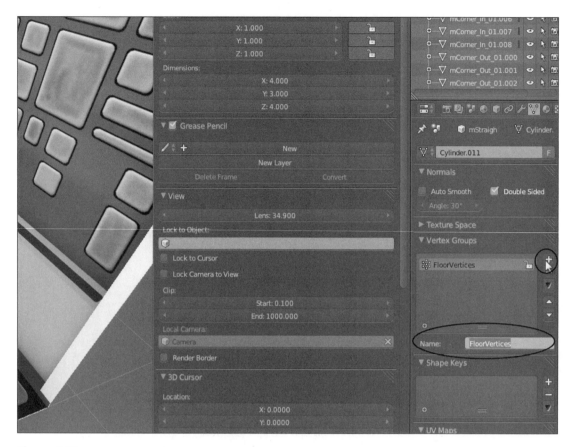

Figure 3.21
Creating a vertex group to contain a vertex selection.
Source: Blender.

After a vertex group is created and selected for the mesh, you can assign a vertex selection
to it by simply selecting the vertices in the mesh and then clicking the Assign button in
the Vertex Groups area of the Data tab in the Properties panel (see Figure 3.22.) You
can then reselect the vertices by clicking the Select button (also shown in Figure 3.22).

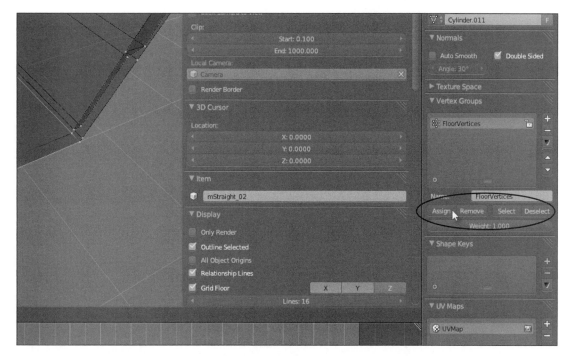

Figure 3.22
Assigning and selecting vertices in a vertex group.
Source: Blender.

Mesh Display Settings

Maybe it's me, but I find it difficult to see and work with vertices in Blender—at least when vertices are shown at their default size and settings. Maybe you feel the same. To work more effectively, I typically change how vertices are rendered in the viewport. Here's how:

1. Select File > User Preferences (see Figure 3.23) to open the Blender User Preferences dialog box.

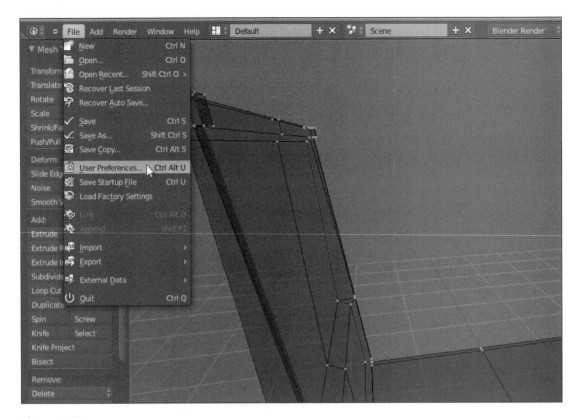

Figure 3.23
Accessing the Blender User Preferences dialog box.
Source: Blender.

2. In the Blender User Preferences dialog box, click the Themes tab.

3. Choose 3D View in the list on the left to show interface options for viewport elements.

4. Choose brighter colors for both the Vertex and Vertex Select options to control the color of vertices when deselected and selected, respectively.

5. Increase the vertex size, perhaps to as high as 8 or 9, to render the mesh vertices larger and bolder in the viewport. For me, these settings make it much easier to see and select vertices while modeling. See Figure 3.24.

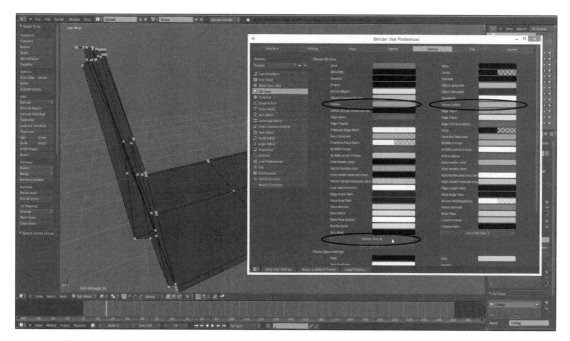

Figure 3.24
Setting the vertex color and size in the Blender User Preferences dialog box.
Source: Blender.

UV Mapping and Texture Creation

Modeling environment pieces in terms of vertices, edges, and polygons is only the first step toward making a complete environment set. The next is to UV map and texture paint the models. This process is achieved in Blender, rather than in Unity, with the help of additional software such as GIMP and Photoshop for painting textures. However, Unity nonetheless comes into the picture. Specifically, it places critical workflow restrictions on you that you'd do well to keep in mind. These issues, and more, are considered in the following sections.

Marking Seams, UV Mapping, and Modeling

UV mapping is, in essence, the process of unravelling the 3D geometry of a model onto a flattened plane. The purpose is to create a two-way mapping relationship between the 3D model and a 2D image. When this relationship is achieved successfully, pixels in a 2D texture can be projected directly onto the surface of a 3D mesh to give its surface any appearance you like. The reverse is also true: Details painted onto a model in 3D can be projected down onto a 2D texture!

Before you can successfully unwrap a model, however, you need to insert splices or cuts into its geometry, marking edges where the model can be opened out and flattened down into 2D. These cuts are called "seams." You should insert them judiciously, because Unity prefers as few seams as possible for performance reasons. That being said, a model will need to have some seams somewhere, because a model with no seams cannot be unwrapped sensibly at all. For every vertex on a seam, Unity will insert duplicate vertices; thus, seams indirectly increase the vertex count of the model.

To insert a seam into a mesh, select the edges that should form the seam and click Mark Seam in the toolbox or choose Mesh > Edges > Mark Seam. (See Figure 3.25.)

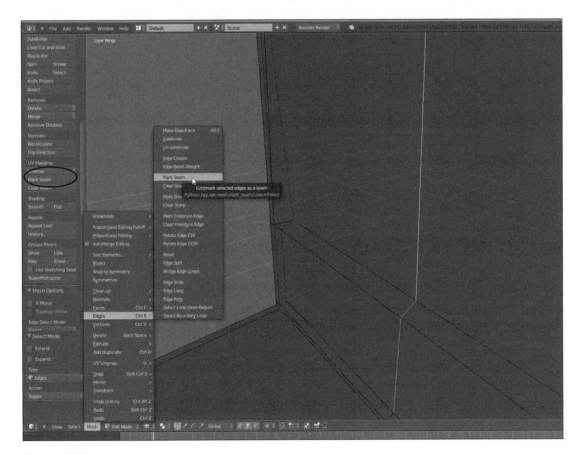

Figure 3.25
Seams should be marked on a mesh before unwrapping. Seams can be inserted via the toolbox or via the Mesh > Edges > Mark Seam menu command.
Source: Blender.

When an edge in a mesh is marked as a seam in Blender, it's highlighted in red in the viewport (unless you change the default color). If you find that seams are not highlighted on your system, this could be because the Seam Display feature is disabled. To enable this feature, open the N panel and select the Seams checkbox in the Mesh Display group. (See Figure 3.26.)

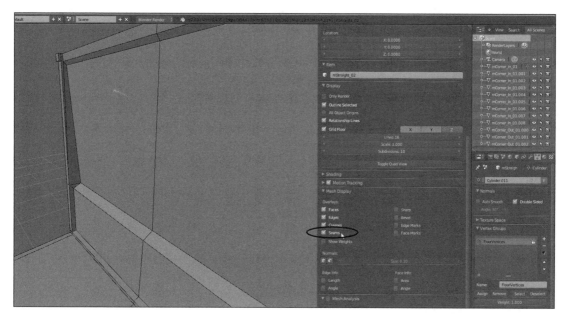

Figure 3.26
Enabling seam display in the N panel to see mesh seams in the viewport.
Source: Blender.

After seams are marked, you can unwrap a mesh using the Unwrap command. Details on unwrapping meshes can be found in the Blender online documentation: http://wiki. blender.org/index.php/Doc:2.6/Manual/Textures/Mapping/UV/Unwrapping.

With seam marking, it's tempting—although one way to waste a lot of time—to think of it as something that comes *after* the modeling phase. Instead, think of seam marking and modeling as simultaneous processes—you mark seams as you model. The reason? Modeling often involves duplication, such as mirroring. If you mark seams as you model rather than afterward, then all your seams will be included in the duplication, saving you from having to spend time after modeling to mark additional seams.

Atlas Textures and UV Overlapping

In Unity, each unique material in a scene carries a render cost or performance burden. Materials increase draw calls. Consequently, more materials lead to more draw calls. The advice, then, for performance, is to reduce draw calls as far as possible. You can help achieve this by reducing the number of materials you use.

Note

_____

In Unity, a *draw call* is an internal cycle or process that Unity performs automatically to display 3D graphics on the monitor. On each frame (and there may be even 100 frames per second), Unity may need to perform one or more draw calls to render the scene correctly. Draw calls place demands on the CPU and GPU. The fewer draw calls that Unity makes to render a scene, the better performance will be. Factors such as the number of materials in the scene will directly affect the number of draw calls performed. For each unique material, there will be at least one draw call.

_____

One way to do this is to reduce the number of diffuse textures you use. From the very outset of UV mapping your environment meshes, think about sharing just one larger texture for all pieces in the set. This kind of texture, onto which multiple meshes map, is known as an "atlas texture."

To UV map for this kind of texture, you'll need to unwrap all meshes in the environment set into the same UV space. To do this in Blender, first join all the meshes into a single mesh. Next, UV map the meshes. Finally, after they've been mapped, separate them back to independent meshes for exporting to Unity.

You can join meshes using the Join command. Just select all meshes to be joined and choose Object > Join, click the Join button in the toolbox, or press Ctrl+J. (See Figure 3.27.)

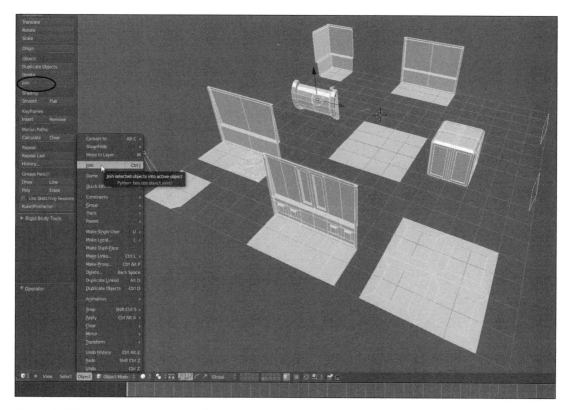

Figure 3.27
Join multiple meshes for unwrapping into single UV space.
Source: Blender.

When the meshes are joined into one, they can be unwrapped as any regular mesh. One tip to keep in mind concerns UV overlapping. If you have two or more areas in the mesh that are structurally similar in terms of topology, and that must look the same in terms of texture—for example, two wall sections or two doorways—consider overlapping their UVs to recycle texture space. That is, consider layering their UVs on top of each other. That means both mesh areas will share the same part of the texture. If this technique is applied for each case where sharing is permissible, the aggregate saving in texture space can be considerable. In fact, there are even technical demos available in which artists have so cleverly recycled texture space through UV overlapping, entire environments map onto just one $1,024 \times 1,024$ texture. Figure 3.28 shows a UV arrangement for the sample modular environment set, provided on the book's companion website (in Chapter03/AssetsToImport). This folder includes a range of meshes for different environment pieces (such as corner pieces, straight sections, T junctions, etc.), which can be fitted together like building blocks, arranged into a complete environment. This set includes a texture, too. Some space has been left in the texture for other game elements, should you add them.

Note

To see the detail and polish that can be achieved using small textures in combination with UV overlapping, consider the sci-fi demo for the UDK here: http://vimeo.com/35470093.

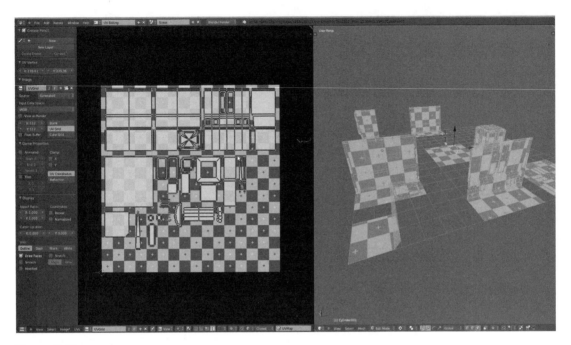

Figure 3.28
Use UV overlapping to recycle texture space.
Source: Blender.

Establishing Texel Density

Textures, being rectangular images, have a width and height measured in pixels. When a UV map is overlaid onto a texture, each UV island or space encompasses an area of pixels inside the texture, mapping the texture to the mesh. The number of texture pixels assigned to each UV island is known as its "texel density."

If you use a checker map (UV grid map) in the UV Editor, you'll get a good proportional indication of the texel density for a mesh based on the sizes of each square in the UV grid. In short, you should UV map your environment pieces so that:

- All squares in the checker map appear square (equal in width and height) when projected on the mesh.
- All squares are the same size across all meshes in the environment set.

Doing this ensures the best texture quality for your meshes because each mesh receives pixels proportional to its physical size in the scene.

Let's consider this further. To generate a UV grid texture map in Blender, do the following:

1. In the UV Editor, choose Image > New Image.

2. Change the Image Generation settings as shown in Figure 3.29. Make sure this texture, once generated, is mapped and applied to your meshes in the viewport. It's important to see the checker map on your models.

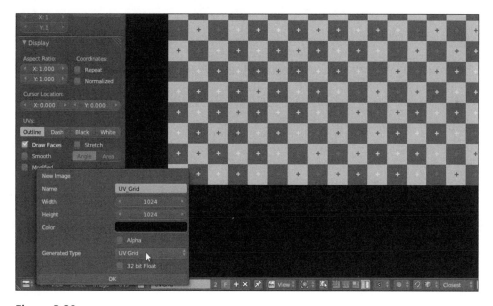

Figure 3.29
Generating a UV grid map to apply a checker map to your models to diagnose texturing and mapping problems.

Source: Blender.

The UV grid, when shown on your models, gives a clear indication of how pixels in the texture project onto the mesh. Keep your eye on two details:

■ If the squares of the grid aren't really squares, but look like long rectangles or skewed parallelograms, then you'll need to adjust the mesh UVs until they look like squares, equal in width and height. If you don't, your texture will look distorted in those regions.

■ Make sure the squares on one model are the same size as the squares on another. If they are not, it means that each model is not receiving pixels proportionally. For example, it could mean that a small object is consuming a lot of texture space, while a large object is consuming very little. This would result in small objects being more detailed than required and larger objects appearing low-res and blurred. Establishing consistency between square sizes in this way is the process of establishing a consistent texel density. See Figure 3.30.

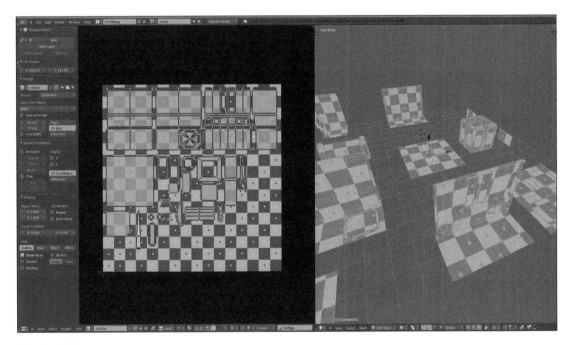

Figure 3.30
Adjust UVs to establish a consistent texel density.
Source: Blender.

IMPORTING AND CONFIGURING ENVIRONMENTS IN UNITY

The modular environment set refers to all the pieces, or modules, taken together. By arranging, duplicating, and combining instances of these pieces into different formations inside a Unity scene, you produce different environments for your game. Typically, each environment piece is exported from Blender as a separate and independent FBX mesh file. The FBX export process was discussed in detail in Chapter 2. See Figure 3.31, where I've imported a collection of environment pieces into a project.

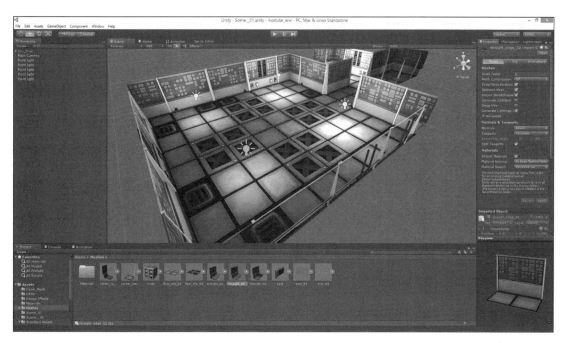

Figure 3.31
Importing environment modules as separate FBX files into a Unity project.
Source: Unity Technologies.

Once imported, consider mesh configuration carefully. Specifically, consider lightmapping and collision detection. If your meshes have only one UV channel or set, then Unity automatically uses this channel for both standard textures, such as diffuse and specular textures, as well as lightmap textures. If this applies to you, leaving these default lightmap settings as is will probably cause your meshes to look like a mess after lightmapping. In response, you can enable the Generate Lightmap UVs checkbox in the mesh properties in Unity. (See Figure 3.32.) This will likely improve the look of your lightmaps, but you may still end up with some issues, especially on spherical or organic-like surfaces.

In these cases, you may need to return to Blender and generate a second UV channel for lightmap UVs.

Figure 3.32
Generating lightmap UVs for a mesh.
Source: Unity Technologies.

In Unity, an easy way to generate collision data for your imported mesh is simply to select the Generate Colliders checkbox in the Object Inspector's mesh properties (also shown in Figure 3.32). When this setting is enabled, every instance of the mesh in the scene will feature a mesh collider component. These components contain collision information that will prevent solid objects, such as the player, from passing through it.

However, the Generate Colliders option, and mesh collider components in general, are computationally expensive—meaning that if your scene features lots of meshes and mesh colliders, your game could underperform. And for mobile devices, it might not perform at all. Consequently, you should use mesh colliders sparingly—only when you need a very high degree of accuracy in collisions. In most situations, an approximation will suffice. In such cases, you can leave the Generate Colliders checkbox unchecked and can use box and sphere collider components to manually approximate the level geometry. The box and sphere collider components are much cheaper than mesh colliders. See Figure 3.33.

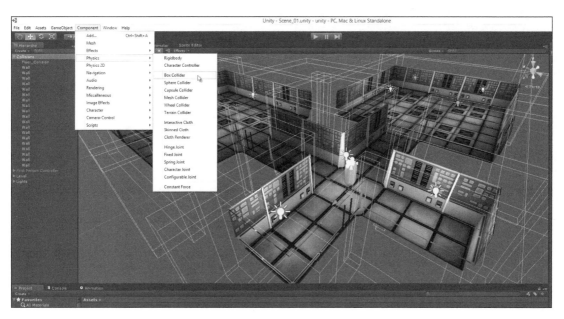

Figure 3.33
Collision data can be added to meshes manually through primitive collider components.
Source: Unity Technologies.

Using Prefabs

The modular pieces of an environment set are meant to be basic and reusable—basic in the sense that complexity and intricacy arise when you combine them with other pieces, and reusable in the sense that no single piece need be used on its own in just one case. But even though environment pieces are reusable, you'll often find (once you start making scenes in Unity) that a level contains many repeated combinations of pieces. There are many configurations, such as corner sections, hallways, tunnels, generic rooms, that—although made from many modular pieces combined—repeat themselves in that particular arrangement throughout the level. Some environments, for example, have multiple rooms based on the same mold or template or multiple corridors that flow in the same way. There is, among these, a higher level of tiling and modularity. You could, of course, just keep reusing and recombining your modular pieces manually every time you needed one of these repeated arrangements in a scene, but often it's easier to use prefabs. With prefabs, Unity lets you group multiple mesh instances to reuse again and again, like a stamp, as though they were all really just one mesh. See Figure 3.34.

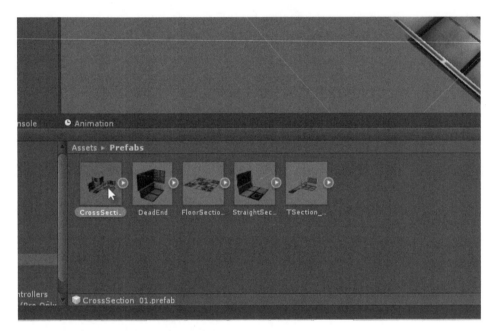

Figure 3.34
A collection of prefabs for reusing modules in common arrangements.
Source: Unity Technologies.

To create a prefab in Unity, simply right-click in an empty area inside the Project panel and choose Create > Prefab from the menu that appears (see Figure 3.35). Then assign the prefab a meaningful name describing the mesh configuration you intend to contain.

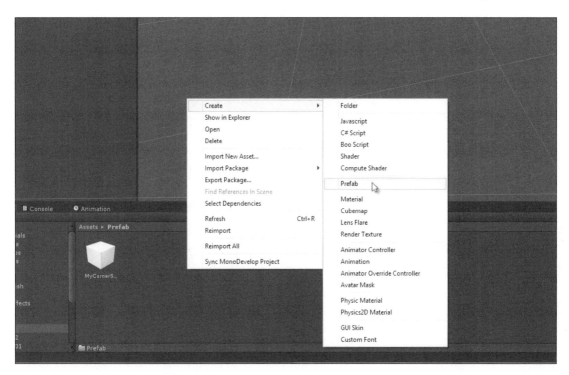

Figure 3.35
Creating prefabs for reusing environment pieces.
Source: Unity Technologies.

After the prefab is created, identify all meshes in the scene that should be included in the prefab. Pick one of those meshes to be a parent game object; then use the Scene Hierarchy to make the remaining meshes children of that parent. When the parent-child hierarchy is established between the objects, select the parent object, and drag and drop it onto the prefab in the Project panel to include all meshes (both parent and children) in the prefab. See Figure 3.36.

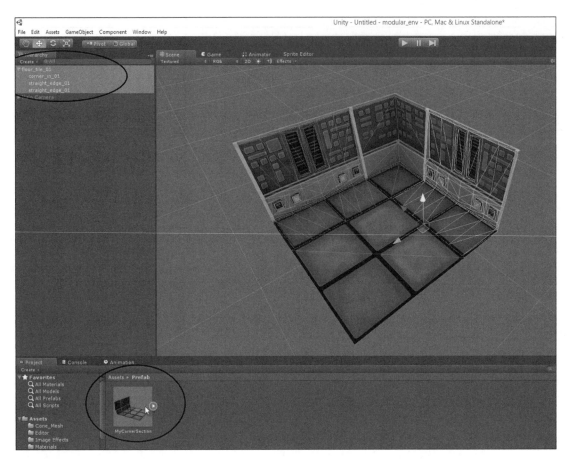

Figure 3.36
Creating prefabs from mesh configurations.
Source: Unity Technologies.

STATIC BATCHING

Most pieces of your environment, such as walls, floors, and ceilings, will probably never move or change during gameplay. They'll always just "be there" as a prop. These kinds of assets and game objects are called "static" because their nature is unchanging. This stands in contrast to dynamic assets, like the player character, enemies, and adjustable props, which do change and move over time.

If you have environment assets that are static and will never move, then you should mark them as such using the Unity Editor. This allows Unity to optimize its renderer using static batching, which can vastly improve the run-time performance of your game across all platforms, both desktop and mobile. To do this, select all objects in the scene that should be static and then select the Static checkbox in the Object Inspector (see Figure 3.37).

Figure 3.37
Activate static batching for all non-moving objects.
Source: Unity Technologies.

SUMMARY

This chapter focused on environment modeling and modularity, examining workflows between Blender and Unity specifically. On the surface, modular environment creation can seem a trivial thing. It looks like it's just about creating building blocks. And it is, in a general sense. But, that process leaves a lot unsaid and conceals a lot of work beneath. In creating modular environment pieces, you must exercise great judgment in sizing and proportioning, ensuring all pieces will match up when arranged together in a Unity scene. In addition, there are issues of UV mapping and prefab workflows to consider. In short, take your time when creating modular environments, and don't expect results to come from rushing. Plan your pieces, decide on sizes and scales, and plan your UV mapping to save time in the long term.

This chapter comes with some companion files: a complete modular environment set for you to explore. These can be found on the book's companion website (visit www .cengageptr.com/downloads and search for this book), in the Chapter03 folder. If you're keen on making modular environments and want more information, I recommend taking a look at my 3DMotive video tutorial, "Making Unity Modular Environments in Blender," which is available online at www.3dmotive.com.

CHAPTER 4

TERRAIN

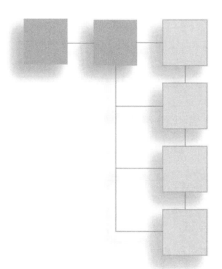

The art of simplicity is a puzzle of complexity.

—Douglas Horton

By the end of this chapter, you should:

- Understand the benefits and drawbacks of the Unity terrain system
- Be aware of terrain alternatives offered by Blender
- Be able to sculpt and texture-paint terrain in Blender
- Understand how to use the Blender sculpting tools
- Be able to create road geometry that conforms to the terrain

Nearly every game featuring exterior environments, such as forests, deserts, plains, mountains, streets, and other landscapes, makes use of terrain—that is, terrain in the technical meaning as opposed to the common-sense meaning. In this sense, *terrain* refers to a large and typically densely tessellated plane-like mesh used to represent the ground, or *terra firma*, of a level.

There are many ways to create terrain meshes like this. Unity offers an easy-to-use and powerful terrain system right from the Unity Editor, which is discussed in a summary fashion in the next section. However, this system has a number of significant limitations, which often leads developers to seek alternative solutions for terrain. One of those solutions is to manually build the terrain in a 3D modeling application. This approach is considered in depth in this chapter using Blender.

CREATING TERRAIN IN UNITY

The Unity Editor ships with an extensive range of terrain tools, targeted at sculpting and painting a large ground mesh to act as the base, floor, or landscape for a scene. These tools and their usage will be considered here in brief, along with some of their limitations as well as general recommendations. The complete documentation on the Unity terrain system can be found online on the official Unity website: http://docs.unity3d.com/ Documentation/Manual/Terrains.html. Figure 4.1 shows the BootCamp scene with a terrain made from the Unity terrain system.

Figure 4.1
Terrain generated for Unity-made BootCamp project. You can download this terrain for free from the Unity Asset Store.
Source: Unity Technologies.

Let's explore a quick and general workflow for using the built-in Unity terrain tools to generate a simple landscape. The instructions here apply to Unity version 4.3; earlier versions used a different workflow. Simply choose GameObject > Create Other > Terrain. Create a new terrain object in the scene, as shown in Figure 4.2. This generates a default terrain mesh at the scene origin.

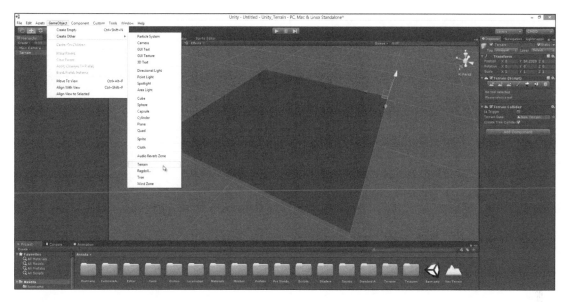

Figure 4.2
Generating a terrain in Unity.

Source: Unity Technologies.

Note

If you are interested in learning how to generate terrain in earlier versions of Unity, see the video course *A Complete Beginner's Guide to Unity 3.5* by Alan Thorn, available at www.3dmotive.com.

Terrain Settings

Before sculpting mountains, chasms, riverbanks, and other details into your terrain mesh, you must configure its settings. You access the terrain settings from the Object Inspector when the terrain is selected. These settings enable you to specify the terrain size, surface area, and general topology.

The default width and length for a terrain is $2,000 \times 2,000$ world units, effectively giving you a surface area of 4,000,000 square meters! Often, you won't need a terrain as large as this; set the terrain to the smallest size necessary. For this sample project, I'll set it to a size of 512×512 world units, and leave all other settings at their defaults. See Figure 4.3.

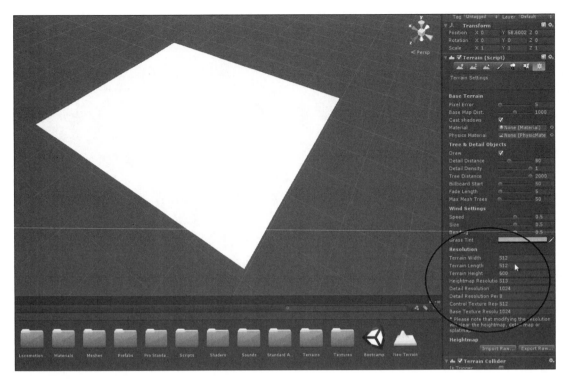

Figure 4.3
Configure terrain size and resolution to control its topology in preparation for sculpting.
Source: Unity Technologies.

Note

As shown in Figure 4.3, when creating terrains, I like to add a directional light to the scene. This will help bring out the forms and shapes when you begin sculpting. This is not an essential step, but useful.

The Heightmap Resolution setting is of special importance. It defines the pixel dimensions of a square texture, which is used under the hood by Unity to deform and sculpt the terrain into shape. The pixels of the square texture are mapped onto the terrain. Whiter pixel values in the texture elevate corresponding areas on the terrain, while darker values depress corresponding areas on the terrain. The higher the Heightmap Resolution value, the more detail and intricacy can be fitted into the texture. This comes with a greater memory and performance footprint, however. So, again, the principles of moderation and balance apply: Use the lowest value appropriate for your project.

Sculpting Terrain

By using the terrain brush tools, you can interactively sculpt the terrain mesh in the viewport in real time. Painting actually works in conjunction with the internal terrain heightmap, discussed in the previous section. That is, painting onto the terrain actually paints pixels onto the heightmap, which in turn deforms the terrain mesh.

When the terrain is selected in the scene, you can access the brush tools via the Brushes panel in the Object Inspector, as shown in Figure 4.4. When a brush is active, simply click the terrain to paint elevations or Ctrl-click to paint depressions. Be sure to use the Brush Size and Opacity settings to adjust the radius of the brush and its strength, respectively. In Figure 4.4, I've used a basic round brush to paint some mountains. You can also smooth out any roughness to the terrain by using the smooth brush.

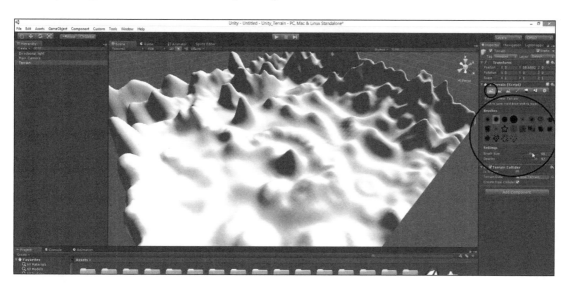

Figure 4.4
Painting terrain elevation using brushes.

Source: Unity Technologies.

Note

You can find more information about sculpting terrain on my YouTube channel: www.youtube.com/watch?v=IhhGWK5VYUs.

Texture-Painting Terrain

After you've sculpted the form of your terrain using brushes and the heightmap, it's time to texture-paint it with terrain textures. That way, the model will look like it's made from real-world materials such as dirt, grass, rock, water, and more. Texture-painting is similar to sculpting the terrain in that you use a brush to do it.

Of course, you would typically create terrain textures for your own games, but Unity does provide some pre-made textures that you can play around with when testing the terrain tools. These are provided in the terrain assets package, which you can import into a project by selecting Assets > Import Package > Terrain Assets. (See Figure 4.5.)

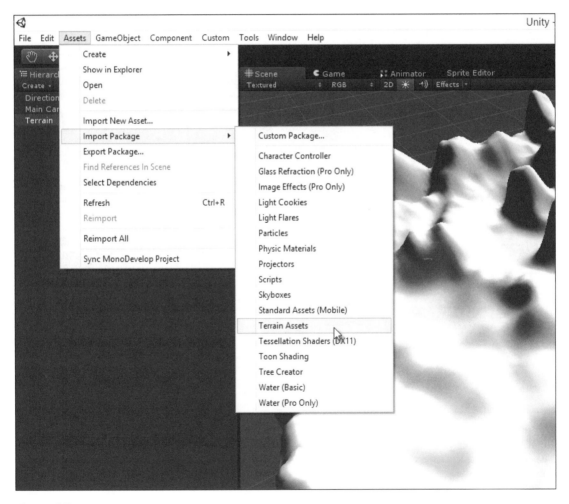

Figure 4.5
Importing the pre-made terrain assets package, which includes textures for quickly getting started on texture-painting terrains.
Source: Unity Technologies.

Before you can texture-paint a terrain, you'll need to build up a palette of textures. Follow these steps:

1. Select the terrain in the scene.

2. Click the Texture Paint tab in the Object Inspector (see Figure 4.6).

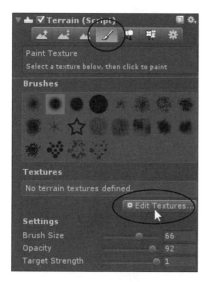

Figure 4.6
Adding textures to the palette for texture-painting.
Source: Unity Technologies.

3. Click the Edit Textures button and choose Add Texture from the menu that appears.

4. The Edit Terrain Texture dialog box opens. Here, you select a texture (and normal map, if required) to add to the palette, set the size, and click Apply. Note that if this is the first texture you're adding to your palette, it will automatically be applied to the terrain mesh as its base, or default, texture. Here, I've chosen a grass texture and set the X and Y size to 100 units (see Figure 4.7). The size here refers to the physical size in world units at which the texture will be tiled across the terrain. Larger values result in less tiling, because the size of each tile is larger.

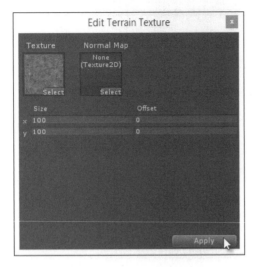

Figure 4.7
Configuring textures in the palette.
Source: Unity Technologies.

5. The terrain is filled with the newly added texture. If you need to go back and adjust the texture and its tiling, simply select Edit Textures > Edit Texture in the Object Inspector (see Figure 4.8).

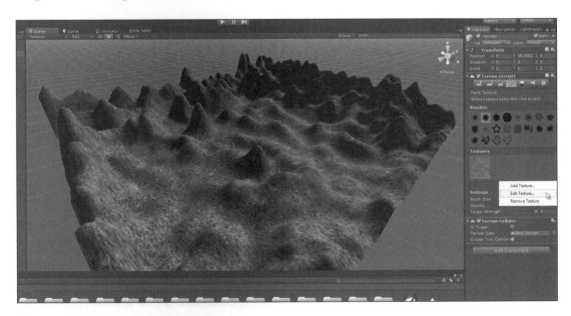

Figure 4.8
You can edit texture properties for the selected texture via the Edit Textures > Edit Texture menu.
Source: Unity Technologies.

6. After you add the base texture, you can add more textures to the palette by again choosing Edit Textures > Add Texture. These textures will not automatically be tiled on the terrain as the base texture was, however. Instead, you'll work with them as brushes, applying them to the terrain wherever they should appear on top of the base.

7. To apply a texture, select it from the palette in the Object Inspector; then choose a brush. Finally, using your mouse, "paint" the selected texture on the terrain. As shown in Figure 4.9, you can use this technique to create complex and intricate terrains.

Figure 4.9
Painting textures from the palette onto the terrain.
Source: Unity Technologies.

EVALUATING UNITY TERRAINS

The Unity Editor offers some truly impressive and versatile terrain tools. In previous sections, you've seen how, with just a few clicks and parameter tweaks, it's possible to generate a completely textured and customized terrain for your scene. But there are some significant drawbacks to using the terrain system, which has caused many developers to seek alternative solutions for their projects. These drawbacks include the following:

■ **Performance.** Traditionally, developers have avoided using Unity terrain objects for mobile projects, such as Android and iOS games. This has primarily been because the tessellation, face count, and general texture requirements for a terrain object made them performance prohibitive. With newer and faster mobile devices offering a greater range of technical possibilities, there have been some changes in this attitude in more recent years, but even so the Unity terrain objects are not always optimal. They often feature more vertices than required and consume more texture memory than needed. This might not prove troublesome on powerful desktop systems, consoles, or even high-end mobiles, but for a wide range of hardware, this cost can still bring down a game if it's not balanced with other optimizations. In short, performance benefits can be gained using a custom solution.

■ **Topology control.** The topology of a mesh, such as a terrain mesh, refers not only to its constituent vertices, edges, and faces, but to their specific arrangement and patterning. Unity terrains are procedurally generated, meaning that Unity builds them on the fly according to the terrain parameters you specify from the Object Inspector's Settings tab. These parameters were discussed earlier in this chapter, in the section "Terrain Settings," and include Width, Height, and Size, among others. However, outside of these parameters, there's practically no flexibility or control over how the terrain is generated or over how its faces are tessellated across the surface. The result almost always tends toward averaging: with an equal and evenly distributed amount of face tessellation and vertex density across the mesh. This can stand in the way of optimization because it's not uncommon to want some terrain areas with fewer faces and detail than others, as those regions will never be seen up close by the gamer. To achieve this kind of topological optimization, a custom solution is required that allows greater control over mesh faces and vertices.

■ **Heightmap limitations.** The elevation and depression of a Unity terrain is determined by a flat, pixel-based heightmap, which has interesting implications for a 3D object. Conceptually, the heightmap is positioned above the terrain and projected downward, where white pixels elevate the terrain and black pixels depress it. Although meaningful and intricate arrangements can be sculpted, this prohibits certain types of terrain formations. For example, you cannot have holes, caves, hollows, caverns, or any sheltered areas where there's empty space between terrain. This is a necessary limitation of using a 2D pixel-based heightmap to generate the terrain. It is possible, however, to overcome these limitations to an extent by an inventive use of separate and additional mesh objects or terrain objects. But for a more thorough solution, it's necessary to build a terrain mesh manually in a 3D modeling application.

Taken together, these three reasons offer solid grounds for considering alternative methods for terrain creation with Unity. While the native tools are serviceable, you may also want to manually model the terrain to get extra control and performance benefits. The following sections explore how Blender can help you in this regard.

BLENDER TERRAIN MODELING

Modeling a terrain in Blender begins with a tessellated plane object, to act as the terrain. In Blender, you can create a plane by choosing Add > Mesh > Plane (see Figure 4.10). The default plane consists of a single face.

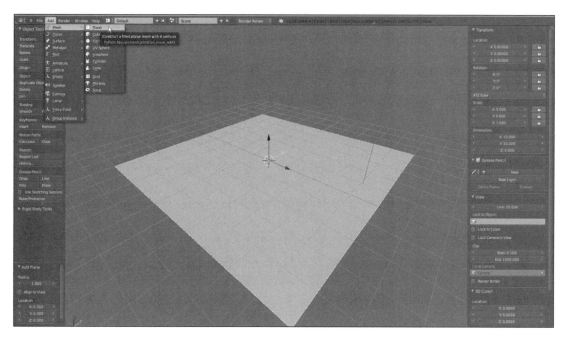

Figure 4.10
Creating a plane object from the Blender Add menu to act as a terrain. Remember to use the N-Panel to specify the width and length of the terrain (1 unit = 1 meter).
Source: Blender.

To add further refinement and tessellation to the plane, thereby increasing mesh detail, use the Subdivide command. Take care not to add more detail than you really need, but incline toward more rather than less. Detail can be reduced both manually and procedurally, as you'll see.

You can access the Subdivide command when the object is selected and in Edit mode. Here's how:

- Choose Mesh > Edges > Subdivide from the menu.

- Click Subdivide in the toolbox.

- If you're using Maya-style controls, Ctrl-right-click (Windows) or Command-right-click the mesh and choose Subdivide from the Specials menu that appears (see Figure 4.11).

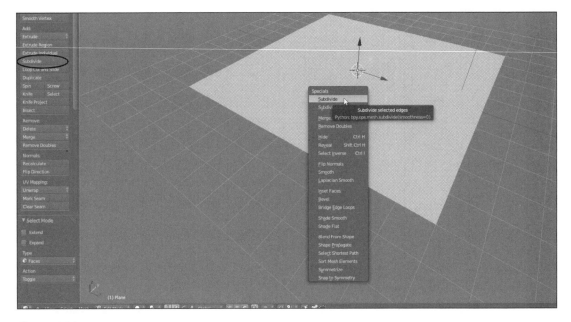

Figure 4.11
Subdividing the mesh for tessellation.
Source: Blender.

You'll probably need to repeat this operation multiple times on all faces to achieve the density you want.

Note

An alternative, non-destructive way to subdivide your mesh is to use the Multiresolution modifier, choosing a Simple Subdivision method. More information on the Multiresolution modifier can be found in the online Blender documentation: http://wiki.blender.org/index.php/Doc:2.6/Manual/Modifiers/Generate/Multiresolution.

Terrain modeling begins with a tessellated plane. From this point, there are three main modeling methods available to you—and none of them are right or wrong, *per se*. Their appropriateness depends not only on your working preferences, but on which method will get the job done best for your circumstances. These methods are as follows:

- The Proportional Editing method
- The displacement-texture method
- The sculpting method

The Proportional Editing Method

This method is so named because of its dependence on the Proportional Editing feature, sometimes known in other 3D modeling programs as Soft Selection. Here, you create mountainous elevations and chasm-like depressions by raising and lowering vertices in the mesh, respectively, allowing Proportional Editing to interpolate or smooth out the edits you make.

Let's try this, working on a flat, tessellated plane. Follow these steps:

1. Click the Proportional Editing toolbar button and choose Connected, as shown in Figure 4.12. This enables Proportional Editing in Connected mode. When activated in Connected mode, Proportional Editing ensures that transformations to selected vertices will cascade outward with declining intensity to affect surrounding vertices within a specified radius. This produces the effect or smoothness or fall-off.

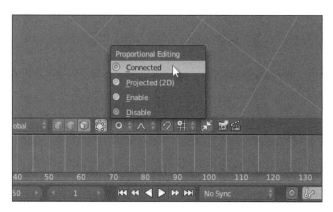

Figure 4.12
Activating Proportional Editing in Connected mode in preparation for terrain construction.
Source: Blender.

2. Before adjusting the vertices, set the fall-off curve. To do so, click the Fall-Off toolbar button and choose Smooth, as shown in Figure 4.13.

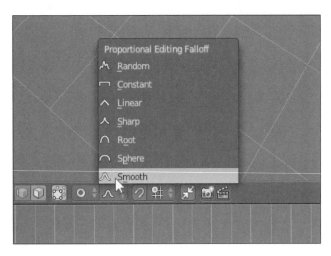

Figure 4.13
Setting the fall-off curve for proportional editing.
Source: Blender.

3. You're ready to start terrain modeling. Simply select a single vertex or multiple disconnected vertices and raise or lower the selected point(s) using the Transformation gizmo. Proportional Editing will take effect automatically to smooth out the transformation. (See Figure 4.14.)

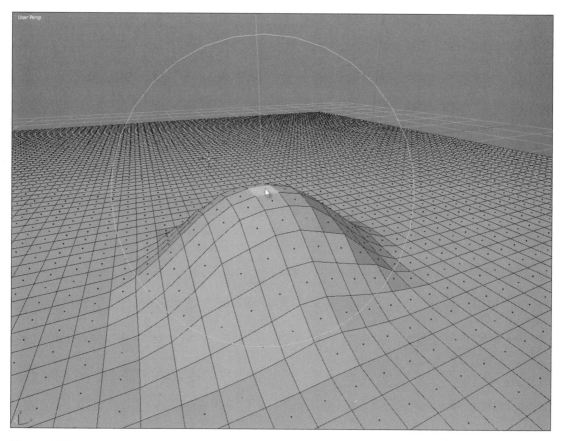

Figure 4.14
Using Proportional Editing to sculpt a terrain. See how in raising just one face, the surrounding faces raise also according to the fall-off radius. This produces a tapering-down effect, resulting in a smooth hill.
Source: Blender.

Note

When you hold down the mouse button over the Transformation gizmo, ready to move a vertex, a white circle appears around your cursor in the viewport. This represents the size or radius of the fall-off that will be applied. With the Maya-style controls active, you can scroll the middle mouse wheel to expand or contract the radius, controlling the extent and strength of proportional editing.

4. Repeat this procedure for all elevations and depressions. Also play around with the Fall-Off modes to create variation in the shapes produced. Try using the Sharp and Random modes. Figure 4.15 shows the terrain I created using this technique.

Figure 4.15
Terrain landscape created using Proportional Editing.
Source: Blender.

The Displacement-Texture Method

The displacement-texture method deforms a tessellated plane object according to the pixel values in a texture (heightmap) to auto-generate a sculpted terrain. This method is, more or less, the approach Unity takes toward terrain.

The heightmap is a grayscale image. Lighter pixels cause terrain vertices to elevate, while darker pixels lower the terrain. The key difference between applying this method in Blender rather than Unity relates to control and power over terrain sculpting after the displacement. In Blender, after displacement has occurred, you can still edit mesh vertices, edges, and faces, and continue to model using the regular modeling tools. Unity, in contrast, offers no direct modeling tools out of the box. There are add-ons, which do offer additional control, but none of these are part of the native package.

Let's try the displacement-texture method here. Follow these steps:

1. From the Textures panel, load a heightmap directly from an image file. Alternatively, generate one automatically. To do so, click the New button, as shown in Figure 4.16.

Figure 4.16
Generating a new texture.
Source: Blender.

2. Click the Type drop-down list and choose Voronoi or Clouds. I've selected Clouds. The Clouds texture is a random waveform generation of grayscale pixels that produces a cloud-like pattern. Using these pixels, you can produce a smooth but natural-looking terrain. Notice that a preview of the Cloud texture appears in the Preview window. This represents the heightmap to be applied to the mesh through displacement. (See Figure 4.17.)

Figure 4.17
Generating a Clouds texture for displacement.
Source: Blender.

3. Ensure the terrain mesh has been assigned UV mapping coordinates using the UV Editor and UV Unwrap. To do this, select all faces in the mesh and choose Mesh > UV Unwrap > Smart Project (see Figure 4.18), accepting the default parameters. You don't have to unwrap through Smart Project; you can use other methods available, as long as the terrain is flattened out across the complete 0-1 texture space.

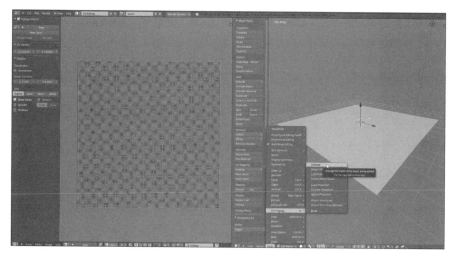

Figure 4.18
Mapping the terrain to texture space.
Source: Blender.

4. Having mapped the terrain, it's time to apply a Displace modifier. This establishes a connection between the terrain mesh and the heightmap texture. Open the Modifiers tab and assign a Displace modifier, as shown in Figure 4.19.

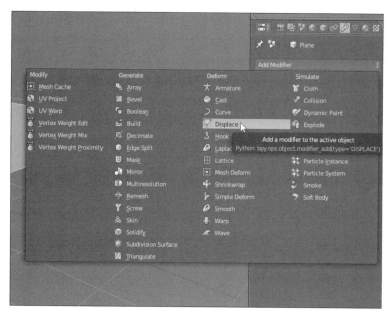

Figure 4.19
The Displace modifier is available from the Modifiers tab.
Source: Blender.

Note

You can find more information on the Displace modifier in the online Blender documentation: http://wiki
.blender.org/index.php/Doc:2.6/Manual/Modifiers/Deform/Displace.

5. Specify the heightmap texture using the Texture field. (See Figure 4.20.) This should automatically displace the terrain object in the viewport, allowing you to see the topological effects of the heightmap straight away. You can also use the Strength field to increase or reduce the intensity of displacement. Negative values (such as −1 or −2) invert the heightmap intensity, effectively treating white pixels as black and black as white. Remember, to bake the changes into the terrain mesh, you must apply the modifier.

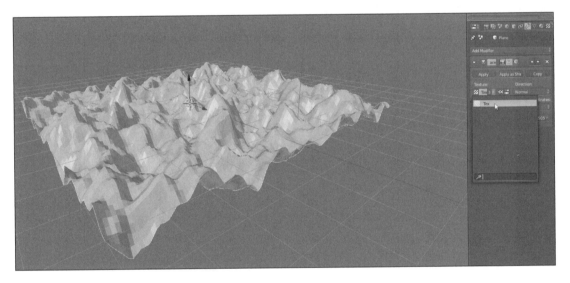

Figure 4.20
Deforming a terrain to a heightmap texture.
Source: Blender.

The Sculpting Method

The final method of terrain modeling considered here is the sculpting method. This method shares a lot with the workflow in Unity for terrains in that Blender allows you to interactively apply brushes to a terrain mesh, shaping and forming it, much like how a sculptor forms clay. The Blender brush system, however, is not heightmap based, meaning that details can be sculpted in true 3D.

This section takes a brief look at how terrains can be sculpted. There is much more to be said about the Blender Sculpt tools, however. Indeed, they would fill an entire book on their own! For those interested in examining the tools in more detail, I recommend the following article: http://wiki.blender.org/index.php/Doc:2.6/Manual/Modeling/Meshes/Editing/Sculpt_Mode.

To sculpt a terrain from a plane mesh, do the following:

1. Select the plane and activate Sculpt mode (see Figure 4.21). The sculpt tools appear in the left toolbox, including brushes and brush options. Remember: if you wish to use them, the sculpt tools work with pressure-sensitive inputs. These include graphics tablets like the Wacom Bamboo, Intuos tablets, or the Huion tablet.

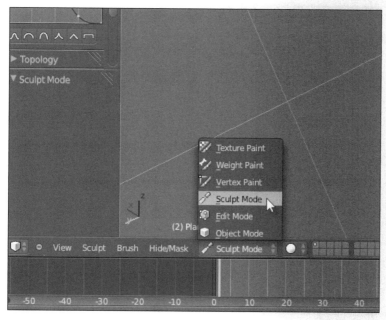

Figure 4.21
Activating Sculpt mode.
Source: Blender.

2. Choose a brush type. There are many brushes to choose from, but for terrains, the Brush and SculptDraw brushes are usually appropriate. To select a brush, click the brush thumbnail preview and choose a brush from the palette that appears (see Figure 4.22).

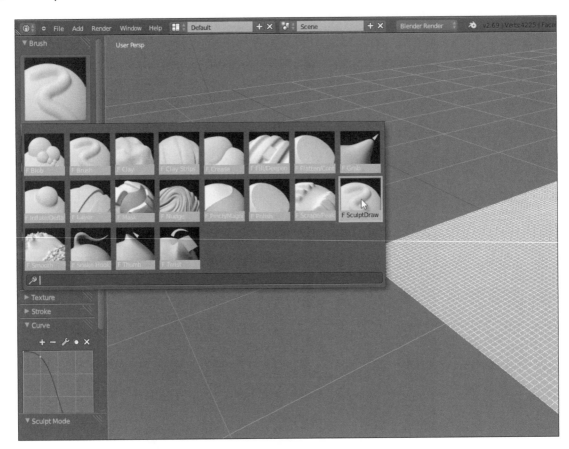

Figure 4.22
Picking a brush type.
Source: Blender.

3. Use the Radius control to adjust how wide an area the brush affects when applied, and the Strength control to adjust the intensity of the effect within the radius. (Look ahead to Figure 4.23.)

4. As shown in Figure 4.23, both the Brush and SculptDraw brushes have two modes: Add and Subtract. The default is Add, meaning that when the brush is active and you click your mouse on the terrain (or apply your pen to the tablet), the terrain will be pulled upward. The alternative mode is Subtract, which you can activate by pressing the Ctrl key (Windows) or Command key (Mac) as you click. This pushes the terrain down.

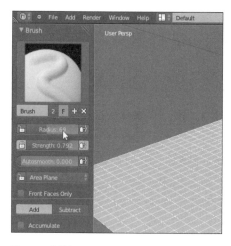

Figure 4.23
Setting the brush size and strength, and specifying whether the brush should use Add or Subtract mode.
Source: Blender.

5. You can hold down the Shift key while painting to quick-select and apply the Smooth brush, which you can also choose manually from the Brush palette. The Smooth brush identifies and averages out disparate faces using their normal vector to create a smoother blending between faces in the terrain. The Smooth brush is especially useful for low-poly terrains. Figure 4.24 shows the final sculpted terrain.

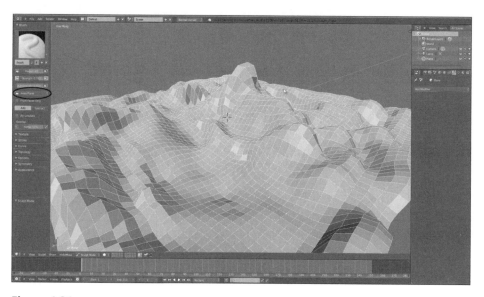

Figure 4.24
Terrain created through smoothing.
Source: Blender.

Note

While sculpting terrain, there may be times when you want to deform a mesh not in the X and Y axes, but in the Z axis to control terrain elevation (up and down). To limit sculpting to the Z axis, select Z from the Area Plane drop-down list, shown in Figure 4.24.

TERRAIN RESOLUTION

Sometimes, when modeling terrain, you'll end up with a mesh that's too detailed for your game. That is, the mesh's vertex, face, and edge count will be considerably more than is acceptable for real-time 3D games. The face count could run into hundreds of thousands or even millions of faces. In these cases, you'll want to reduce the face count for all or part of your mesh.

You *could* remove faces and edges manually using the Blender modeling tools, such as Cut, Delete, and Merge. But Blender offers the Decimate modifier to automate this process to some extent. It reduces the faces and triangles in a mesh procedurally. Like all modifiers, you apply the Decimate modifier from the Modifiers tab, shown in Figure 4.25.

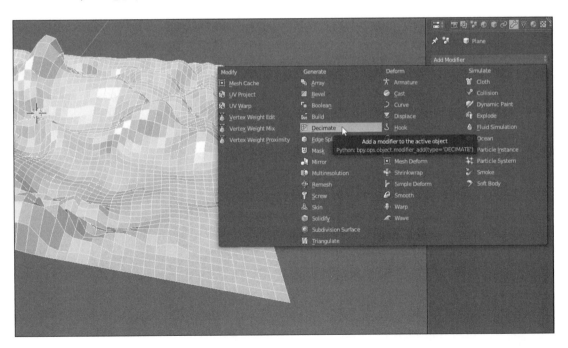

Figure 4.25
Applying Decimate to a mesh, reducing face count.
Source: Blender.

Caution

Reducing the faces of a mesh changes its topology and structure. For this reason, the degree of face reduction is directly proportional to mesh fidelity. The greater the face reduction, the more mesh quality is lost, and the further it degrades from the original.

The Decimate modifier works largely by a ratio parameter. The default ratio of 1 means the mesh remains unchanged and maintains all its original faces. A ratio 0.5 produces a mesh that is approximately 50% less detailed, with around half the original faces. The mesh in Figure 4.26 shows the result of decimating the mesh in Figure 4.25 to around 20% of its original detail.

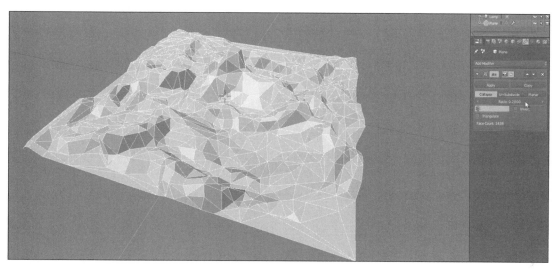

Figure 4.26
Reducing mesh detail with the Decimate modifier can result in optimized meshes and face counts, but it can also damage mesh quality. Use with caution!
Source: Blender.

TEXTURE-PAINTING TERRAIN

After you've modeled a terrain surface using any of the aforementioned techniques (or others), it's time to paint the terrain—that is, to apply a texture to the mesh, making it look like a real terrain made from rocks, grass, or snow, or a blend of types. There are many methods for doing this. One is to assemble the terrain as a regular texture in a separate image-editing application, like GIMP or Photoshop, and then apply it to the terrain through its UVs—in other words, the normal mesh-texture paradigm. But Blender offers some additional texture-painting features that make texturing more intuitive and fun for terrains. This section examines those features further.

UV Mapping Terrains

Before working with any texturing workflow, it's important for your mesh to have good UVs and mapping. For details on generating UVs, see the section "UV Mapping and Texture Creation" in Chapter 3, "Modular Environments and Static Meshes." In short, UVs define a two-way correspondence or map between a texture in 2D space and a mesh in 3D space. Using the Blender UV Image Editor, you can easily generate a UV grid texture that renders on the mesh as a checkerboard pattern, allowing you to easily assess the quality of the UV mapping in the viewport.

With good, solid, and predictable UV mapping, the UV grid should render on the mesh in squares (equal in width and height). Further, all squares should appear the same size across the model, reflecting a consistent texel density. Of course, UV mapping may not always appear in that ideal way when first generated; but by using the Blender UV Editor and its toolset, you can work and edit the UVs into the ideal setup for your model. For complex models, this process may take a lot of time. But the success of texturing cannot be greater than the quality of the initial UVs, so you want to make sure the UVs look good before the texture phase. Figure 4.27 shows a sculpted texture with a UV grid applied, ready for texturing.

Note

Texel density is an issue for textures in real-time games. Each texture has a pre-defined number of pixels in terms of width and height in the image file. But textures are not typically shown onscreen at their true size or in their original perspective. They're usually squashed or stretched (resampled) onto 3D meshes of varying sizes in game, like wrapping paper around a gift. Texel density describes this relationship. When a large texture is squashed into a smaller space, it produces a high texel density. When a smaller texture is stretched to fit in a larger space, it produces a low texel density.

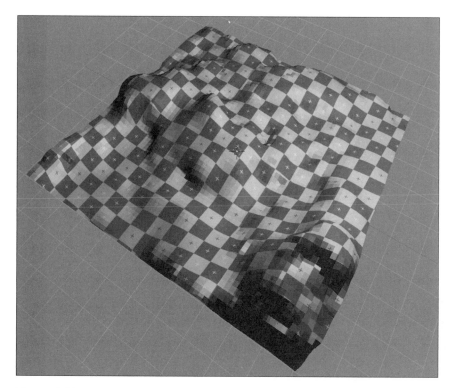

Figure 4.27
Making sure a terrain has appropriate UVs in preparation for texture-painting.
Source: Blender.

Generating a Texture for Painting

So you've made a terrain with suitable UVs and are ready for texture-painting. This process begins inside Blender, with the UV Image Editor. To texture-paint a model, a new and blank texture should first be created, which contains all pixels for painting. To begin, click the New button in the Image Editor's bottom toolbar (see Figure 4.28).

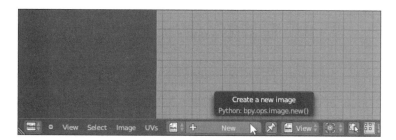

Figure 4.28
Creating a new texture using the UV Image Editor.
Source: Blender.

I've named the texture TerrainTexture, and have accepted the default pixel dimensions of 1,024 × 1,024. You can go larger for your terrains, depending on your needs. I usually change the background color from black to a neutral mid-tone (0.5, 0.5, 0.5). Finally, I disable the Alpha value because terrain textures typically have no alpha requirement. Note that these values are all preferences, not requirements. It's important always to be mindful of your needs and your project, so take time to choose appropriate settings. Keep in mind the texture-creation guidelines considered in the previous chapter. See Figure 4.29.

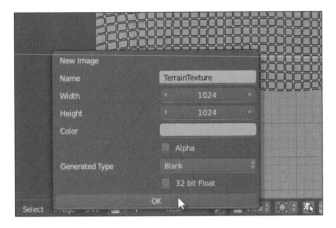

Figure 4.29
Specifying texture-creation settings.
Source: Blender.

Painting from the UV Image Editor

There are two main methods for texture-painting in Blender:

- Through the UV Editor interface
- Through the standard 3D viewport

These methods are not mutually exclusive; you can use both methods together. In this section, the first method is considered.

1. Activate Paint mode from the Image Editor's bottom toolbar. (See Figure 4.30.) This changes the options and tools available in the Image Editor's left toolbox (look ahead to Figure 4.31). Available tools include the brush and other related tools for texture-painting. These work much like the sculpting tools for terrains, except the texture-painting tools paint pixels onto the texture rather than deforming the mesh.

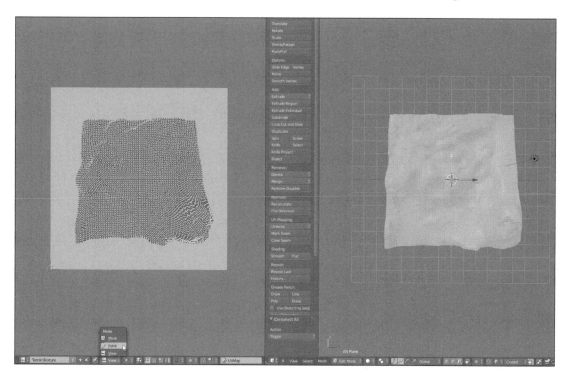

Figure 4.30
Enabling Paint mode.
Source: Blender.

2. Select a brush and choose a color, size, and intensity. Then paint! As with the sculpt
   tools, pressure sensitivity from pen tablets can be applied.

In terms of the interface layout, I prefer to have the UV Image Editor alongside the 3D
viewport so I can immediately see the results of my painting on the mesh. When working
this way, be sure the 3D view is shaded in Textured mode as opposed to Solid or Wire-
frame mode; otherwise, the texture will not be rendered on the mesh. (See Figure 4.31).

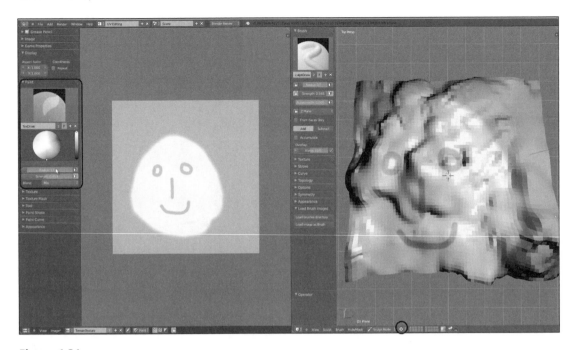

Figure 4.31
Texture-painting to a mesh from the Image Editor.
Source: Blender.

It's worth mentioning that all the texture-painting brush tools offer blending modes. That is, each and every brush stroke can have a separate blend mode applied. Available modes include the following:

- Add
- Subtract
- Multiply
- Lighten
- Darken
- Mix

You select these modes alongside the brush tools in the toolbox, before you apply the stroke to the texture. See Figure 4.32.

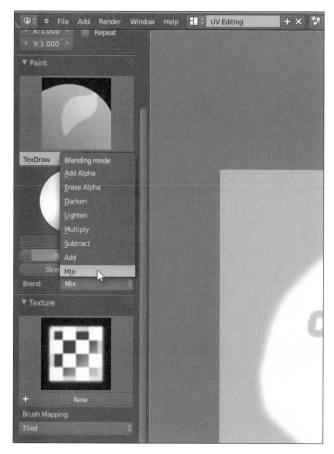

Figure 4.32
Texture-paint brushes can be applied with blend modes.
Source: Blender.

By default, Blender doesn't (at the time of this writing) offer a native layer system for texture-painting. The result is that all brush strokes are applied and baked into a single layer on the texture, meaning no single stroke or paint operation can be separated or independently adjusted once applied. There is, however, a workaround add-on, called Texture Paint Layer Manager, that offers layer functionality. You can easily install this add-on into Blender via the User Preferences dialog box. Follow these steps:

1. Choose File > User Preferences.
2. The Blender User Preferences dialog box opens. Click the Add-On tab.
3. In the Categories list, select Paint.

4. Click the Paint: Texture Paint Layer Manager checkbox to install the add-on. (See Figure 4.33.)

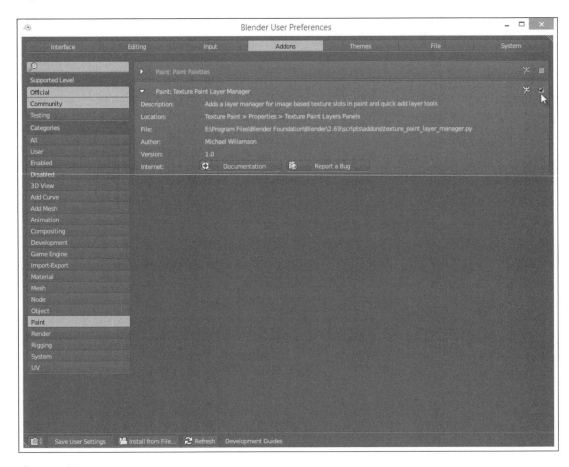

Figure 4.33
Enabling the Texture Paint Layer Manager add-on for handling texture layers.
Source: Blender.

The details of using this add-on are not covered here, because it's not a native part of Blender. If you wish to use the add-on, details on how to do so can be found here: http://wiki.blender.org/index.php/Extensions:2.6/Py/Scripts/3D_interaction/Texture_paint_layers.

Painting from the 3D View

The alternative way to texture-paint is directly from the 3D view, just as an artist working with a real-world sculpture or model might paint. Using this method, you apply pixel-based brush strokes to the model with either your mouse or a tablet. The strokes are projected from the 3D view onto the model and baked into the associated texture. Using this method, your viewing angle on the model is of critical importance; be sure to get a clear and comfortable viewing angle on the mesh before painting.

1. To activate texture-painting in the 3D view, select the Texture Paint mode from the Mode list in the bottom toolbar. See Figure 4.34.

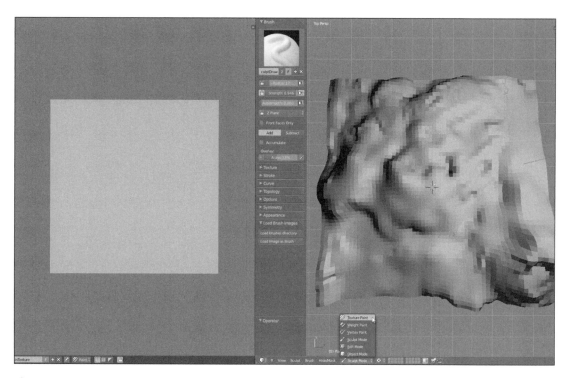

Figure 4.34
Activating Texture Paint mode in the 3D view.
Source: Blender.

2. When Texture Paint mode is activated, the left toolbox displays a range of brush options. These can be used in just the same way as texture-painting in the UV Editor. Select a brush, set a size and strength, and then paint! See Figure 4.35.

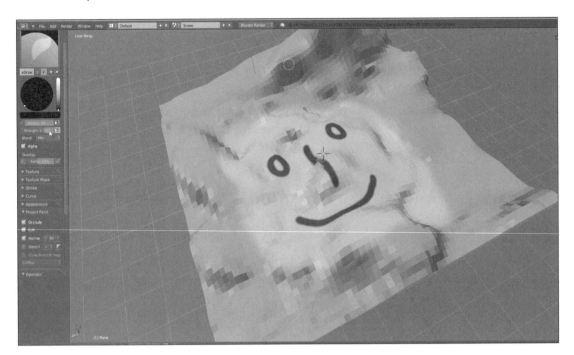

Figure 4.35
Painting directly from the 3D view.
Source: Blender.

When using this method, there are some issues related to projection that should be considered. For example, how should a face be painted when it falls within the radius of your brush but is facing away from you? Or how should a face be painted when it's within the brush radius and is facing you, but is occluded from view because it's behind something else nearer to the camera? These are questions that Blender has for you. The default behavior in both cases is not to paint on and affect such faces, but you can change this behavior using the Project Paint settings on the toolbar (see Figure 4.36). Deselecting the Occlude checkbox allows occluded faces (faces that are hidden from view because they are behind other faces nearer to the camera) to be painted. Deselecting the Cull checkbox allows faces pointing away from the camera to be painted. And deselecting the Normal checkbox means that all faces—whether facing you or not, or occluded or not—will be painted with equal brush intensity.

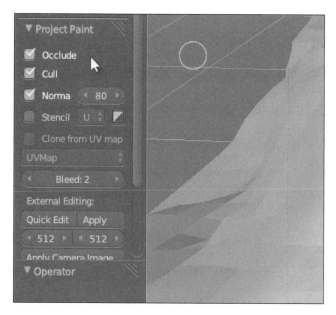

Figure 4.36
Use the Project Paint options to control how faces respond to brushes and the camera.
Source: Blender.

Painting with Textures

So far in this chapter, whether texture-painting from the Image Editor or the 3D view, you've painted only with bold colors selected from the color picker using brushes. In some cases this might be enough (for example, for cartoon terrains), but typically you'll want your brushes to paint with pre-made photo textures, such as grass and rock textures, so your terrain looks like real-world terrain. This is achieved in Blender through the Texture group, in the left toolbar, which appears in both the UV Editor and the 3D view. This group allows you to select any valid, pre-loaded texture as a brush.

1. To load new textures into Blender, access the Properties panel and choose the Textures group.

2. Click the New button to generate a new and valid texture. See Figure 4.37.

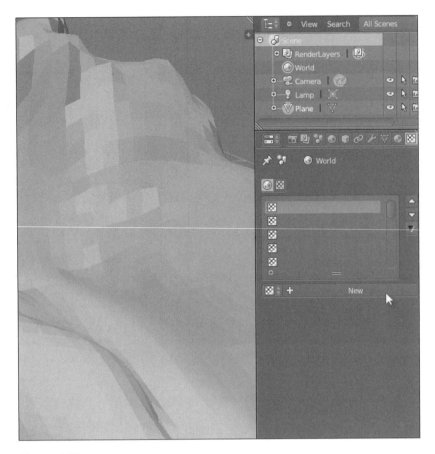

Figure 4.37
Generating a new texture.
Source: Blender.

3. After a new texture is created, you need to tweak a few more settings to associate it with a pre-made image file on your hard drive. By default, newly created textures are of the Clouds type or some other procedural type. To change this, click the Type drop-down list and select Image or Movie. This allows you to choose an image or movie file to use as the texture. See Figure 4.38.

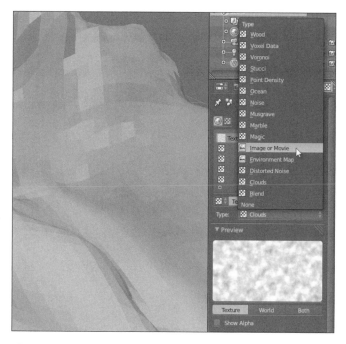

Figure 4.38
Changing the texture type to Image or Movie.
Source: Blender.

4. Scroll down and click the Open button in the Image group (see Figure 4.39). Then select a file from your system to use for the texture.

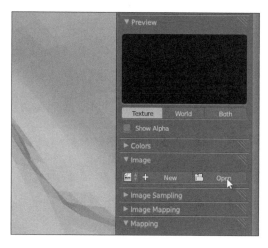

Figure 4.39
Selecting an image file for the texture.
Source: Blender.

5. Now you're ready to paint with the loaded texture. In Texture Paint mode, switch back to the N-Panel on the left side and, from the Textures group, select a texture to use. (See Figure 4.40.) The selected texture is loaded into the active brush, meaning that all subsequent brush strokes will paint pixels from the texture.

Figure 4.40
Painting with the selected texture.
Source: Blender.

Note

Blender mixes or combines the texture with the selected brush color from the color palette. For example, if you've chosen the color red, then your texture will be tinted red when you painted. The same goes for all other colors. If you just want to paint from the texture using its default colors, make sure your brush color is set to white (1.0, 1.0, 1.0).

6. When you're finished painting with the selected texture and need to unload it from the active brush, click the Unlink DataBlock icon beneath the texture thumbnail in the Brushes N-Panel. See Figure 4.41.

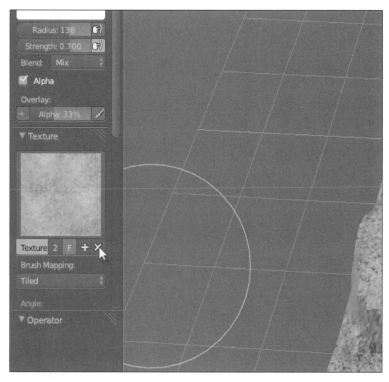

Figure 4.41
Unloading a texture from a brush.
Source: Blender.

WORKING WITH ROADS AND PATHS

One of the most frequently asked questions I encounter with regard to terrain concerns how to create roads, paths, and other details that should conform to the topology of the terrain. Roads, for example, don't just sit on the terrain like discrete objects such as cars, people, and houses, which have a clearly identifiable position and center of gravity. Instead, roads extend across large regions of the terrain, snaking, winding, and conforming to its contours and surface. It's not enough for the road to just be positioned on top of the terrain; the road shape and topology must conform to the underlying terrain. This distinction suggests that road/path construction is intimately connected to the terrain. One solution is simply to model the road in the terrain, as part of the terrain itself. But doing this can be tedious. If a road is particularly long, complex, and/or winding, you can end up with poly-modeling headache. Instead, it's much to separate the road-modeling phase from the terrain-modeling phase, merging them together only at the end. This section discusses the tools Blender offers for doing this.

Creating Roads

Earlier sections of this chapter demonstrated three methods for creating terrain meshes: Proportional Editing, texture displacement, and sculpting. Together or separately, these methods can build large and complex terrains for practically any game type. This section considers the separate process of road/path modeling, and in such a way that the roads you make will always conform to the terrain you've built. Follow these steps:

1. Switch to the Top viewport to get a bird's eye (topographical) view of the terrain. (Note: I'm assuming you've already created a terrain!) See Figure 4.42.

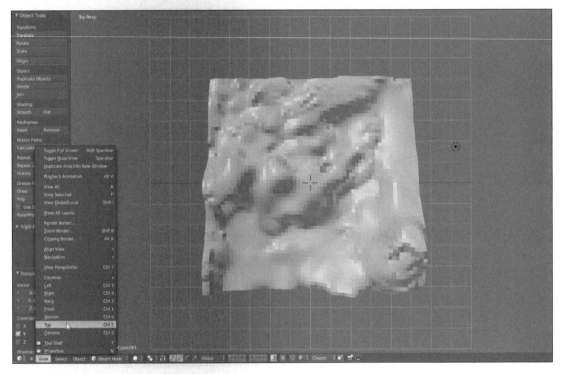

Figure 4.42
Use a top-view of your terrain to plan and create a road.
Source: Blender.

2. There are many ways to create a road. One is to use curves. Using curves, you only need to draw the border or edges of the road as it winds through the terrain. At this stage, you don't need to worry about the vertical ups and downs or its conformity to the terrain. Just concentrate on the horizontal (planar) arrangement of

the road in a Top viewport. To add a curve, choose Add > Curve > Bezier, as shown in Figure 4.43.

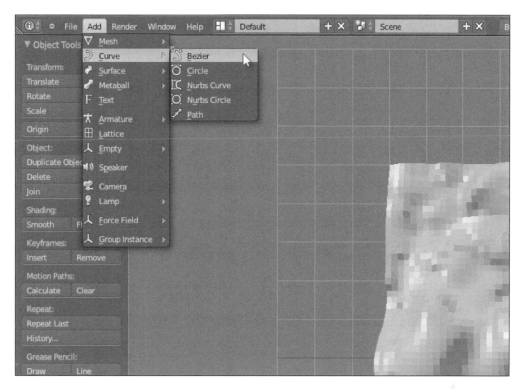

Figure 4.43
Creating a Bezier curve.
Source: Blender.

3. Seen from above, the first curve you add represents one edge of the road, either the left or the right side (it doesn't usually matter). You will soon create the other edge through duplication. First, however, you'll use the Curve Extrude feature (Alt+X in Edit mode) to add connected points to the curve, laying them down one after the other, adjusting the Bezier handles to shape and angle the road as required across the terrain. Remember: Don't worry about the control point elevation in the Z (up/down) axis in relation to the terrain. Terrain conformity will be handled automatically later.

4. After you add the final control point, you may need to connect the last point to the first, forming a completely enclosed curve. You'll need to do this if the first and last points can be moved separately from one another. To fix that, select the curve in the

scene, enter Edit mode, and, from the viewport menu, choose Curve > Toggle Cyclic. It's also useful (in Object mode) to center the object pivot to the Curve Center by choosing Object > Transform > Origin to Geometry, as shown in Figure 4.44.

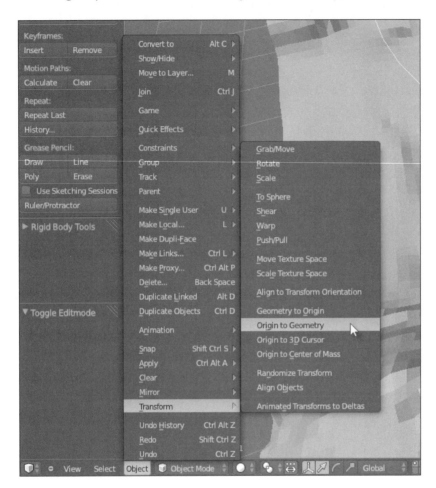

Figure 4.44
Centering the pivot to the curve.
Source: Blender.

5. After you've made one curve, representing one edge, you're ready to create the road's other edge. To do so, just duplicate the first curve and scale it up or down to form the other edge. Figure 4.45 shows the completed road. When you have two sides, you can join the curves together by selecting both curves and choosing Object > Join from the viewport menu.

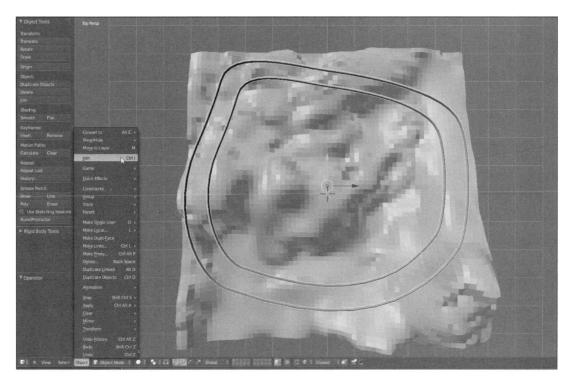

Figure 4.45
Creating a complete road using joined curves. Here, I've used the Geometry group for the curve (in the Properties window) to add a bevel effect, giving the curve some depth. This is only to improve its visibility in the screen shot.

Source: Blender.

6. As a final step, embed the road into the terrain mesh itself so the road conforms to the surface both horizontally and vertically. You can achieve this using the Knife Project tool. This tool uses the viewport's current viewing angle to project the selected object's outline onto the terrain surface, making cuts and incisions in the terrain mesh wherever intersections occur from the projection. Essentially, it cuts the road outline into the terrain beneath. To use the Knife Project tool, make sure you're using a Top viewport, located directly above the terrain. Position the road outline over the terrain in the scene, as it should appear on the terrain if it were projected downward (refer to Figure 4.45). Then it's time to use Knife Project. To do so, first deselect everything. Then take care to select objects in the proper order. First, select the object to be projected (the road curves). Then select the object to be cut by the projection (the terrain). Finally, enter Edit mode (press the Tab key) and select the Knife Project tool from the toolbox on the left in the 3D view. See Figure 4.46.

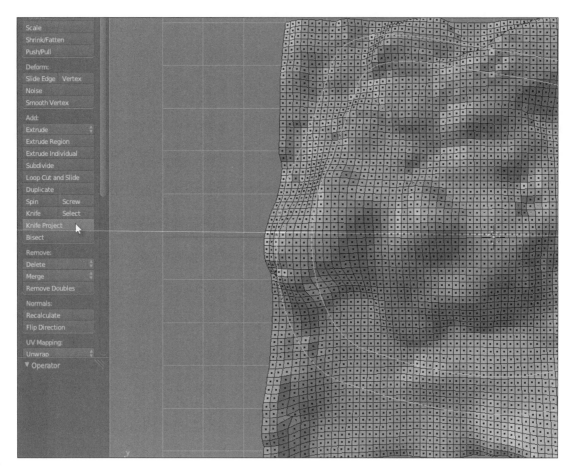

Figure 4.46
Knife Project can project road outlines from curves onto a terrain mesh below.
Source: Blender.

Selecting Knife Project cuts the road into the terrain, and the cuts will conform to the terrain elevation! This gives you a really easy method for adding roads to your terrain. See Figure 4.47. Of course, there may still be work to do. For example, you may want to tweak the roads to improve their appearance in the mesh. Nevertheless, the Knife Project tool offers a solid basis for adding road layouts to a terrain surface. Congratulations! You can now make custom terrains, complete with roads and paths.

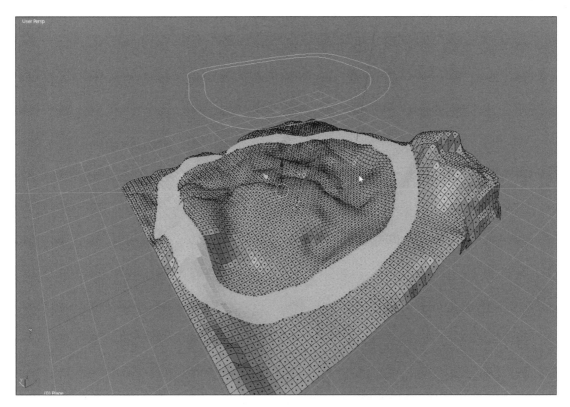

Figure 4.47
Custom-sculpted terrain with a basic road system, created using Knife Project.
Source: Blender.

SUMMARY

This chapter focused on terrains and game environments. It began with an exploration of the Unity terrain system—specifically, on how Unity terrains are sculpted from internally maintained heightmap textures describing vertical elevation. The limitations of this system led us to examine the options Blender offers for creating terrains. These terrains can be created as static meshes and imported back into Unity, replacing the native terrains. Blender offers three main methods for terrain modeling, as well as texture-painting options and even convenient tools for cutting road and path systems into the terrain. The next chapter considers animation workflows in Blender—specifically, techniques and tips for exporting animations to Unity.

CHAPTER 5

ANIMATION WORKFLOWS

There's only two things that limit animation. One is the ability to imagine and the other is to draw what you imagine.

—Eric Larson

By the end of this chapter, you should:

- Understand how to animate in Blender for importing to Unity
- Be able to work with keyframes
- Understand blend shapes and shape keys
- Understand Blender rigging and bones for use in Unity Mecanim
- Be able to import animated assets from Blender into Unity

Animation for games is essentially about describing change over time, whether it's a change in the position of a character or a change in a character's fundamental structure and morphology. In this general sense, animation involves a specific kind of relationship or mapping: a ratio between time and value, or between the time at which a change occurs and the change itself that happens when the time arrives. For this reason, every time you want an object to move or change in your game, you'll need to resort to animation by defining the motion you need in terms of a relationship between time and value. This mapping is typically achieved through the concept of keyframes, and the other, related concepts that follow. Before considering animation further in Blender and Unity, keyframes are explored in more depth.

ANIMATION UNITS: THE KEYFRAME

As mentioned, animation involves change over time. This definition relies on the concepts of both change and time. Both Blender and Unity package these concepts together into the keyframe structure.

Specifically, a complete animation sequence may contain one or more keyframes. A *keyframe* defines the properties for an object (such as a character) at a specific point in time. These properties might include its position, rotation, and scale, among others (known as channels). For meaningful changes to occur in animation, there must be at least two keyframes, each defining the state of the object at a unique time in the animation sequence. Both Unity and Blender use these keyframes to play back an animation smoothly by way of tweens (short for in-betweens). Tweens are auto-generated frames of animation that are inserted between user-defined keyframes to create a smooth transition over time between the first and last keyframes in any pair. Tweens are calculated automatically by a process called interpolation, which is controlled by a mathematical structure known as an F-curve (short for function curve). The horizontal axis describes time and the vertical axis describes the change. See Figure 5.1.

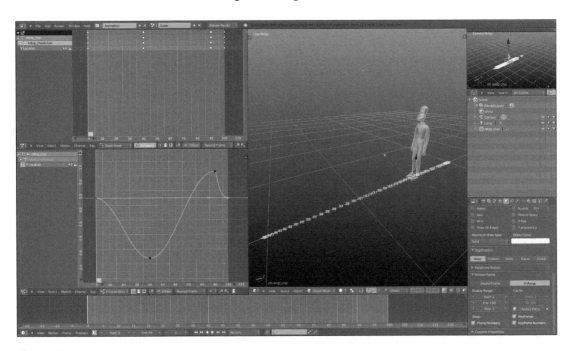

Figure 5.1
The Animation Editor with F-curves and keyframes in view, inside the Graph Editor (lower-left corner).
Source: Blender.

The speed at which an animation plays back is typically defined in Blender by frames per second (FPS). But as you'll soon see, Unity offers import controls for scaling animation time, allowing animations to be made faster or slower according to your needs. This speed can even be changed at run time. Even so, it's helpful to define an appropriate frame rate in Blender as a preliminary step to creating animation to help you visualize how it will appear in-game. To set the frame rate in Blender, switch to the Render tab in the Properties panel and type a value in the Frame Rate field, as shown in Figure 5.2. The most common values are 25 and 30 FPS.

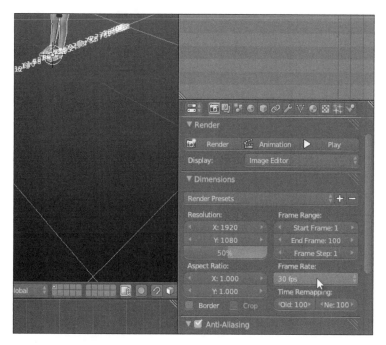

Figure 5.2
Specifying an animation frame rate in Blender.
Source: Blender.

PREPARING FOR ANIMATION IN BLENDER

The general animation workflow between Blender and Unity works as follows:

1. You make an animation in Blender.

2. You export the animation from Blender.

3. You import the animation into Unity.

4. You test and tweak the import, performing any re-importing if required.

Thus, animation details must be planned and created first in Blender. Before you get started with animation, however, there are some helpful working practices, gotchas, and guidelines to keep foremost in your mind concerning the Blender UI and general preferences. These are considered in subsequent sections.

Use a Dedicated Animation Layout

Animation is not simply an adjunct procedure or afterthought that follows the modeling and UV mapping phases of mesh creation. Rather, it's a distinct process that requires much thought, dedication, and time. For this reason, you must adjust the Blender interface to support an animation workflow that's intuitive for you. You can create your own custom UI layouts, but Blender ships with a pre-made Animation layout. You can activate this by choosing Animation from the UI Preset drop-down list at the top of the Blender UI, as shown in Figure 5.3.

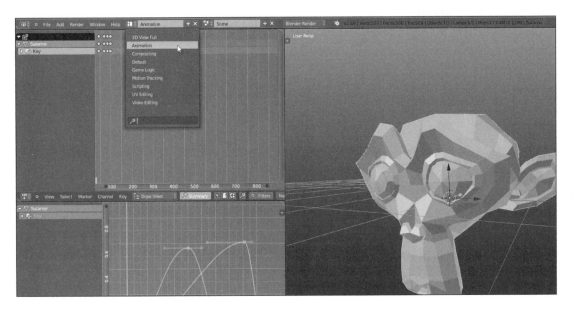

Figure 5.3
Using the Blender Animation UI layout.
Source: Blender.

Beware of Auto-Key

Auto-Key is a toggle-able feature in Blender that's deactivated by default. If you activate it (by clicking the Auto-Key button in the animation timeline toolbar; see Figure 5.4), Blender will monitor all transformations and edits made to meshes in the scene.

When an edit is detected, Blender automatically generates appropriate animation key-frames for the edits, inserting them at the currently selected time on the animation time-line. It effectively pieces together an animation for you as you edit objects, saving you from having to create keyframes manually. It does this by making educated guesses as to which properties you want to animate and about how you'd like the keyframes to be interpolated.

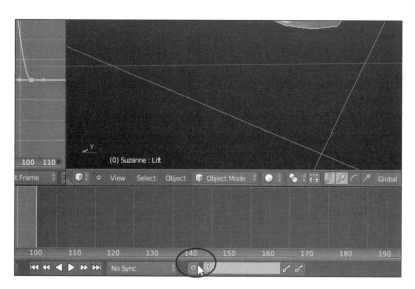

Figure 5.4
You can toggle Auto-Key on and off to help with building animations.
Source: Blender.

Auto-Key is supposed to save you time and work, creating keyframes automatically. How-ever, Auto-Key can easily produce more keyframes than is necessary, resulting in clutter and mess in your animation data. This is damaging to an efficient workflow, leading to larger files sizes. It can also affect in-game performance when the animation is imported into Unity because Unity will need to process more frames. For this reason, I recommend avoiding Auto-Key in most situations. That way, you ensure that you work only with the data you need. However, there may be times, such as when working with many objects or rigged characters, when it's especially convenient and intuitive to use Auto-Key. In these cases, I recommend enabling the Only Insert Available option in the Editing tab of the Blender User Preferences window (see Figure 5.5). This option requires you to always set the first keyframe for all objects on only the needed channels. Thereafter, the Auto-Key feature will be restricted to setting keys for only those channels. Thus, this option ensures that Auto-Key cannot create new keyframes for additional and unneeded channels.

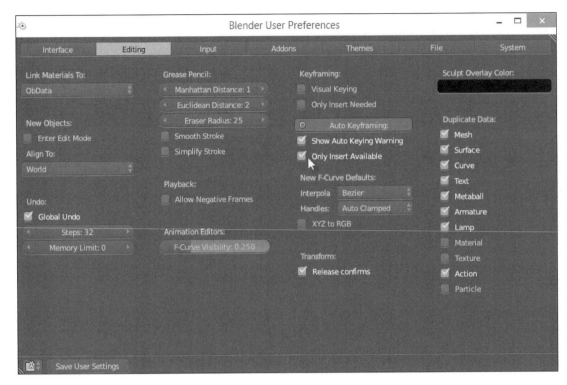

Figure 5.5
Placing limits on the Auto-Key feature.
Source: Blender.

Insert Single Keyframes

Often, the most efficient method for creating keyframes is to insert them manually. This gives you control of exactly which keyframes are created in the sequence, making it easier to limit the keyframes to only what you need. To manually insert a keyframe for any valid field at any time during the animation sequence, right-click the field and choose Insert Single Keyframe from the menu that appears (using the Maya style controls). See Figure 5.6.

Figure 5.6
Manually inserting keyframes into an animation.
Source: Blender.

Animation Length

Every animation has a total duration in terms of frames. By default, Blender sets the animation length to 250 frames, but you can easily change this. When importing animated files into Unity, however, it's important to specify the animation length in a specific way in Blender. Otherwise, your animations may be imported with more or fewer frames than you expected. This can leave wasted spaces of time at the start or end of your animations.

One method for setting animation length is to set the end frame limit in the Timeline window, as shown in Figure 5.7. However, if the Use Alternative Start/End Frame option is activated in the toolbar, it's possible for the animation length, as shown in the Timeline window, to be different from the scene animation length, which is imported into Unity. The result is that the Timeline window can only be guaranteed to show you a selected portion of the total timeline. Often, it will display the complete animation timeline, but not always. The end frame value will not always refer to the total animation length in the file. For this reason, animation length should be specified using a different method, which I'll discuss next.

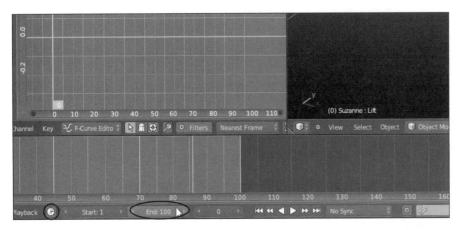

Figure 5.7
Setting animation length from the Timeline window can be unreliable for exporting animations to Unity.
Source: Blender.

The second (recommended) method for specifying total animation length doesn't suffer the limitations of the previous method. It always specifies the total number of animation frames in the file. To achieve this, do the following:

1. Click the Render tab in the Properties panel.

2. Specify the final frame number in the End Frame field, under the Dimensions Group. See Figure 5.8.

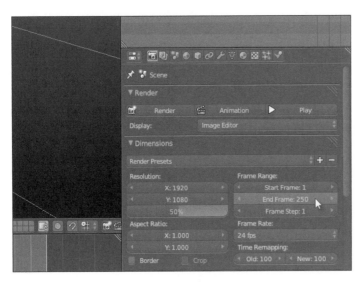

Figure 5.8
Setting the animation length in terms of total frames.
Source: Blender.

Exporting Animations to FBX

Chapter 2, "Blender-to-Unity Workflow," detailed how to export meshes from Blender into the FBX and Collada format, suitable for importing into Unity. You can export meshes to FBX using the Blender FBX Exporter, by selecting File > Export > Autodesk FBX. That chapter, however, considered only static and non-animated meshes. The general workflow for exporting animated meshes is, thankfully, similar. But take care about the settings in the FBX Exporter, ensuring all relevant animation options are enabled. Specifically, make sure Include Animation, All Actions, Include Default Take, and Optimize Keyframes are checked. See Figure 5.9.

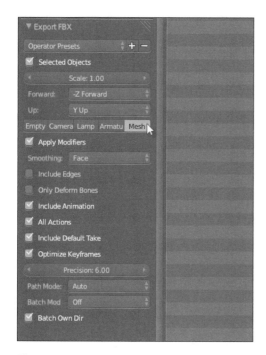

Figure 5.9
Using the Blender FBX Exporter to export the selected mesh, complete with animation data.
Source: Blender.

Note

You don't have to use the FBX format to export meshes and animations to Unity. An alternative export format is Collada (DAE). You can export Blender files to this format by choosing File > Export > Collada.

Working with Multiple Animations

Often, you'll need to assign multiple animations to a single object—for example, when animating a single character through multiple poses and motions, including walking, running, and jumping animations. There are two main methods for handling multiple animations like this in Blender that work well with Unity. Let's examine these in a specific case: the case of exporting a character model with multiple poses.

Exporting Animations and Characters Separately

One method is to export your character mesh separately as a single, rigged, and non-animated FBX mesh, and then to export each separate animation in a different FBX file. This configuration produces one mesh file along with several additional files that include the animation data to be applied to the mesh. Each of these files represents one complete animation—walk, run, jump, etc. In this method, each mesh and animation is segregated across multiple files. The primary disadvantage is that it produces lots of files, especially if you're working with many objects and animations.

Exporting Animations and Meshes Together in a Single File

The second method is to export both the character mesh and its animation data (all poses) into a single FBX file. In this scenario, the multiple animations don't span multiple files. Instead, they are incorporated into a single timeline, back to back. The timeline is extended to include all animations together, and each separate animation spans only a smaller subset of the timeline, one after the other.

Exporting a mesh with all its animation data is convenient because it means you only have to import one file into Unity. Unity still allows you to share the animation data in one file with meshes in other files, as you'll see. The disadvantage here is that, with lots of meshes and animations included in a single file, the file can grow large and cumbersome.

Note

When working with animations, you'll need to reach a decision about which export workflow is best for your game.

KEYFRAME ANIMATIONS FROM BLENDER TO UNITY

This section walks through the process of creating a basic keyframe animation and exporting it from Blender to Unity. You can use your own file or use the Chapter05/KeyFrame Start.Blend file, available on this book's companion website. (To access the site, visit www .cengageptr.com/downloads and search for the title of this book.)

To get set up, follow these steps:

1. Start with an Animation GUI layout. Then open a file that contains an object. This can be any object—a cube mesh or whatever you like. Again, feel free to use the Chapter05/KeyFrameStart.Blend file, available on this book's companion website.

2. Set the Animation Length to 100 frames.

3. Set the Timeline End Frame and the Scene End Frame settings to 99, as discussed in the "Animation Length" section.

4. Set the Start Frame setting to 0. By default, Blender sets the Start Frame setting to 1. Unity, however, recognizes the start frame as 0, so it's convenient to match up the frame numbering between Blender and Unity. See Figure 5.10.

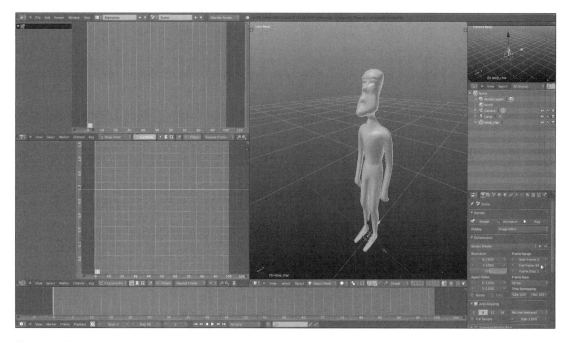

Figure 5.10
Configuring frame numbering for animation.
Source: Blender.

For this simple animation, the mesh will simply move forward, backward, and then forward again across frame 0 to frame 99. To create this animation, follow these steps:

1. Position the Time slider in the animation timeline at frame 0. (If you're using the Maya style controls, right-click.)

2. Create the first, starting keyframe with the mesh at the origin position in the scene. To do so, select the mesh. Then, from the Object Data tab in the Properties panel, right-click the Y field (or X field, depending on where you want to move) and select Insert Single Keyframe from the menu that appears. This marks the initial mesh position at animation start. An animation track is created in the Graph Editor and Dopesheet views, as well as a marker in the Timeline view. (See Figure 5.11.)

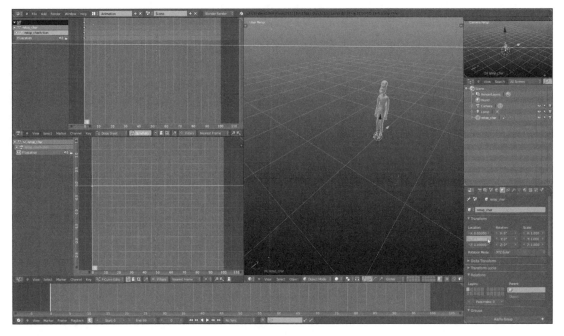

Figure 5.11
Setting the first keyframe for the animation.
Source: Blender.

3. Insert additional keyframes for the mesh throughout the animation timeline. In this case, I moved the mesh forward to Y −1.96168 for frame 20, backward to Y 1.24381 for frame 55, forward to Y −1.29317 on frame 80, and backward one more time to the origin for frame 99. Be sure to set a keyframe for each move or else use Auto-Key. (If you use Auto-Key, read the section "Beware of Auto-Key" first.) See Figure 5.12.

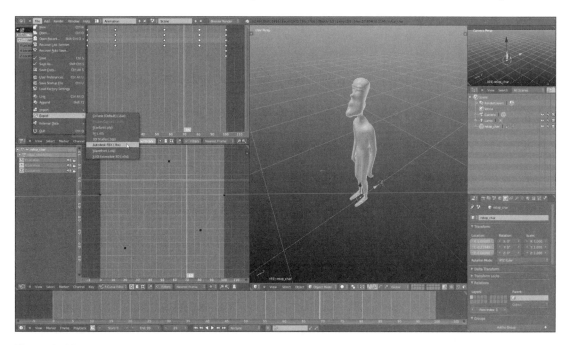

Figure 5.12
Completing the animation sequence.
Source: Blender.

4. When the animation is complete, select the animated mesh and choose
   File > Export > Autodesk FBX to export the file as an animated mesh, using the
   export settings shown in Figure 5.9. This creates an animated FBX file, which
   includes both the mesh and animation data. (This corresponds to the second
   export method discussed in the section "Working with Multiple Animations.")
   After export is complete, import the mesh into Unity, as shown in Figure 5.13.

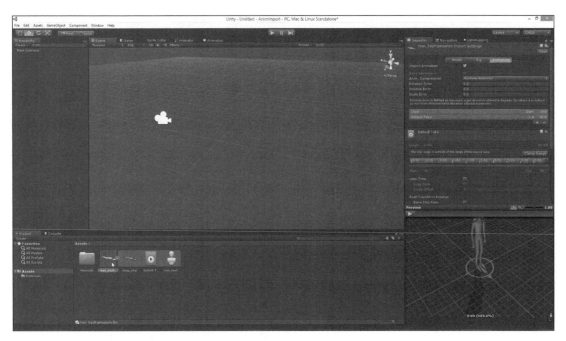

Figure 5.13
Importing an animated FBX file into Unity.
Source: Unity Technologies.

In Unity, when an imported mesh is selected in the Project panel, its data and configuration is displayed across three tabs in the Object Inspector:

- **Model.** The Model tab lists all settings that pertain to the structure, vertex, and UV information that is part of the mesh itself.

- **Rig.** The Rig tab defines an underlying skeletal structure beneath the mesh that is associated with animation (more on this later).

- **Animations.** The Animations tab defines all animation data associated with the mesh file.

It's important to note that the mesh, rigging, and animation data in Unity are separate from each other. That means animations embedded in one mesh file need not animate the mesh in the same file. Animation data from one file can be applied to a mesh in a different file, or even to multiple meshes across many files. This process is known as *retargeting*. See Figure 5.14.

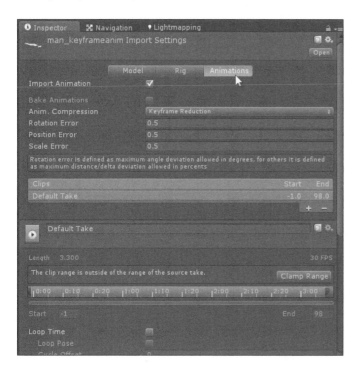

Figure 5.14
Imported mesh data is divided across three groups: Mesh, Rig, and Animations.
Source: Unity Technologies.

The next steps explain how to configure an imported mesh in Unity, ready for use in a scene. This involves configuring the skeletal rig and bone structure that will deform the mesh, and also creating animation clip data from the animation timeline in the file.

1. Click the Rig tab in the Object Inspector and ensure the Animation Type field is set to Generic. This specifies that the mesh is a non-humanoid rig, compliant with Mecanim.

Note

Mecanim refers to a range of animation features introduced in Unity 4. These features make it simpler to import, configure, and use animated character meshes that have been created in 3D modeling applications, such as Blender. You'll make use of Mecanim throughout this chapter and beyond. For an introductory look at Mecanim, I recommend my book *Unity 4 Fundamentals* (ISBN: 978-0415823838).

Note

The character in Figure 5.14 is, in fact, a humanoid in commonsense terms, but not in the narrower and specific sense understood by Unity. In Unity, a humanoid is a mesh that features a specific kind of skeletal rig, with a minimum number of bones in a specific relationship. The model featured in Figure 5.14 has no explicit rig at all, so it is classified as a generic type.

2. Click the Animations tab. Notice that it features the DefaultTake clip, which contains all animation on the timeline in the file, from frame 0 to 99. Later, you'll see how to divide this timeline into separate clips. For the file here, however, you need only one clip. Simply rename the clip BasicAnimation and use the Start and End fields to set the start and end frames for the animation, if needed. This timeline represents the complete animation, as created in Blender.

3. Select the Loop Time checkbox to make the animation loopable—that is, to force Unity to play the animation on a loop.

4. If you like, click the Play button in the animation preview window to see the animation in action, applied to the mesh in the file. (See Figure 5.15.)

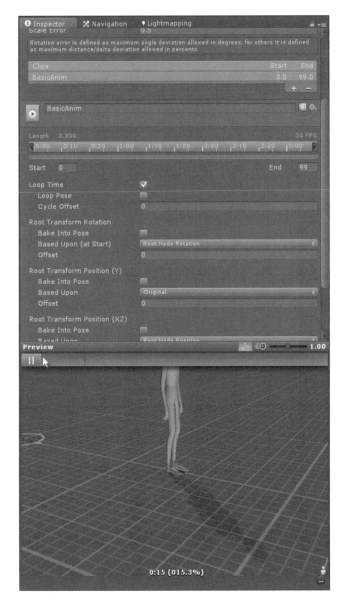

Figure 5.15
Configuring an animation clip.
Source: Unity Technologies.

5. After you specify the settings, click the Apply button to confirm the changes. This updates the animation clip data.

If you add the mesh to the active scene as a GameObject and then click Play on the Unity toolbar to run your game, you'll notice the mesh remains static and no animation is automatically applied to the mesh. To have the animation play automatically on the mesh using the animation clip settings, you'll need to use an AnimatorController asset. Nearly every kind of imported mesh in Unity is instantiated in the scene with an Animator component attached. This component features a Controller member, referencing an AnimatorController asset defining when and how the animation should play, if it all. By default this member is unassigned, or given the value of None—which is why no animation plays automatically on the mesh. See Figure 5.16.

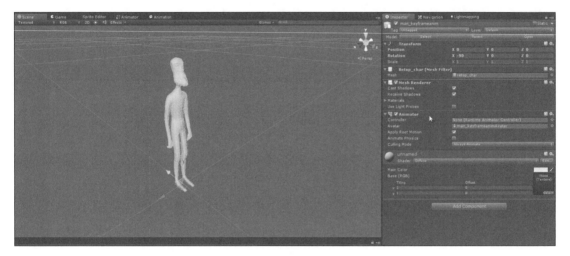

Figure 5.16
A mesh instantiated in the scene with an Animator component attached. Remember, the mesh Scale Factor has been set to 1 in the Object Inspector, ensuring the mesh is set to an appropriate size in the scene. (See the section "Scale Factor" in Chapter 2.)

Source: Unity Technologies.

To create an AnimatorController asset, right-click in the Project panel and choose Create > AnimatorController from the menu that appears. You can edit an AnimatorController through the Animator window—not to be confused with the Animation window. To open the Animator window, choose Window > Animator. See Figure 5.17.

Figure 5.17
Creating an AnimatorController to define animation playback.
Source: Unity Technologies.

The AnimatorController is a special kind of asset, defining a finite state machine (FSM) for the selected mesh. It is, essentially, a form of visual scripting. Using the controller and its features, you can put the selected mesh into multiple states of animation and define connections between the states determining when some animations become active and others inactive. You can even allow for weighted blends between multiple animations playing simultaneously, such as firing a weapon while walking.

Here, we'll apply only the BasicAnimation clip to the mesh, created earlier. To do so, simply drag and drop the BasicAnimation animation clip, embedded inside the mesh asset, from the Project panel into the Animator window. This automatically adds the animation clip to the Animator graph, where it appears as an orange node. (Orange indicates the default node—the initial animation state of the mesh when the scene begins.) Thus, the Animator graph sets it so that, as the scene begins, the mesh will be animated using the BasicAnimation clip.

When the BasicAnimation node is selected in the Animator graph, you can adjust its speed from the Object Inspector, controlling how quickly or slowly the animation will play. A speed of 1 leaves the animation at its default speed, as defined in the Blender file; a value of 2 means double speed; a value of 0.5 means half speed; and so on. For this example, I'll leave the speed at 1. See Figure 5.18.

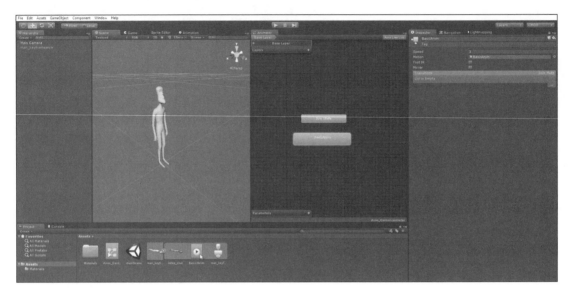

Figure 5.18
Building the Animator graph.
Source: Unity Technologies.

Having created the Animator graph, you can now assign it to the mesh through its Animator component. Follow these steps:

1. Select the mesh in the scene.

2. Drag-and-drop the AnimatorController onto the Controller field of the Animator component.

3. Click the Play button on the toolbar and see the animation take effect on the mesh. This works because, on scene start, the mesh will always enter the animation state defined by the default (orange) node in the Animator graph. See Figure 5.19.

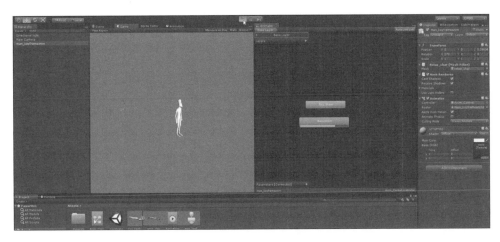

Figure 5.19
Object with animation playing.
Source: Unity Technologies.

Follow-Path Animations and Animation Baking

One common animation requirement for games is to move objects, such as people, cars, and spaceships, along a pre-determined path (see Figure 5.20). Perhaps the most intuitive approach to this is to draw out a path using the Blender curve tools and have the object follow the curve, allowing the curve to define the path across a complete animation time-line. This approach, however, introduces the issue of animation baking, also referred to as animation conversion.

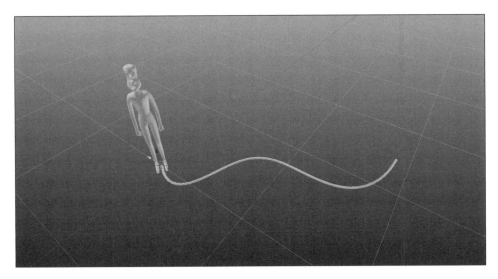

Figure 5.20
Animating objects along a path.
Source: Blender.

Let's explore this issue by creating an animated object that moves along a path. You can create your own Blender scene and object to follow along with this exercise or use the Follow_Path.blend file, available from this book's companion website, as a starting point. Follow these steps:

1. In Blender, you can draw paths using curve objects. To create a curve, simply choose Add > Curve > Path. See Figure 5.21.

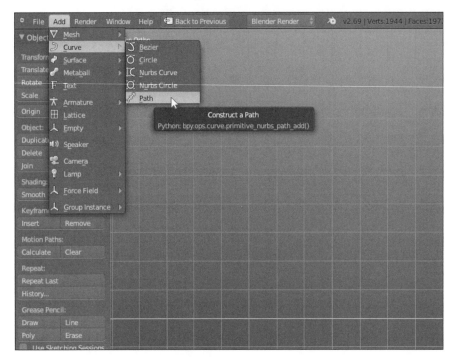

Figure 5.21
Creating a curve for defining an animation path.
Source: Blender.

2. To shape and define the path, you use Edit mode (press the Tab key). In Figure 5.22, I've created a sample zig-zagging path. Remember, with paths, the control points do not rest on the curve itself. Instead, they define the limits or extremities of a curve, which is interpolated between them.

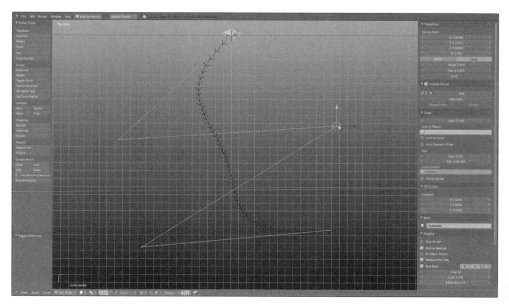

Figure 5.22
Using control points to define a path.
Source: Blender.

3. To heighten the visibility of the curve in the viewport, click the Curve Data tab in the Properties panel. Then increase the Bevel Depth setting in the Geometry Group. See Figure 5.23.

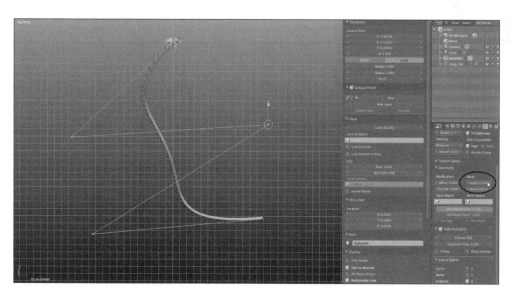

Figure 5.23
Bevel depth can increase curve visibility in the viewport.
Source: Blender.

4. To make an object follow the created path, select the object and apply a Follow Path constraint. To do so, choose Follow Path from the Constraints tab in the Properties panel, as shown in Figure 5.24.

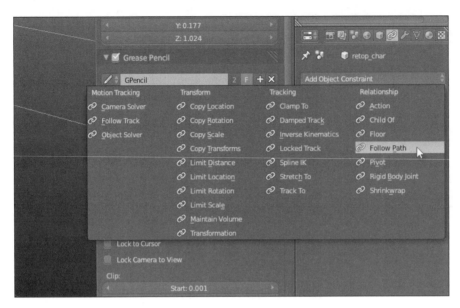

Figure 5.24
The Follow Path constraint allows objects to follow selected curves as a path.
Source: Blender.

Note

For more information on the Follow Path constraint, see the Blender online documentation: http://wiki.blender .org/index.php/Doc:2.6/Manual/Constraints/Relationship/Follow_Path.

5. In the Follow Path Constraint settings, click the Target field and select the curve object as the target to use for the path.

6. Use the Forward field to align the forward vector of the object to the path—that is, to align the nose (the front of the object) to face the path. That way, as the object traverses the path in animation, it'll be facing in the direction of movement. See Figure 5.25.

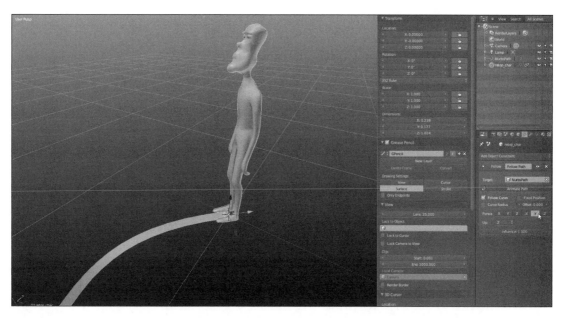

Figure 5.25
Aligning objects to their target path.
Source: Blender.

7. Click the Animate Path button. This will generate the needed animation data internally to move the object successfully along the path. To test this, scrub the slider across the Timeline window to preview the animation in the viewport. You should see the object traverse the path, beginning on the first frame and ending on the last. Notice how the object remains aligned (facing forward) as it moves along the curve. See Figure 5.26.

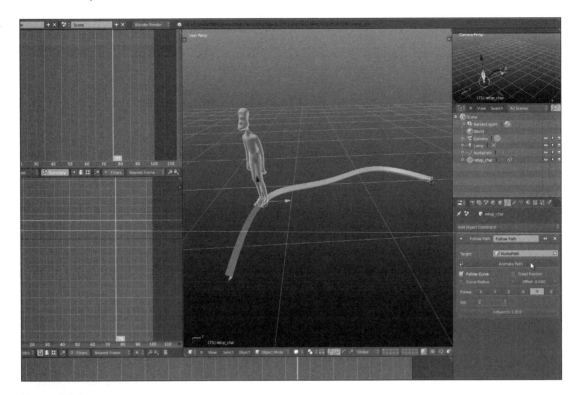

Figure 5.26
Animating and object along a path.
Source: Blender.

When it comes to exporting to Unity, there is a problem with the animation created thus far. You may have noticed in Figure 5.26 that, although the mesh is animated along the path, no keyframes exist in any of the animation views—neither the Graph Editor nor the Dopesheet view. This is because object constraints (like the Follow Path constraint) don't generate keyframes by default. They control the movement and motion of objects, but they don't do so through keyframing. Unity, however, can accept animation only through keyframing, shape keys, and rigging—and none of these are involved in this case. That means if you try to export the mesh and animation right now, none of the path animation data will be carried into Unity, leaving you with a static mesh. To make this animation Unity-compliant, you'll need to convert it to keyframes. This process is known as *animation baking*.

To perform animation baking, follow these steps:

1. Select the mesh in the 3D View and choose Object > Animation > Bake Action. See Figure 5.27.

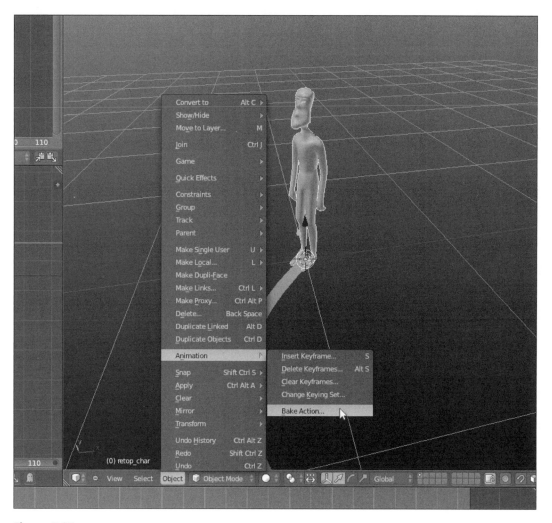

Figure 5.27
Preparing to bake constraint animations.
Source: Blender.

2. The Bake Action dialog box opens. Set the animation's start and end frames. (For path-follow animations, these will typically be the first and last frame,

respectively). This represents the active section of the timeline to be baked (converted) into keyframes.

3. The Frame Step value determines the accuracy of the animation, with lower values producing greater fidelity to the original path animation. Take care, however: If, for example, you choose a value of 1, a keyframe will be created for every frame, between the animation's start and end. The general aim is here to apply a value that leads to the greatest accuracy with the fewest keyframes. (Fewer keyframes means less animation data, and thus better performance in Unity.) To generate this animation, I set Frame Step to 4, resulting in a keyframe every four frames.

4. Select the Visual Keying and Clear Constraints checkboxes to bake in the animation data from the Follow Path constraint. See Figure 5.28.

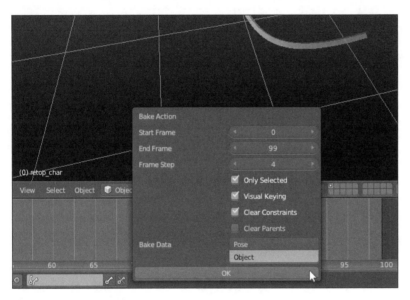

Figure 5.28
Configuring Bake Settings.
Source: Blender.

After baking, keyframes will be generated, as shown in the Animation Editors in Figure 5.29. With the keyframe data generated, the mesh can now be exported as an FBX file with the default take for the scene. This file can then be imported as a regular, animated mesh into Unity, as explained earlier in the section "Keyframe Animations from Blender to Unity." Congratulations! You can now export path animations from Blender to Unity!

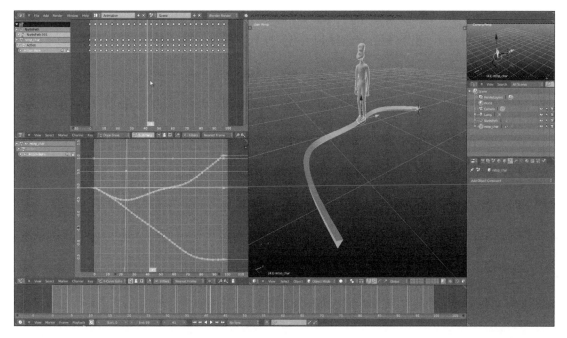

Figure 5.29
Animation bakes generate keyframes from constraint animations.
Source: Blender.

BLEND SHAPES AND SHAPE KEYS

Unity 4.3 introduced support for morphing animation, known as blend shapes (in Unity and Maya). Blender names this feature shape keys. The animation types considered so far in this chapter operate at the object level—that is, you've animated movement and motion for a discrete object, such as a character. Blend shapes, however, operate at the sub-object or component level. They allow you to animate the motion of vertices, edges, and faces within a mesh. This kind of animation is useful for creating facial expressions, mouth movements, blinking eyes, and other kinds of morph-style animation where an object remains in place but its structure changes.

Shape keys in Blender work by allowing you to model a character into different poses, saving each unique pose as a shape key. Each shape key can then be assigned its own weighting value (between 0 and 1 in Blender and 0 and 100 in Unity), representing how strongly that pose features in the mesh at any time during animation.

Let's look at a concrete example. Open the blendshape_start.blend, available from the companion website. This file features the standard Blender monkey head (see Figure 5.30), which you can create by choosing File > Add > Mesh > Monkey. The objective here will be to model the head into different forms and poses—in other words, different shape keys—for importing into Unity using blend shapes.

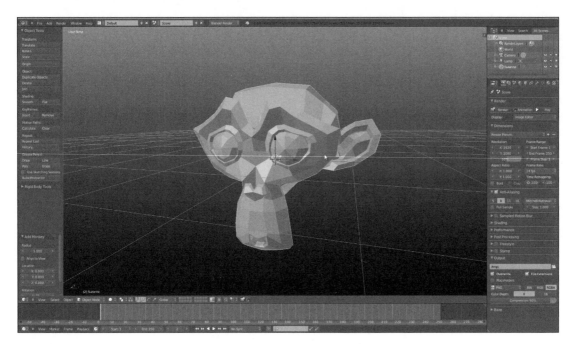

Figure 5.30
Getting started with shape keys.
Source: Blender.

The first step to working with shape keys is to create the base, or basis, pose. This represents the mesh's neutral or default configuration—that is, how it looks when no other pose or state is being applied, or the default arrangement of vertices in the mesh. Follow these steps:

1. Select the monkey head object in the viewport.

2. Click the Object Data tab in the Properties panel.

3. Click the plus (+) icon under the Shape Keys field to add the first basis shape key. See Figure 5.31.

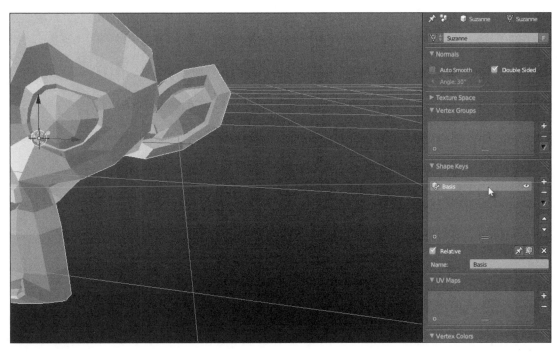

Figure 5.31
Adding the basis shape key.
Source: Blender.

4. Adding the basis shape key is the equivalent of recording a copy of the mesh and its current state. To create a new state, you create a new shape key and then deform the mesh using the standard modeling tools. (Don't do this the other way around! That is, don't deform first and then add a key.) To create a new shape key, click the plus (+) icon in the Shape Keys group located in the Properties panel's in the Object Data tab (see Figure 5.32). The edits you make will be stored in the selected shape key in the shape key list. I've created two new states, Raised and Lowered, to edit the shape of the monkey head. Notice that as you exit Edit mode and return to Object mode, all edits to the mesh in the shape keys appear to vanish in the viewport and the basis state is shown.

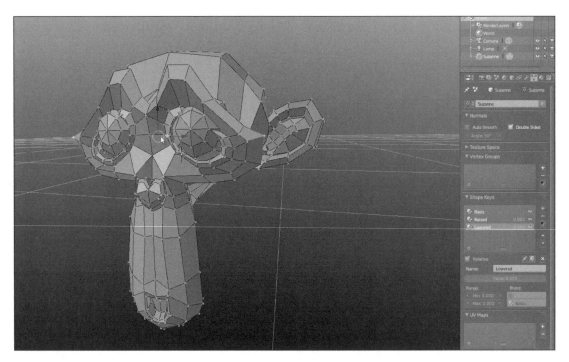

Figure 5.32
Defining shape keys.
Source: Blender.

5. When all shape keys are created, apply one or more of the states, blended onto the basis state, by using the shape key's Value field. Each shape key has its own Value field, specified in the range of 0 to 1, defining how strongly the key should be blended onto the basis along with any other keys being applied. The mesh then becomes a weighted average of all applicable shape keys. A value of 0 means the key has no influence on the final mesh, while a value of 1 represents the strongest and most complete influence a key can have. See Figure 5.33 for an example of shape key blending.

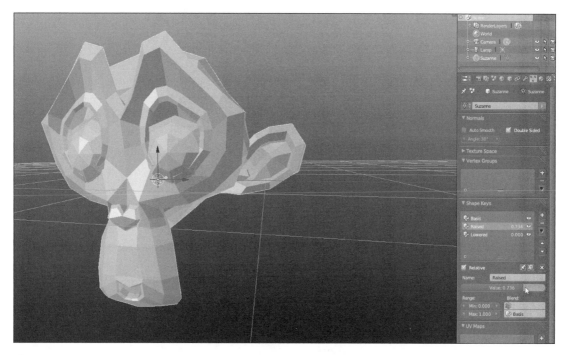

Figure 5.33
Use the Value slider for the Raised shape key to morph the basis mesh.
Source: Blender.

Note

It's possible also to animate the Value field of the keys in Blender to produce morph animation between the states—that is, to change (or keyframe) the *numbers* in the Value field smoothly over time to produce continuous morphing animation in the mesh. However, at the time of writing, the major limitation to using shape keys is that shape key animation does not migrate into Unity, even though the shape keys themselves do. As you'll see soon, there are some workarounds for this. For now, though, the monkey head created so far with its shape keys can be exported to a standard FBX file and imported into Unity.

6. Before importing the mesh featuring shape keys into Unity, make sure the Import BlendShapes checkbox in the Object Inspector is selected. See Figure 5.34.

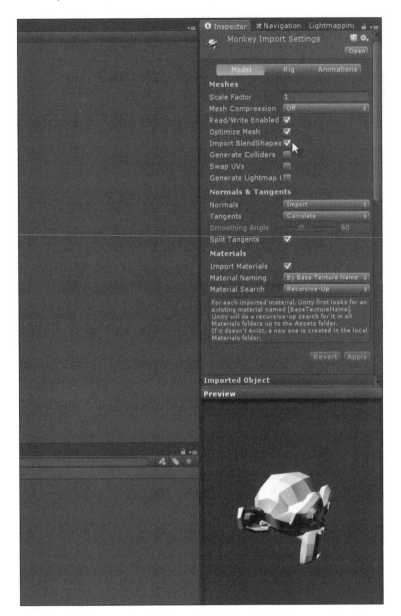

Figure 5.34
Enable the Import BlendShape option for Blender shape key meshes.
Source: Unity Technologies.

7. Add the imported monkey mesh into the scene, select it, and then examine its components in the Object Inspector. It features a SkinnedMeshRenderer component, which lists all specified shape keys under the BlendShapes group. Each group has its

own unique entry, with a floating-point value ranging from 0 to 100 (not 0 to 1), each of which starts at 0 by default. You can raise the value for each group to apply the blend shape morph to the basis mesh, just as it worked in Blender. See Figure 5.35.

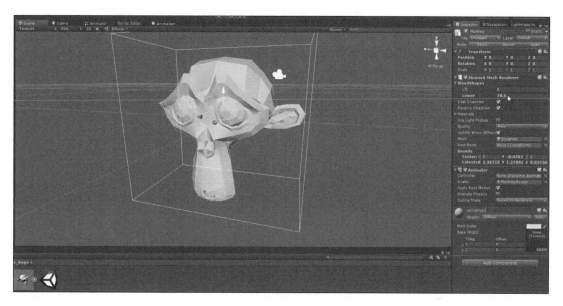

Figure 5.35
Applying blend shapes in Unity from imported Blender meshes.
Source: Unity Technologies.

As mentioned, Blender keyframes for shape keys don't migrate into Unity like regular keyframes—at least not at the time of writing. In practice, that means blend shapes cannot be imported with animation data. This leaves two main methods or workarounds:

- Create all keyframe animation for blend shapes inside Unity using the Legacy Animation Editor. To access this, choose Window > Animation.

- In Blender, animate an empty object with keyframe animation on one only axis (such as the Y axis), constraining its values between 0 and 100. Then, import that object into Blender, using its animation curves on that axis to directly control the input fields for the blend shapes on the SkinnedMeshRenderer. The connection between the dummy object transform and the blend shapes would need to be scripted.

BONES AND RIGGING

The third and final major animation type supported by both Blender and Unity is bones, sometimes known as skeletal animation. With this form, artists use Blender to construct a custom skeleton (a hierarchical arrangement of bones), approximating the joints and connection points of their model. This structure is termed a *rig* (Unity) or an *armature* (Blender). The rig/armature is then associated with the model through skinning, and is animated to deform the model. See Figure 5.36.

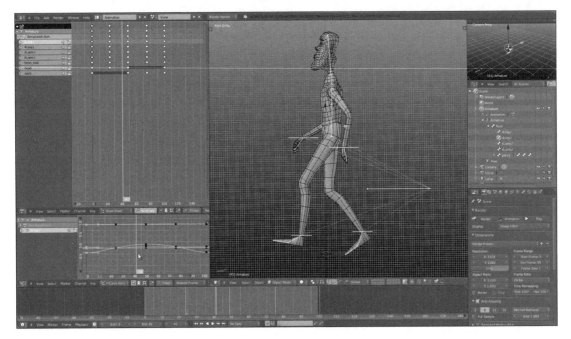

Figure 5.36
A character model with a skeleton rig and a walk-cycle animation.
Source: Blender.

The basic details and specifics of bones and rigging are outside the scope of this book. Here, I'll assume you're already familiar with the basics and instead focus on tips and techniques for working with bones and rigs in Blender specifically for use in Unity.

Always Name Bones

You should get into the habit of manually assigning meaningful and appropriate names to bones in a rig because both Blender and Unity often require you to specify or identify bones by name. Don't leave the naming process as an afterthought, either. Instead, name the bones as you create them in Blender.

In addition, adopt a naming convention when creating bones for humanoid characters or creatures in general. The normal standard is to post-fix every symmetrical bone with either .l or .r (or _left and _right), depending on whether the bone is located on the left or right side of the body, respectively. Thus, hand bones will be named hand.l and hand.r, thigh bones named thigh.l and thigh.r, and so on. Using this convention is not simply a matter of helping the artist or programmers on the team; it serves a purpose in both Blender and Unity. Blender uses symmetrical names for its X-Axis Mirror feature (see the next section), and Unity uses them to determine how bones should be auto-configured in a character avatar (see the upcoming section "Importing Rigged Meshes into Unity"). See Figure 5.37.

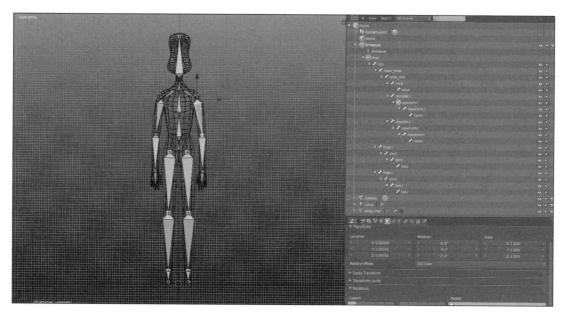

Figure 5.37
Assign meaningful names to bones within a skeleton.
Source: Blender.

Use X-Axis Mirror for Character Rigs

Many character rigs, such as human and humanoid skeletons, are in many respects symmetrical. For example, thinking of the spine as the vertical line of symmetry, humans have an arm and a leg on each side. They are not, of course, *truly* symmetrical in real life, but they appear symmetrical enough to treat them as being so for computer graphics.

Now, it's possible to create all bones individually and to rig each side separately, but you can save time and work by using Blender's X-Axis Mirror feature. This enables you to create bones for only one side of the character and have the other side auto-generated using mirroring.

The success of this feature depends on your use of conventional bone naming while creating the rig. X-Axis Mirror only works after you create the first arm or leg bone on each side, and post-fix the bone names with .l and .r. To enable X-Axis Mirror, select the X-Axis Mirror checkbox in the left toolbox while in Edit mode for the armature. See Figure 5.38.

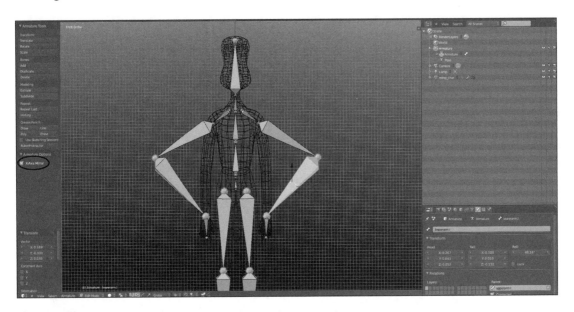

Figure 5.38
Enabling X-Axis Mirror to symmetrically construct a skeletal rig for a character.

Source: Blender.

Note

Remember: You can specify bone names in the Outliner, the N-Panel, and from the Bone Data tab in the Properties panel. (Refer to Figure 5.38.)

Forward and Inverse Kinematics

When working with long bone chains, like arms, legs, or octopus tentacles, a common animation problem arises with regard to posing. Typically, animators need to move the hands or feet (the ends of the bone chain) to specific positions in the game world—for example, moving hands to grab a coffee cup or moving feet to walk on the steps of a staircase.

By default, all Blender rigs use forward kinematics. In practice, this makes such posing difficult and tedious because you need to manually rotate and position not just the end of the bone chain, but every other bone in the chain, until the pose looks correct. For arms, this would include the hand, forearm, elbow, and upper arm, and perhaps even the shoulder.

If you instead use inverse kinematics (IK) for animation, you'll only need to position the final bone in the chain—for example, the hand or foot. Blender will calculate the rotations and movements for all other bones upward in the chain, ensuring they're transformed correctly while remaining in place at their sockets or joints. Note however that enabling inverse kinematics requires some additional configuration for bones at the rigging stage, as you'll see shortly.

Adding inverse kinematics to a leg or arm is generally similar. Let's consider the leg here. To add inverse kinematics to a leg, follow these steps:

1. Select the shin bone in Pose mode.

2. Add an Inverse Kinematics constraint from the Bone Constraints tab in the Properties panel. (See Figure 5.39.)

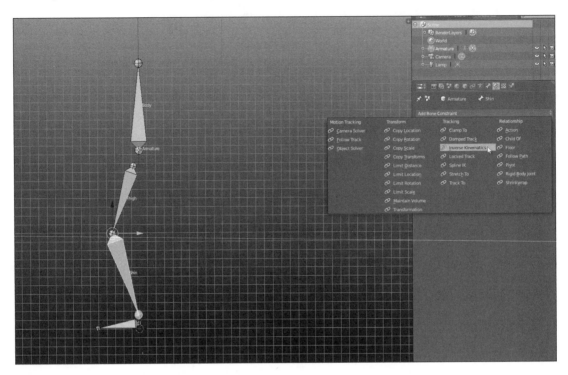

Figure 5.39
Inverse kinematics is added to bones as a bone constraint.
Source: Blender.

3. In the Inverse Kinematics (IK) properties, specify the foot bone as the IK target for the leg—that is, the end of the bone chain you want to move and animate.

4. In the Chain Length field, which indicates how many bones long the IK chain is, indicate how many bones the shin is from the top of the leg. For a leg that has two bones—the shin and the thigh—the Chain Length setting should be 2. (See Figure 5.40.)

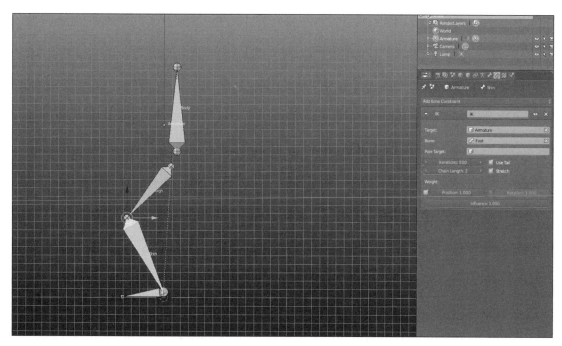

Figure 5.40
Configuring a leg with inverse kinematics.
Source: Blender.

That's it! In performing these steps, you've successfully configured an IK Leg. If you transform either the foot bone or the body, the leg will automatically bend at the knee joint to accommodate the repositioning.

Note

Unity Free lacks support for IK, but that doesn't mean you can't import IK-rigged characters; IK is typically baked down into keyframes on export from Blender. It just means characters in Unity cannot be animated in real time using IK through scripting.

Deform and Control Bones

There are two main bone types in rigging:

- **Control bones.** Control bones are those that animators directly access and move when keyframing a rig for animation. Typically, control bones include all ends of an IK chain (such as feet and hands), as well as others, such as the head, chest, and hip bones.

- **Deform bones.** Sometimes known as mechanism bones, deform bones are intermediary bones that bend or deform automatically as a result of IK when the control bones are transformed, but that animators do not directly access or keyframe. In other words, animators will never need to see or edit deform bones, only the control bones.

These are not officially recognized or understood by Blender or Unity; rather, they are types that developers distinguish when rigging because of the distinct ways in which bones are used during animation.

Once your rig is created, it's good practice to hide deform bones on a separate layer, leaving only the control bones visible for animators to use. This produces a cleaner animation workflow. To hide deform bones, follow these steps:

1. Select all deform bones in the rig.

2. Press the M key on your keyboard to open the Move to Layer dialog box.

3. Select an unused layer. This moves the selected deform bones to that layer. (Moving bones to a different layer affects only their visibility in the viewport, not their functionality.) See Figure 5.41.

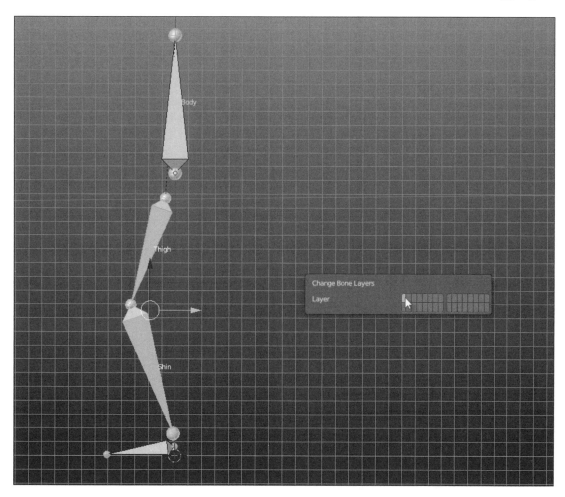

Figure 5.41
Hiding deform bones on an unused layer.
Source: Blender.

Exporting Rigged Characters

Both the FBX (.fbx) and Collada (.dae) format support rigged and animated characters. You can export FBX files via the File > Export > Autodesk FBX command, and export Collada files via the File > Export > Collada command. Figure 5.42 shows the standard FBX options to enable when exporting character rigs, and Figure 5.43 shows the Collada options. If using Collada, be sure your mesh is exported while its armature is in Rest pose.

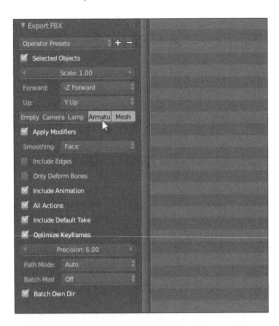

Figure 5.42
Exporting a rigged mesh with FBX.
Source: Blender.

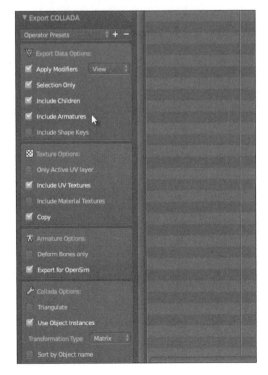

Figure 5.43
Exporting a rigged mesh with DAE.
Source: Blender.

Importing Rigged Meshes into Unity

The Mecanim animation system, introduced in Unity 4, offers a range of impressive features for animating and otherwise working with rigged characters. You import a rigged character much like you import any regular mesh—by dragging and dropping the mesh file from Windows Explorer or the Mac Finder into the Unity Editor Project panel. After the rigged character is imported, however, you must make an additional tweak in the Mesh Importer in the Object Inspector. To do so, select the Rig tab. Then click the Animation Type drop-down list and choose Humanoid (see Figure 5.44). This indicates to Unity that the imported mesh is not only rigged and animated, but is a humanoid rig. Because you've specified this more narrow type, Unity offers additional features that makes working with characters easier. (See the upcoming sidebar for more information.)

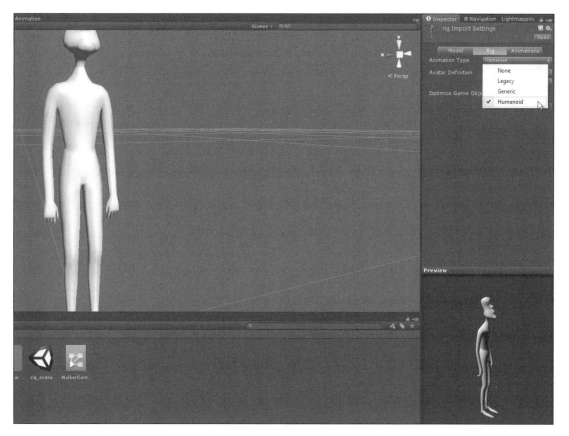

Figure 5.44
Importing a rigged character mesh into Unity.

Source: Unity Technologies.

Options for Humanoid Rigs

When you select Humanoid in the Animation Type drop-down list, Unity generates an avatar or, more fully, an avatar definition. This is a special asset type embedded into the mesh. Essentially, it is a map or database, defining how each bone in a complete skeletal rig or system should match up with and deform the surrounding character mesh. This mapping is called Muscles. When working with a rig and mesh that have been imported together in a single file, it can be difficult to see how the avatar could be useful, because the bone and skinning data will have already been specified in Blender through armatures and vertex weights. But when you use avatars, a powerful feature, known as retargeting, becomes possible. That is, by using different avatars for different characters, it becomes possible to reuse a skeletal rig and its animations on different humanoid models. The avatar enables you to control how one skeletal rig should map to a model. Doing this is important because it allows you to use, for example, a skeletal rig for a skinny character on a much larger character, simply by redefining how the skeletal rig maps to the Muscles.

To preview and edit a character avatar, use the Avatar Editor, available from the Object Inspector. To do so, click the Configure button. Provided your skeletal rig is in a general and standard humanoid form, with appropriate bones, Unity will prove itself efficient at auto-detecting the bones in the rig and configuring the avatar for you. This often means you'll have no extra work to do with the avatar. See Figure 5.45.

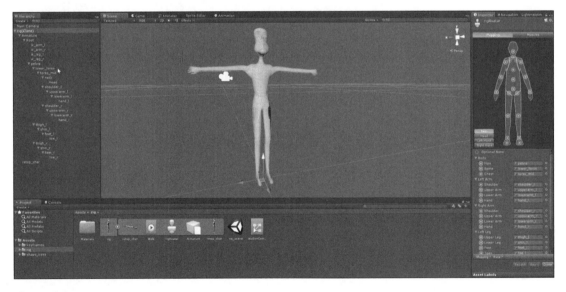

Figure 5.45
Previewing the avatar.
Source: Unity Technologies.

The Avatar Editor displays the rigged model in the Scene viewport and shows the complete Blender bone hierarchy in expanded form in the Scene Hierarchy panel. The Object Inspector displays the mesh bone mapping and muscle definitions. The humanoid mapping in the Object Inspector should appear in green. Red indicates a bone mapping problem, and typically requires you to manually specify the bone mapping. You can do this by dragging and dropping bones from the Scene Hierarchy panel into the appropriate anatomy field in the Object Inspector, mapping hip bones, arm bones, head bones, and leg bones to their proper places to complete the avatar. Only after the bone definitions are correct will the avatar work in the scene as intended; take time to define it fully.

SUMMARY

This chapter covered the intricate and extensive field of computer animation with Blender and Unity. Blender offers three main animation forms that can be exported successfully into Unity: basic keyframe animation (including path animation), shape keys, and skeletal rigs. Together, these three animation types allow for both rigid body animation (such as when an object changes its scene position or rotation) and sub-object or vertex animation (such as when an object remains in position but changes its structure by bending or morphing—for example, when a character moves his mouth). Taken together, these two forms allow for almost any animation type conceivable in a computer game, and this makes Blender and Unity a powerful combination.

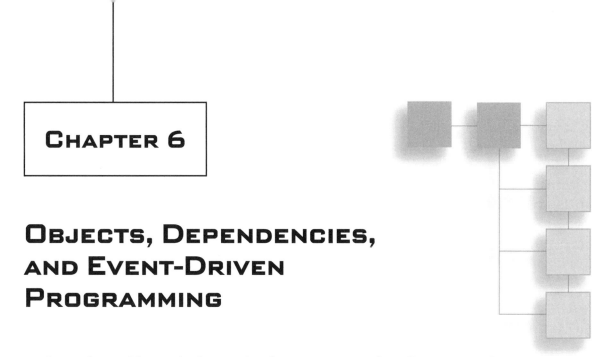

CHAPTER 6

OBJECTS, DEPENDENCIES, AND EVENT-DRIVEN PROGRAMMING

The complexity of things—the things within things—just seems to be endless. I mean nothing is easy, nothing is simple.

—Alice Munro

By the end of this chapter, you should:

- Understand hard-coded dependencies and their solutions
- Be able to work with components and messages
- Understand event-driven programming
- Be able to create an event and notification system
- Understand parent and child relationships for objects

So far in this book, most chapters have focused primarily on workflows in Blender that are compatible or useful for Unity. Thus, the focus has been mostly on how to create assets in Blender that work with Unity, such as modular environments, terrains, and animated meshes. This chapter, however, represents a departure from that approach. It focuses on game-development practices pertaining mostly to Unity. Specifically, it focuses on hard-coded dependencies and on ways to solve them. Let's begin by first considering what hard-coded dependencies are and on how they arise.

Hard-Coded Dependencies

A video game is a form of software, and is the result of software engineering. In most fields of engineering, some kind of structure or complexity is assembled and built, whether it's an engine, a bridge, a tunnel, a building, or a piece of software. In nearly all these cases, the thing being made is, technically speaking, the sum of its parts. There might be disagreements about this point artistically and aesthetically speaking, but structurally speaking, the whole is made from its constituent pieces. The decision as to which pieces to use and how those pieces should be connected during manufacture is of utmost importance for the reliability and strength of the thing being made. Not only that, but the quality of the parts relates to the ease of maintaining the structure once made.

Consider the simplified case of an "ideal" clock, run from interconnected cogs forming part of a complete mechanism. (Think of a giant, classical clock like Big Ben in London, England, or Abraj Al-Bait in Mecca, Saudi Arabia.) Here, the cogs rotate regularly and systematically. If a malfunction occurs, an engineer can scan through the cogs to identify where the fault lays. When the problematic cog is finally found, it can be replaced seamlessly by a new and identically shaped cog that integrates with the others in exactly the same way as the original cog, allowing the system to resume running as though it had never stopped at all.

This kind of isolated repair is possible because, although all cogs work together as part of a complete system, each cog is nevertheless isolated and independent enough to stand alone. This allows for a cog's replacement without it affecting or compromising other parts of the system. If, however, an inventor were later to design a modified cog for the clock—a super-cog, with extra parts and integrated appendages, forming embedded connections and links to other parts in the system—then repairing and replacing it would be a more complex and expensive affair. This is because the cog has deep-rooted connections to other pieces. It doesn't stand in isolation like a regular cog. It has dependencies on other parts. Thus, during its manufacture, a dependency has been created.

In game development, hard-coded dependencies most often occur with object-oriented programming, when one class is made to depend on another either directly or indirectly. Perhaps you're making a wizard character for an RPG game, coded in C# as a Wizard class, as is typical with pure object orientation. However, in developing this class, dependencies to outside functionality can soon arise: When casting offensive spells, for example, the wizard will need to deal damage to enemies. Likewise, when being attacked by enemies, the wizard will need to receive damage. Similarly, events and actions during gameplay, such as completing quests and defeating enemies, will increase the wizard's score and experience points.

For that functionality to happen successfully, the `Wizard` class will need to know when those events happen—but none of those events or actions are native to the `Wizard` class itself. They happen outside of it. In short, then, the `Wizard` class—and nearly every other class in your game—does not and cannot stand in complete isolation to outside functionality. At some point during development, a connection and relationship between classes must be engineered. The question is, can connections like these be engineered while avoiding hard-coded dependencies?

Hard-coded dependencies are generally bad because of the interconnections they establish between classes and objects. These interconnections make it difficult to change, remove, or edit any one of the classes without also affecting another. Consider the case of a wizard object dealing damage to an enemy through spell-casting. Listing 6.1 shows a C# example, creating a connection between a wizard and enemy with hard-coded dependencies.

Listing 6.1: `Wizard` Class with Hard Code Dependencies

```
public class Wizard
{
        //Reference to enemy class
        public MyEnemy Enemy;

        //Function called when wizard casts a fireball spell
        public void OnCastFireBallSpell()
        {
                //deal 20 points of fire damage to enemy
                 Enemy.DealDamage(20);
        }
}
```

Listing 6.1 is a classic case of hard-coded dependencies. The `Wizard` class maintains a direct and internal reference to an enemy object and deals damage to that enemy through the `DealDamage` function. Of course, there's nothing strictly *wrong* with the code, if it works. The problem is that it's really easy to break. That is, you don't have to try very hard to achieve malfunction. For example, if you later decided to remove the `Wizard` class completely, then the enemy character would no longer receive fire damage because there would be no `OnCastFireBall` function to cause it. There might, of course, be another class elsewhere that also deals fire damage to enemies, but if there were, it would only be duplicating what the `Wizard` class already did (and duplication is bad too because it leads to needlessly lengthy code). Furthermore, if you were to change the `Enemy` class by replacing the `DealDamage` function with a more specifically named function, `DealFireDamage`, then a compilation error would result because the wizard character would be calling a `DealDamage` function that no longer existed.

The point is, due to connections between the two classes because of their implementation, you can't easily change one without affecting the other. This might not seem especially troublesome when you consider simple cases like Listing 6.1. But, when such dependencies and connections are multiplied within the same class and across all classes in a game, leading to a spaghetti nightmare of interconnections, then it can make code maintenance unmanageable in the long term. Thankfully, there are solutions to hard-coded dependencies.

SOLVING DI: COMPONENT-BASED DESIGN AND MESSAGES

Traditionally, hard code dependencies have been solved, as far as practically possible, within an object-oriented framework in C# by using virtual functions, interfaces, and polymorphism. More recently, however, some new methodologies outside object orientation have been used. Unity uses these newer methods by offering components and messages. To achieve good performance with Unity, it's important to understand how to work effectively with both. The following sections detail these two related aspects separately.

Component-Based Design

In Unity, a level or environment is called a *scene*. A scene is composed from a hierarchy of game objects, all of which are listed in the Hierarchy Panel of the user interface whenever a scene is open in the editor. In Figure 6.1, the scene features only a camera object and a cube object, centered at the world origin.

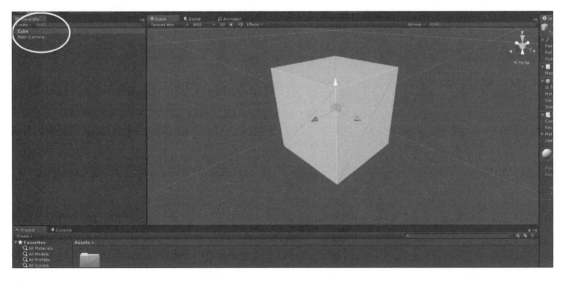

Figure 6.1
A scene is composed from a hierarchy of game objects.
Source: Unity Technologies.

Just as a scene can be broken down into game objects, so can each game object be broken down further. Specifically, each game object is made up of components. All game objects must have at least one component: a Transform component. This is a compulsory component that specifies an object's position, orientation, and scale in world space. Typically, however, game objects feature more than one component. The cube, shown in Figure 6.2, is composed of four components: Transform, Mesh Filter, Box Collider, and Mesh Renderer. The Transform component defines an object's transform data; the Mesh Filter component contains mesh information (vertices, edges, and polygons), the Collider component defines an approximate bounding volume for use with collision detection, and the Mesh Renderer component allows the mesh filter data to be displayed onscreen during gameplay.

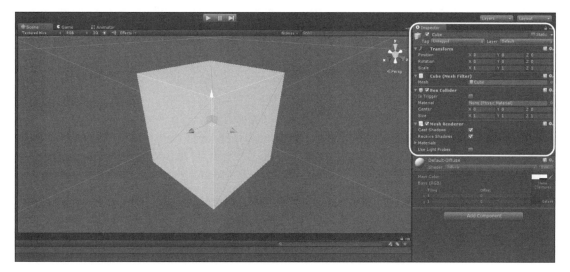

Figure 6.2
Every game object is made of components.
Source: Unity Technologies.

Defining game objects in terms of modular components, as Unity does, is distinctly different from the traditional object-oriented approach. With object-orientation, there would normally be an attempt to encapsulate the whole cube, transform, and mesh data into a single class using inheritance. With component-based design, however, each component is conceived as a smaller and less-encompassing block. It serves a dedicated function independent of any larger classes or objects. Objects in their entirety simply arise from a specific collection of components attached to a single game object.

Here, game objects are seen as emergent entities—hence the reason component-based design is sometimes called an *entity system*. The cube mesh becomes what it is simply because four components together (Transform, Mesh Filter, Box Collider, and Mesh Renderer) make it so. If you were to remove one of those components (except Transform), you'd still be left with a game object—just a different one. If you removed the Mesh Renderer component, for example, you'd get an invisible cube. If you instead removed the Box Collider component, you'd get a substance-less cube that you couldn't ever bump into. And if you removed the Mesh Filter component, you'd get a formless collider.

In short, by defining and thinking about objects in terms of related components, you are extricated to a degree from the trap of hard-coded dependencies. You stop thinking about the game object as a complete and discrete element with multiple parts rolled into one; instead, you think about an object as a being borne from combinations of components. This technique applies not just to the cube considered here, of course, but to all objects.

Messages

In Listing 6.1, a `Wizard` class directly called upon an `Enemy` class to deal damage. This approach requires the `Wizard` class to know something about the implementation details of the `Enemy` class—specifically, that it has a `DealDamage` function. In practice, then, for Listing 6.1 to compile and work successfully, the `Enemy` class must always implement a `DealDamage` function. This dependency is limiting and restrictive.

Using the component system in Unity, it's possible to transcend this problem. Components may interact and communicate with other components, without any knowledge of their internals or implementation. That means one component can talk to another without knowing what the other does or how it works. Let's see an example of this by creating two custom C# components for the cube object in Figure 6.2. (To create the cube object, choose GameObject > Create Other > Cube.) One component will be Wizard, and the other Enemy. We'll make them talk.

Remember: You create script files in Unity by selecting Assets > Create > C# Script. (See Figure 6.3.) Unity also supports the JavaScript and Boo languages, but these are not discussed in this book.

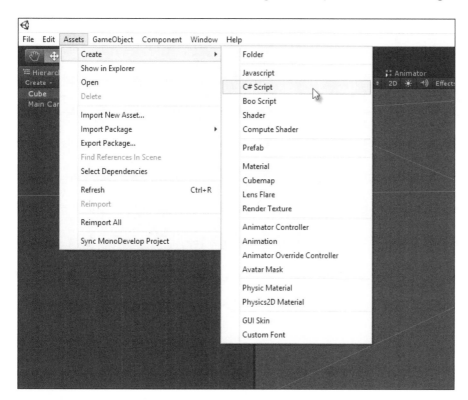

Figure 6.3
Creating C# script files.
Source: Unity Technologies.

The code for the Wizard class is listed in Listing 6.2, and the code for the Enemy class in Listing 6.3. Comments follow these classes. Both classes should be attached to the same game object in the scene. For this example, I've attached them to the same cube object, as shown in Figure 6.4.

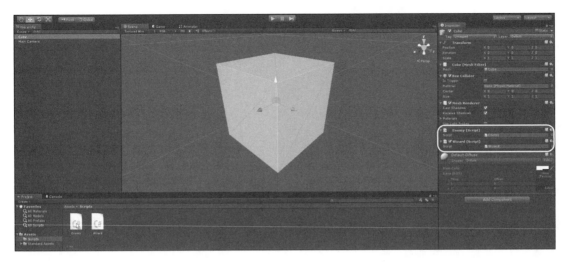

Figure 6.4
Attaching C# script files to a game object.
Source: Unity Technologies.

Note

To attach the scripts as components to a game object, just drag and drop the script file from the Project panel onto the object in the scene.

Listing 6.2: Wizard.cs

```
using UnityEngine;
using System.Collections;

public class Wizard : MonoBehaviour
{
    // Update is called once per frame
    void Update ()
    {
        //If player presses fire button
        if(Input.GetButtonDown("Fire"))
        {
        //Now deal damage to any enemy components attached to this object
            SendMessage("ApplyDamage", 10.0f,
SendMessageOptions.DontRequireReceiver);
        }
    }
}
```

Listing 6.3: Enemy.cs

```
using UnityEngine;
using System.Collections;

public class Enemy : MonoBehaviour
{
     //Function called to deal damage to enemy
     public void ApplyDamage(float Damage = 0.0f)
     {
          Debug.Log ("Damage Dealt - ouch!");
     }
}
```

Here are some comments pertaining to Listing 6.2 and Listing 6.3:

- Class `Wizard` uses the `SendMessage` function to dispatch an `ApplyDamage` message to the game object (the object to which the wizard component is attached). All components attached to the object will receive this message.

- Components will receive the message in the form of a function call. If the component has an `ApplyDamage` function, then it will be called for that component. If the component has no such function, then nothing will happen for that component.

- The function argument `SendMessageOptions.DontRequireReceiver` acts as a type of fail-safe. It indicates that, should any component not implement an `ApplyDamage` message, an error will not be generated.

Note

You can find more information on the `SendMessage` function in the Unity documentation: http://docs.unity3d.com/Documentation/ScriptReference/GameObject.SendMessage.html.

The great benefit of using messages and components together is that one component (the sender) can send messages to another (the receiver) without knowing the receiver's implementation details. The receiver has the option (or not) to respond to the sender's message. By using this system as a basis for sending and receiving events, components can work together while avoiding the pitfalls of hard-coded dependencies.

Note

There are important performance issues related to the component message system. Specifically, the `SendMessage` function (as well as the `BroadcastMessage` function, discussed shortly) rely on a programming concept known as *reflection*. In short, each time `SendMessage` is called, Unity must internally use a function lookup table to compare the argument string against a list of function names to see which component and function should be invoked (if any). This process, when called frequently across many objects, can be the cause of performance problems, especially on mobile devices. In short, use `SendMessage` and `BroadcastMessage` with minimalism in mind.

Taking Messages Further: `BroadcastMessage` and Hierarchies

There may be times when you want to invoke behaviors and functionality on many related objects in one batch at the same time. For example, maybe a group of enemies must be destroyed together in an explosion, or maybe your wizard character casts a group-affecting spell, such as mass-healing, where multiple people are affected together. To achieve this, you could use the `SendMessage` function multiple times across many objects, but it might be more convenient to use `BroadcastMessage` instead. The `BroadcastMessage` function enables you to send a message to a specified game object and to all its child objects in the scene hierarchy. In other words, it works like `SendMessage`, except its call cascades downward through the hierarchy of objects. So if you have a parent object with multiple children and need to send a message to them all, then `BroadcastMessage` can be your friend. Listing 6.4 demonstrates its usage.

Listing 6.4: Broadcasting an `ApplyDamage` Message to the Current Object and All Its Children

```
BroadcastMessage("ApplyDamage", 10.0f, SendMessageOptions.DontRequireReceiver);
```

If you arrange game objects into a scene hierarchy with careful planning, then the `BroadcastMessage` function can be very powerful. One helpful application here is to create an empty, root game object in your scene of which everything else is a child or descendent. (See Figure 6.5.) By doing this, you can easily send a message to every object in the scene by broadcasting a message to the root. This can be especially helpful to distribute system-wide notifications, such as `Exit-Game`, `Load-Game`, and `Save-Game` notifications.

Note

To create empty game objects, choose GameObject > Create Empty. Empty game objects act like dummies in 3D software. They feature only a Transform component.

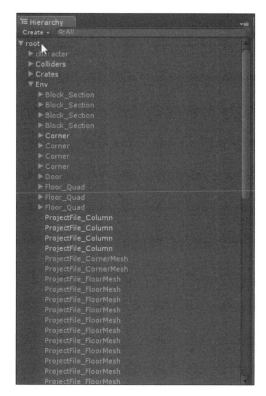

Figure 6.5
Creating scenes with a root game object can simplify message broadcasting.
Source: Unity Technologies.

SENDING MESSAGES TO SELECTED OBJECTS

So far, you've seen how to send a message to a single object and to a hierarchy of objects. But what about an array of selected objects? Perhaps you need to send a respawn message to all dead enemies in the scene or to all expired power-ups. Or maybe you need to lock all doors due to an intruder alarm being activated. Or possibly you need to temporarily disable all player weapons, preventing them from attacking.

There will be times when you want to send messages to only a select group of objects that may not share the same hierarchy. In these cases, you'll need to use SendMessage on each object. There are ways to make this process easier, however. Listing 6.5 shows how to generate an array of all components in the scene of a specified type, and then how to send a message to the array.

Listing 6.5: Sending Messages to Selected Objects

```
//Get all objects of specified type in the scene(get all enemies)
Enemy[] Enemies = Object.FindObjectsOfType<Enemy>();

//Loop through enemies in array
foreach(Enemy E in Enemies)
      E.SendMessage("ApplyDamage", 10.0f, SendMessageOptions.DontRequireReceiver);
//Apply Damage
```

Note

You can find more information on the FindObjectsofType function in the official Unity documentation: http://docs.unity3d.com/Documentation/ScriptReference/Object.FindObjectsOfType.html. Avoid calling this function during update or frame-based events.

SENDING MESSAGES TO PARENTS

There might be times during development when you need to pass a message upward, rather than downward, through object hierarchies. For example, an end-of-level boss character for a side-scrolling space-shooter game might feature multiple gun turrets, all of which must be destroyed. These turrets might be implemented as separate game objects, all attached as children to a common parent object. When a turret is destroyed by the player, the parent object should be notified. To enable the child to notify a parent, you can use the SendMessageUpwards function. This function works like BroadcastMessage, except it dispatches messages upward through the hierarchy to parents rather than downward to children. Take care, however, as this function doesn't simply stop at the first parent object encountered; rather, it moves upward recursively to the topmost parent object in the scene until no more parents are found. See Listing 6.6.

Listing 6.6: Sending Messages Upward to Parents

```
SendMessageUpwards("ApplyDamage", 10.0f,
SendMessageOptions.DontRequireReceiver);
```

NOTIFICATION SYSTEM

Using the SendMessage and BroadcastMessage functions between objects can be useful for avoiding logical dependencies and interconnections, but it can still leave you wanting better. For example, if a wizard character deals damage directly to an enemy using the SendMessage function, there might be additional objects in the scene that'll want to know about that event. For example, the GUI classes might want to know to update health and status bars after the attack. Other enemies might also want to know the same thing in case it influences their AI handling, such as fleeing behavior. In short, there's a potentially unknown number of classes that could need to know about any event that may occur in-game—and not just once, but every time the event happens.

If you use `SendMessage` and `BroadcastMessage` on an object-to-object basis as you've done so far, where one object sends a message directly to another without any kind of mediation between them, then event handling could become complex and unwieldy for larger projects. For this reason, early in development, it's good practice to create a dedicated and centralized event-handling class that manages event notifications across all objects in the game. This event-handling system effectively allows an event-causer (a sender or poster) to notify the system about the occurrence of an event type (such as enemy damage). Then, once posted, the system will immediately pass that notification on to all other classes (listeners) that have explicitly registered to be notified about that event type.

Listing 6.7 displays the full source code for a complete event-handling system (called `NotificationsManager`) in C#. Subsequent sections explain how it can be used in practice and how it works.

Note

> `NotificationsManager` and its usage in a Unity project, with wizard and enemy objects, is included with the book companion files in the Chapter06 folder.

Listing 6.7: `NotificationsManager`

```
//EVENTS MANAGER CLASS - for receiving notifications and notifying listeners
//-------------------------------------------------
using UnityEngine;
using System.Collections;
using System.Collections.Generic;
//-------------------------------------------------
public class NotificationsManager : MonoBehaviour
{
        //Private variables
        //---------------------------------------------
        //Singleton property access
        public static NotificationsManager Instance
        {
```

```
            get{
                    if(!instance) instance = new NotificationsManager();
                    return instance;
                }
        }
```

```
    //Internal reference to object instance
    private static NotificationsManager instance = null;
```

```
    //Internal reference to all listeners for notifications
    private Dictionary<string, List<Component>> Listeners = new Dictionary
<string, List<Component>>();
```

```
    //Methods
    //-------------------------------------------------
    //Called a start-up
    void Awake()
    {
            //If instance already active then remove this instance
            if(instance) {DestroyImmediate(gameObject); return;}

            //Else make this single instance
            instance = this;
    }
    //-------------------------------------------------
    //Function to add a listener for a notification to the listeners list
    public void AddListener(Component Sender, string NotificationName)
    {
            //Add listener to dictionary
            if(!Listeners.ContainsKey(NotificationName))
                    Listeners.Add (NotificationName, new List<Component>());

            //Add object to listener list for this notification
            Listeners[NotificationName].Add(Sender);
    }
    //-------------------------------------------------
    //Function to remove a listener for a notification
    public void RemoveListener(Component Sender, string NotificationName)
    {
            //If no key in dictionary exists, then exit
            if(!Listeners.ContainsKey(NotificationName))
                    return;

            //Cycle through listeners and identify component, and then remove
```

```
            for(int i = Listeners[NotificationName].Count-1; i>=0; i--)
            {
                    //Check instance ID
                    if(Listeners[NotificationName][i].GetInstanceID() ==
Sender.GetInstanceID())
                            Listeners[NotificationName].RemoveAt(i); //Matched. Remove
from list
            }
        }
        //-------------------------------------------------
        //Function to post a notification to a listener
        public void PostNotification(Component Sender, string NotificationName)
        {
                //If no key in dictionary exists, then exit
                if(!Listeners.ContainsKey(NotificationName))
                        return;

                //Else post notification to all matching listeners
                foreach(Component Listener in Listeners[NotificationName])
                        Listener.SendMessage(NotificationName, Sender,
SendMessageOptions.DontRequireReceiver);
        }
        //-------------------------------------------------
        //Function to clear all listeners
        public void ClearListeners()
        {
                //Removes all listeners
                Listeners.Clear();
        }
        //-------------------------------------------------
        //Function to remove redundant listeners - deleted and removed listeners
        public void RemoveRedundancies()
        {
                //Create new dictionary
                Dictionary<string, List<Component>> TmpListeners = new Dictionary<string,
List<Component>>();

                //Cycle through all dictionary entries
                foreach(KeyValuePair<string, List<Component>> Item in Listeners)
                {
                        //Cycle through all listener objects in list, remove null objects
```

```
                for(int i = Item.Value.Count-1; i>=0; i--)
                {
                        //If null, then remove item
                        if(Item.Value[i] == null)
                                Item.Value.RemoveAt(i);
                }

                //If items remain in list for this notification, then add this to tmp
dictionary
                if(Item.Value.Count > 0)
                        TmpListeners.Add (Item.Key, Item.Value);
        }

        //Replace listeners object with new, optimized dictionary
        Listeners = TmpListeners;
    }
    //-------------------------------------------------
    //Called when a new level is loaded; remove redundant entries from dictionary; in case
left-over from previous scene
    void OnLevelWasLoaded()
    {
        //Clear redundancies
        RemoveRedundancies();
    }
    //-------------------------------------------------
}
```

NotificationsManager In-Depth

To summarize, NotificationsManager allows listener objects to register for events using the AddListener function. For any event type (such as enemy attack events, level restart events, player-die events, or others), there may be none, one, or more listeners; all registered listeners for an event will be notified when the event happens. When a component causes an event during gameplay, it must notify NotificationsManager using the PostNotification function. When PostNotification is called, NotificationsManager cycles through all listeners for the event, notifying each one. Using NotificationsManager, an Enemy class can register for and respond to ApplyDamage events as shown in Listing 6.8.

Listing 6.8: Enemy Class Registering with `NotificationsManager`

```
using UnityEngine;
using System.Collections;

public class Enemy : MonoBehaviour
{
    void Start()
    {
        NotificationsManager.Instance.AddListener(this, "ApplyDamage");
    }

    //Function called to deal damage to enemy (will be invoked automatically by
NotificationsManager)
    public void ApplyDamage(Component Sender)
    {
        Debug.Log ("Damage Dealt - ouch!");
    }
}
```

In Listing 6.8, the `Enemy` class uses the standard `Start()` event to register with `NotificationsManager` for all `ApplyDamage` events. Registering is something each listener has to do only once; `NotificationsManager` will notify the listener when the event happens by using `SendMessage` to call a function on the listener. The function name should match the name of the event being listened for. In Listing 6.8, the event is `ApplyDamage`, and the `Enemy` class implements the function `ApplyDamage` to handle this event. As long as a class adheres to this protocol set by `NotificationsManager`, any event can support any number of listeners—and thus multiple enemies can listen for and respond to the `ApplyDamage` event, or others.

Let's now see some code showing how `NotificationsManager` works from the perspective of an event causer that should post a notification to be propagated to listeners. See Listing 6.9.

Listing 6.9: Sample `Wizard` Class That Invokes an Attack on Enemies

```
using UnityEngine;
using System.Collections;

public class Wizard : MonoBehaviour
{
    // Update is called once per frame
    void Update ()
    {
```

```
        //If player presses fire button
        if(Input.GetButtonDown("Fire1"))
        {
            //Notify enemies in level
            NotificationsManager.Instance.PostNotification(this, "ApplyDamage");
        }
    }
}
```

There's little that needs commenting on Listing 6.9 in terms of event handling (although a noteworthy feature is discussed in the next section). Here a class posts notification to NotificationsManager whenever an event happens.

Note

To see NotificationsManager at work, see the Unity project files associated with this chapter, in the Chapter06 folder.

Singletons

NotificationsManager is a special kind of object. Typically, a class or component is scripted with the intention that it will be instantiated many times throughout the scene. Both the Wizard and Enemy classes created so far—even as sample classes for the purpose of demonstrating concepts—can be instantiated more than once in the scene, giving you multiple wizards and multiple enemies if you need them. This often makes sense. But NotificationsManager is a centralized object by nature. That is, there should be only one instance of the class in the scene, and all other game objects interact with the event system through that single instance.

In practice, NotificationsManager should be attached to one game object in the scene, and there will never be any reason to have more instances than this. Now, in practice, we could simply just acknowledge this to ourselves and then move on to more interesting issues. But there's good reason not to stop here, and indeed NotificationsManager, as shown in Listing 6.7, takes additional steps in this regard. Consider, for example, the class member instance, Instance, and the Awake event. And consider also how the Enemy and Wizard classes interacted with NotificationsManager in Listing 6.8 and Listing 6.9, using the convention NotificationsManager.Instance.

Specifically, the NotificationsManager has been implemented as a singleton object. A singleton object is one whose class has been defined so that multiple instances are not possible. The singleton object is not simply one that just happens to be instantiated only once;

rather, it's an object that cannot be instantiated more than once. The restriction is built-in. This is made possible by the use of static member variables. In practice, that means any class in any scope, anywhere in the Unity project, can always access the single and only instance of NotificationsManager through the convention NotificationsManager.Instance. With this convention, every class has convenient and full access to the event-handling system! The famous sci-fi author Arthur C. Clarke once said, "Any sufficiently advanced technology is indistinguishable from magic." Indeed, the singleton has a feeling of magic about it. I recommend using singletons to effectively solve your overarching class-management problems.

MESSAGES AND ACTIVE OBJECTS

NotificationsManager depends on the SendMessage function, discussed earlier, to dispatch notifications to listeners. However, it's important to qualify the conditions under which SendMessage operates successfully in Unity. Specifically, SendMessage, BroadcastMessage, and SendMessageUpwards are effectual only on active game objects—that is, objects whose activeInHierarchy member is set to true. This value can be toggled on and off directly in the Unity Editor via the Object Inspector (see Figure 6.6). It can also be changed in code through the SetActive function. (See http://docs.unity3d.com/Documentation/Script Reference/GameObject.SetActive.html for more information.) If activeInHierarchy is set to false, then the object will automatically ignore all messages, acting as though they were never sent. For this reason, if you want your objects to play nice with NotificationsManager and the messaging system generally, be sure they're active when you need them to be.

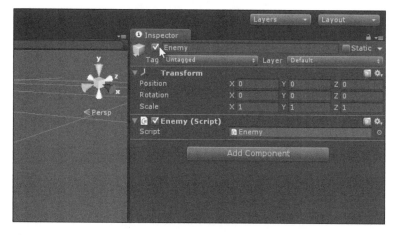

Figure 6.6
Toggling the active state of a game object from the Editor.
Source: Unity Technologies.

TRAVERSING GAME OBJECT HIERARCHIES

In addition to sending messages and events automatically across collections of game objects, it can also be useful to manually navigate the game object hierarchy from code, as well as to change it. For example, suppose your RPG features an inventory object, where collected items like flasks, armor, weapons, potions, and others are added as child objects to an inventory parent for as long as they remain in the inventory. In cases like these, it's useful to add and remove children to and from parents dynamically, and to enumerate all child objects of a parent. Let's see how to do that here. Listing 6.10 adds an object to a new parent.

Listing 6.10: Assigning an Object a New Parent

```
//Search Scene. Find object of name
GameObject Child = GameObject.Find(ObjectName);

//If object was not found, then exit
if(Child == null) return;

//Reparent
Child.transform.parent = Parent.transform;
```

See in Listing 6.10 that game object parenting data is stored inside the object's Transform component—specifically, transform.parent. For more information on the Transform component, see http://docs.unity3d.com/Documentation/ScriptReference/Transform.html.

Now let's consider the case of enumerating through all children of an object—that is, looping through each and every child object of a parent. See Listing 6.11. For each child, this example will retrieve the Transform component, but this technique can be applied to retrieve any component attached to the game object.

Listing 6.11: Get Transform Component for All Child Objects

```
//Loop through children
for(int i=0; i<Parent.transform.childCount; i++)
{
        //Get child object
        GameObject ChildObj = Parent.transform.GetChild(i).gameObject;

        //If child is valid
        if(ChildObj == null) continue;

        //Get Transform component of child
        Transform TransComp = ChildObj.GetComponent<Transform>();
}
```

Summary

This chapter focused narrowly on Unity game objects and their relationship to events and messages. This is a subject area commonly overlooked and dismissed as only marginally important by many newcomers. But this chapter has shown that kind of dismissal to be premature, and also why game objects and their arrangement into hierarchies are critically important for messages and event-handling systems. Further, it explored the implementation of a `NotificationsManager` class as a singleton object, which allows only one instantiation at any one time. Using this structure and static members, every class in a Unity project can provide direct and easy access to a fully featured event-handling system, capable of dispatching event notifications to any and every kind of listener.

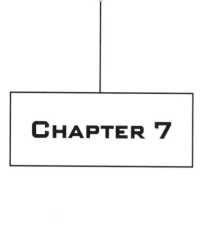

CHAPTER 7

RETOPOLOGIZING

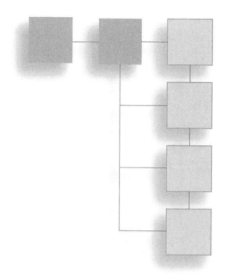

Simplify, simplify.

—Henry David Thoreau

By the end of this chapter, you should:

- Understand what retopologizing is and why it's used
- Learn how to use the Blender sculpting tools in more depth
- Understand surface snapping and the Shrinkwrap modifier
- Be able to manually retopologize a mesh
- Be able to reduce mesh detail using the Decimate modifier

In the early days of 3D graphics for video games, most meshes were modeled in 3D software using the famous box-modeling method. This method is so named because, using it, the artist almost always begins with a standard box mesh, just as a sculptor begins with a formless lump of clay. From that starting point, the artist can make almost anything from the box by extruding, cutting, subdividing, beveling, and tweaking faces, edges, and vertices.

Details of the box-modeling method are covered in almost every fundamentals course for Blender, and so needn't be reiterated here. However, in more recent times, the box-modeling method has been adapted and integrated into a larger workflow that includes mesh sculpting and high-polygon modeling (or *high-poly modeling* for short). What do these terms mean? What is their significance for creating models in Blender? And what is their impact for exporting models into the Unity engine? These questions are considered throughout the rest of this chapter, and answering them involves the subject of retopologizing, as you'll see.

High-Poly Meshes and Subdivision Surfaces

The resolution or detail of a mesh is specified in terms of vertices. Technically, the more vertices a mesh has, the more detailed it is, because each vertex represents a control point on the surface by which detail can be defined. Typically, when importing a mesh into a game engine, the vertex count should be kept as low as possible for performance reasons. (Of course, that advice is meant within reasonable limits that are consistent with your design.) However, that doesn't mean you must minimize the vertex count when modeling in 3D software, before exporting the mesh. Many artists actually begin with a low-poly model and then procedurally increase the detail of the mesh using subdivision. The result is a high-poly mesh—sometimes known as a *subdivision surface* (see Figure 7.1). Figure 7.2 shows how a simple cube object (A) can be subdivided into a denser surface (B), from which more detail can be added and defined.

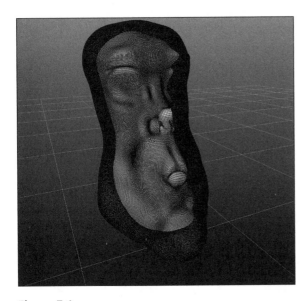

Figure 7.1
High-poly head mesh. High-poly meshes give you a denser mesh surface into which detail can be sculpted instead of using traditional box-modeling methods.
Source: Blender.

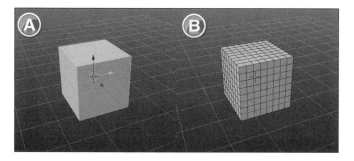

Figure 7.2
Low-poly meshes can be subdivided into denser meshes.
Source: Blender.

The chief purpose of mesh subdivision is to increase the number of vertices so that more detail can be added to your models. These details might include creases, chinks, cloth folds, rough surfaces, bumpiness, cracks, hairs, fibers, and more. This subdivision has implications for the artist in his or her modeling workflow, however. Specifically, it reduces the suitability of the box-modeling method because box modeling requires the artist to work directly with vertices and faces. That approach works as long as the poly count is low because it's easier to manipulate individual faces. But with subdivision surfaces, the density of the mesh makes it impractical to model at the vertex level. The solution to this problem is to sculpt models using dedicated sculpting and brush tools, analogous to real-world sculpting tools. You considered these tools in Chapter 4, "Terrain," when you created terrains for Unity. (See Figure 7.3.)

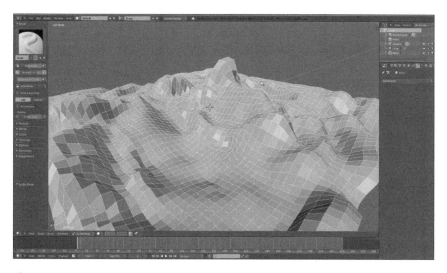

Figure 7.3
Blender sculpting tools are suitable for modeling and deforming high-poly meshes.
Source: Blender.

In short, high-poly meshes open up a vast new world of detail for the artist. With more powerful hardware and more efficient 3D software, including Blender, the artist can now work with highly tessellated meshes, using sculpting tools to carve in and extrude out details that were formerly possible only through texturing. But, despite the greater detail available in meshes, there's a big logistic problem, considered next.

HIGH-POLY MESHES AND REAL-TIME GAMES

The main problem with high-poly meshes for games is their high-poly nature—that is, their level of detail. The high-poly mesh may indeed render and work acceptably in most cases when sculpting in Blender using the modeling tools, but the same cannot be said for the mesh once it's imported into Unity and rendered in real time, complete with textures, shaders, and other meshes. In Unity, the high-poly mesh will likely cause serious performance issues, resulting in lag or even crashes—not just on mobile devices and legacy hardware, but on desktop and console platforms. The level of detail of high-poly meshes is simply not compatible with contemporary consumer hardware for real-time games. This situation may, and probably will, change in the future, but that future has not yet arrived. So the question arises as to the point and value of high-poly meshes for games if their very nature is such that they cannot be imported successfully into real-time game engines. Surely, if high-poly meshes cannot be imported into a game engine, they must be a waste of time!

The answer to this question is less simple than you'd think. That's because artists can use a technique known as *normal mapping* to sculpt high-poly models and then save, or *bake*, an approximation of their surface detail into a special kind of image file, or texture, called a *normal map*. After the normal-map detail is generated from the high-poly mesh, it can then be projected onto a low-poly (and game-suitable) version of the mesh to simulate or fake the detail that was present in the high-poly original. The aim of this technique is to give developers the best of both worlds: to simulate high-poly detail on low-poly meshes. If used effectively, low-poly meshes can imitate the look of high-poly meshes. In other words, they can appear far more detailed than they really are.

To produce these two meshes—the original high-poly mesh and the low-poly mesh that will be exported to game engines, along with a normal map—artists in Blender typically use a very specific workflow. They begin by creating the original high-poly mesh with the sculpting tools. Then, on the basis of that completed mesh, they generate the low-poly version either manually or automatically. The process of generating the low-poly version is known as *retopologizing*. This is because in creating the low-poly version, artists must use box-modeling techniques to rebuild the mesh topology so it effectively approximates the high-poly model.

RETOPOLOGIZING IN PRACTICE

The rest of this chapter considers a specific case study for a retopologizing workflow—specifically, how to create a high-poly game character that'll evolve into a low-poly (game-ready) version compatible with normal mapping. The project files for this chapter are included in the Chapter07 folder, and the work is detailed step by step throughout subsequent sections. Figure 7.4 shows the high- and low-poly versions of the character, side by side.

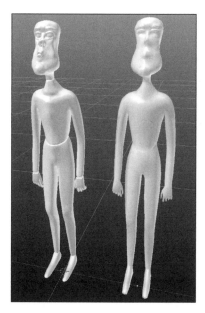

Figure 7.4
High-poly model (left) with a retopologized low-poly version (right).
Source: Blender.

Step 1: Use Box Modeling to Create a Low-Poly Start

Whether you're building a high-poly character, vehicle, weapon, organic structure, or something else, you'll typically start by creating a low-poly approximation or starting point using box-modeling techniques—namely, extruding and tweaking faces. This low-poly model marks out the basic form and structure your model will have. It needn't feature any fine details, just the basic shape and silhouette of your model. This starting point should be low-poly rather than high-poly. As such, you can use nearly all the box-modeling tools available to create it. These are accessible from the Mesh menu when the mesh is in Edit mode. (See Figure 7.5.)

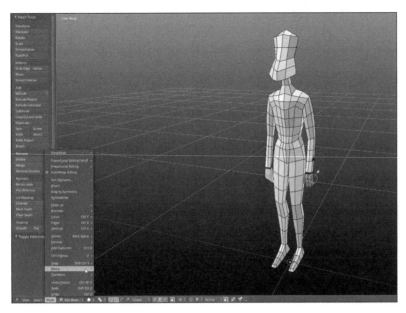

Figure 7.5
Start by creating a low-poly base mesh from which sculpting can begin. You can form the mesh using box modeling. You can access most box-modeling tools from the Mesh menu when the mesh is in Edit mode.
Source: Blender.

Note

For symmetrical models with one line of symmetry (such as a humanoid model), you'll probably need to build only one half or side of the model. You can then duplicate the remaining side using the Mirror modifier. See http://wiki.blender.org/index.php/Doc:2.6/Manual/Modifiers/Generate/Mirror for details.

The base mesh being created here (refer to Figure 7.5) represents a starting point. Soon, you will subdivide or tessellate this mesh (that is, make it denser in terms of vertices) without compromising its original shape and structure. This process will ensure that the mesh has sufficient detail for the sculpting process to come. However, because the mesh will be subdivided, there are three important tips to remember when modeling:

- **Use only quads (and triangles where absolutely necessary).** That is, create the model to feature only four-sided polygons, with three-sided polygons only where necessary. Triangles can cause unseemly creases or sharp edges. Avoid *n*-gons, as they can cause tessellation problems with the subdivision process, resulting in messy geometry. (See Figure 7.6.)

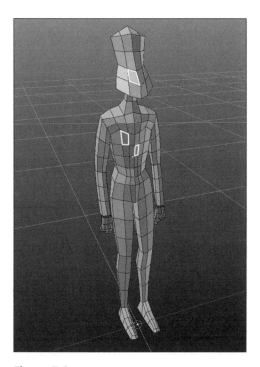

Figure 7.6
Create base meshes from quads. Use tris only if unavoidable. Don't use *n*-gons.
Source: Blender.

- **Normalize quad size.** Try to keep all faces in your model a similar size in terms of surface area. The process of subdivision causes all faces to be sliced into equally sized segments, or smaller faces. If your mesh has similarly sized faces throughout, then you can guarantee that subdivision (when it happens) will have a predictable and consistent effect across the entire surface of your mesh. If some faces are significantly larger than others—for example, arm faces are longer than chest faces—then the subdivision process will divide the model unequally, resulting in some areas being more detailed and tessellated than others. (See Figure 7.7.)

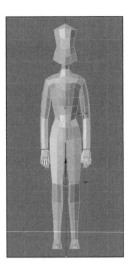

Figure 7.7
Use evenly spaced quads throughout the model. Pinpoint precision is not required here.
Source: Blender.

■ **Follow the model contours.** Identify the prominent contours of your model, such as the waistline, knee lines, neck line, lower and upper chest, arm sockets, ankle lines, eye sockets, nose, etc. Then conform your geometry to these contours. In practice, this means lining up your edges and edge loops to follow and flow along those contours in clean and neat lines. This will make it easier to model and emphasize these regions, as well as to animate the model cleanly at appropriate joints, such as the knees and arm sockets, without incurring distortion and ugly deformations. (See Figure 7.8.)

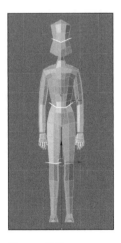

Figure 7.8
Arrange edge loops to conform to model contours.
Source: Blender.

Step 2: Subdivide

After you create the base mesh, the next step is to subdivide in preparation for high-poly sculpting. It's important to subdivide the mesh sufficiently to allow for the detail you need. Otherwise, the mesh will look rigid and angular rather than smooth and organic. In addition, you'll probably want to collapse the modifier stack for your mesh before subdividing, baking in modifiers such as the Mirror modifier (if you have one applied). This prevents a hard seam along the line of symmetry, allowing the smoothing algorithm to work across the entire mesh rather than just half of it. Also, this allows for asymmetrical sculpting to create differences in detail across each side of the model. To bake the Mirror modifier, just click its Apply button in the Properties panel. (See Figure 7.9.)

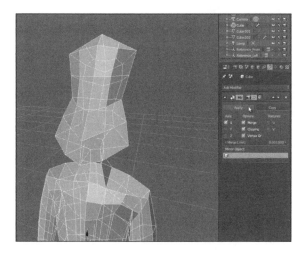

Figure 7.9
Baking the mirror modifier into the mesh.
Source: Blender.

In Blender, there are many ways to *up-res*—that is, to increase the vertex count. Perhaps the simplest method is to select all faces in the mesh and then choose Mesh > Edges > Subdivide. This method applies no true smoothing to the mesh, however; it simply maintains the mesh form and shape while increasing the number of faces. This might be what you need in some cases, such as when modeling hard-surface vehicles, but for organic structures like flowers, people, mushrooms, and other tissue surfaces, you'll probably want smoothing applied as well as subdivision. (See Figure 7.10.)

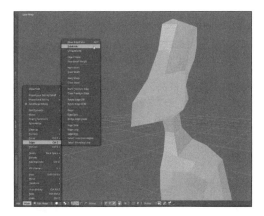

Figure 7.10
The Subdivide command maintains the mesh shape but increases the internal tessellation of each selected face.
Source: Blender.

Another way to increase resolution—this time with smoothing—is to use the Subdivision Surface modifier. (See Figure 7.11.) This modifier both subdivides and applies smoothing to surfaces. You control the strength of these settings using the View and Render properties. The View property defines the amount of smoothing and division to be applied to the model in the viewport, while the Render property allows you to specify separate values for the model if you're rendering it using the Blender Internal Renderer (discussed in Chapter 9, "Baking") or the Cycles Renderer. Typically, for games, only the View property is critical here, because real-time game models are not rendered with Blender, but with Unity. The main issue with this modifier for sculpting is that it doesn't offer support for viewing multiple subdivision levels between sculpting and non-sculpting modes. The subdivision preview is controlled only on a view/render basis. For this reason, there's a more suitable alternative for sculpting, considered next.

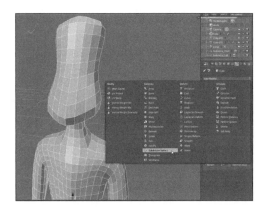

Figure 7.11
The Subdivision Surface modifier.
Source: Blender.

The preferred subdivision and smoothing method for sculpting high-poly meshes is the Multiresolution modifier. (See Figure 7.12.) In short, you apply this modifier to your mesh using the Modifiers tab in the Blender Properties panel; then click the Subdivide button for the modifier to add an extra level of subdivision to the selected mesh, with smoothing included. For the high-res character model in Figure 7.4 (the one on the left), a subdivision level of 7 has been specified.

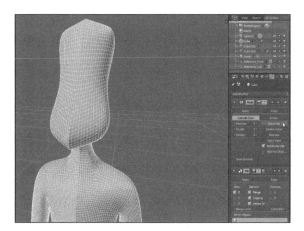

Figure 7.12
The Multiresolution modifier applied with three levels of subdivision active.
Source: Blender.

The higher the subdivision level, the more densely tessellated your mesh will become, and the more detail will be added. The Preview, Sculpt, and Render fields enable you to adjust the subdivision visibility separately for those three specific modes in case you need to lower the display levels to improve performance on your computer while sculpting or viewing. Take care when adding subdivision levels, as high levels can affect system performance and lead to sluggish behavior. Find a maximum that works for you on your system and keep within those limits.

Step 3: Sculpt and Subdivide

After you add a Multiresolution modifier to your base mesh using the Modifiers tab in the Properties panel, you're ready to start the process of sculpting. The way I usually handle this process is to sculpt and subdivide in stages. This ensures that I get the best performance from my computer possible. Subdividing your meshes to the highest levels initially can result in slower performance in the long term, so subdivide to the maximum extent only when the time is suitable.

To sculpt and subdivide, follow these steps:

1. Access the sculpting tools. To do so, select your model and switch into Sculpt mode. (See Figure 7.13.)

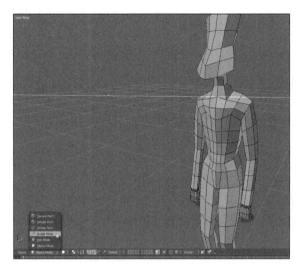

Figure 7.13
Accessing Sculpt mode with your mesh selected.
Source: Blender.

2. Add your first level of subdivision with the Multiresolution modifier by clicking the Subdivide button.

3. Use the sculpting tools to block in some extra detail.

4. Add another level of subdivision by clicking the Subdivide button, and sculpt more detail.

5. Repeat this process of sculpting, subdividing, and sculpting again until you reach the highest level of subdivision for your model, sculpting in the final polish and details. (See Figure 7.14.)

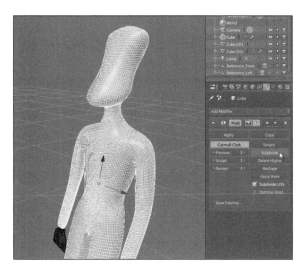

Figure 7.14
Subdivide and sculpt together.
Source: Blender.

When sculpting, keep the following tips in mind:

■ **Use a pen tablet when sculpting (rather than a mouse), if your budget allows.**
A tablet is more responsive to pressure sensitivity, enabling you to incorporate more
nuanced and graduated detail into your sculpting strokes. You can control which
fields and properties of the sculpting brush are affected by pen sensitivity from the
left toolbox, as shown in Figure 7.15. (First, you must select the Enable Tablet option,
located to the right of each field.)

Figure 7.15
Activating pen sensitivity for sculpting.
Source: Blender.

■ **Use mirroring for symmetrical sculpting.** If you need to sculpt the same details across both sides of a model, enable the Mirror Axis options. This bakes all sculpting changes to both sides of the mirror axis. In Figure 7.16, deformations are applied to both of the model's cheeks using mirroring. Using mirroring can save lots of sculpting time, so be sure to enable it for symmetrical models.

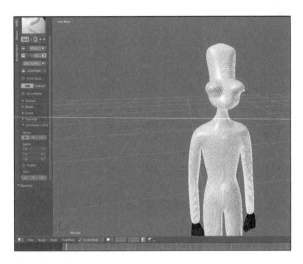

Figure 7.16
Mirrored modeling with sculpting tools.
Source: Blender.

■ **Pick the right brush for the job.** Users often stick with only one brush type, trying to force it to do things it was never designed for. But there are several tools available, each with its own specialty (see Figure 7.17). Make sure you explore them all. The Brush and SculptDraw brushes are especially useful for pulling and pushing soft, rounded sections of the model inward or outward to contribute smooth organic details like lumps, bumps, holes, and crevices. Although it's technically possible to achieve virtually every kind of detail and pose with these brushes, they can sometimes be inconvenient—especially for creating folds, creases, and crevices, such as fabric folds or facial wrinkles. In these cases, it's often more intuitive to use the Crease, Nudge, or Pinch brushes. I used these brushes to create skin folds for my character around the mouth, nose, and nostrils.

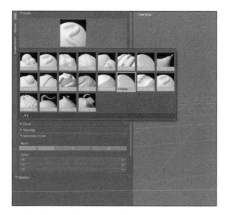

Figure 7.17
Take advantage of all the brushes on offer.
Source: Blender.

■ **Use the Texture brush.** This brush is excellent for creating pores, hairs, fabric roughness, lip and knuckle wrinkles, and more. The Texture brush varies or attenuates the strength of its deformations based on color values in a specified texture image. You simply pick a valid texture, and the Texture brush does the rest. To use this brush, you'll first need to create and configure a new texture—either a procedural texture such as Clouds or a texture from a selected image file. You achieve this by using the standard Texture tab, found in the Blender Properties panel. From here, click the Type drop-down list to select the texture type required for the texture, and then select the generated texture from the Texture picker in the left toolbox for the Texture brush options. See Figure 7.18. There, I've used a cloud-patterned texture to sculpt in the roughness for the character's eyebrows.

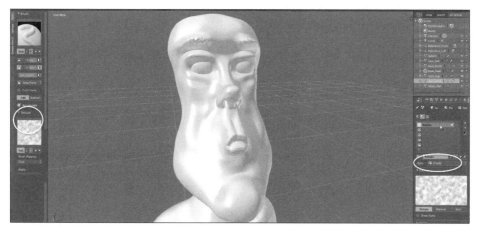

Figure 7.18
Sculpting finer details, like eyebrows, with the Texture brush.
Source: Blender.

Step 4: Retopologize

After you've sculpted your high-poly model, you're ready to begin the process of retopologizing—that is, creating a low-poly version of the high-res original. There are many methods for retopologizing meshes in Blender, some available out of the box with the native tools and some commercial add-ons. Here, I'll detail two manual methods that are part of the main Blender software. These methods are perhaps tedious compared to the more automated and time-saving tools on offer (such as the Contours Retopology tool), but once you've grasped the manual methods, you'll be in a position to retopologize whether you have access to additional third-party tools or not. There's a famous adage, "Give a man a fish and he'll eat for a day. But teach him how to fish and he'll eat for a lifetime." So here, I want to teach you how to fish. To do this, I'll cover surface snapping and the Shrinkwrap modifier, starting with the former.

Retopologizing with Surface Snapping

When you use the surface-snapping technique, you effectively create a low-poly mesh on a face-by-face basis. You start the process by entering Local view on the selected mesh. That means only the selected mesh will be visible in the viewport (as opposed to other mesh pieces), enabling you to work more quickly because Blender has to render fewer faces. To enter Local view, select your mesh and press Shift+I (Maya controls) or choose View > Global/Local (see Figure 7.19).

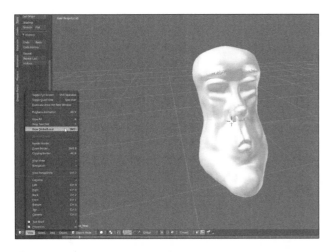

Figure 7.19
Entering Local mode isolates the selected mesh in the viewport.
Source: Blender.

If required, you can control face visibility even further to improve performance even more. Specifically, you can use Edit mode to select specific faces to show and hide temporarily. This can be useful for hiding backfaces and other mesh areas that are not directly relevant at the moment. To hide selected faces, press Ctrl+H or choose Mesh > Show/Hide > Hide Selected. To unhide any hidden faces, press Shift+Ctrl+H or choose Mesh > Show/Hide > Show Hidden (see Figure 7.20). The point here is to view only the area of the mesh you plan to retopologize.

Figure 7.20
Showing and hiding selected faces.
Source: Blender.

Tip

You may, of course, plan to retopologize the whole mesh, but you should do so in stages. That is, retopologize one part, then move onto the next region, and so on, showing and hiding the relevant areas as you progress. Doing this will make your work a lot easier.

Next, you'll create the beginnings of your new low-poly mesh. Follow these steps:

1. Switch to a front view of your mesh.

2. Create a new plane object in the scene. To do so, click the Plane button in the toolbox on the left side of the interface (see Figure 7.21) or choose Add > Mesh > Plane (in Blender versions before 2.7).

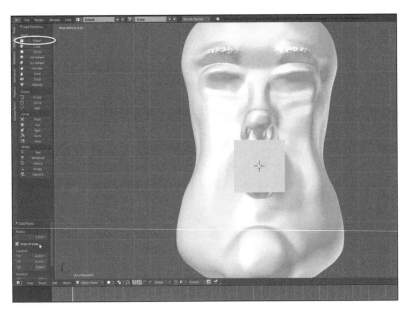

Figure 7.21
Create a plane as the first polygon for a low-poly mesh.
Source: Blender.

3. Enable the Align to View setting in the plane's creation parameters to orient it toward the viewport camera.

4. Scale the plane down or up as required.

5. Position the plane object at a convenient place in the viewport, on top of your underlying high-poly mesh. There's no need to rotate it. The plane represents the first polygon for the low-poly mesh.

6. You'll be working with this plane a lot, so it's important for it to be clearly visible in the viewport in relation to the underlying high-poly mesh. To improve visibility, select the plane object in the viewport, and enable the following settings in the Object Data tab of the Properties panel:

   ■ X-Ray (this causes the plane to always render in front of the high-poly mesh)

   ■ Wire

   ■ Draw All Edges

   In addition, set Maximum Draw Type to Wire to render the mesh in wireframe. This allows the wireframe structure or cage of the low-poly mesh to be drawn around the high-poly version. See Figure 7.22.

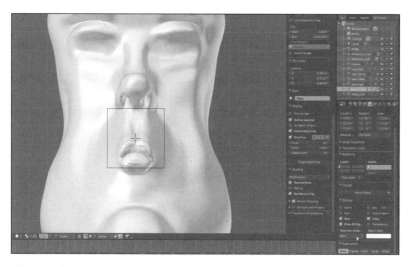

Figure 7.22
Improving visibility of the low-poly mesh.
Source: Blender.

To prepare for the retopologizing process, you'll enable surface snapping. That way, every time you move a vertex in the low-poly mesh, it will *snap*—or automatically move—to the nearest point on the underlying high-poly surface. This enables you to build a low-poly mesh, face by face, that automatically conforms in 3D dimensions, to the high-poly mesh, giving you the best low-poly approximation of the original.

To enable surface snapping, follow these steps:

1. Activate the Snapping option. To do so, click the Magnet icon in the 3D view toolbar.

2. Click the Snapping drop-down list and choose Face as the snapping target, because you want your low-poly mesh to conform to the high-poly mesh faces.

3. To make sure you'll be snapping the active or selected element, choose Active from the Snap Target list.

4. Enable the Project Individual Elements on the Surface of Other Objects option. This allows the snapping process to take effect between multiple and separate meshes, meaning you can snap the vertices of the low-poly mesh to the faces of the high-poly mesh. See Figure 7.23 for the complete snapping configuration.

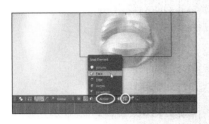

Figure 7.23
Enabling surface snapping involves activating several snapping options.
Source: Blender.

Finally! Everything is in place for retopologizing. Follow these steps:

1. Enter Edit mode for the plane mesh.

2. In the front orthographic view, position the mesh's vertices at critical points over the high-poly mesh. Try to preserve the shape and contours of the original, keeping the edge loops where you'd expect to find them if you had box-modeled the entire mesh from the beginning. As you position and move the vertices, they'll automatically snap to conform to the high-poly version. Continue this process, using the box modeling techniques, such as extrude, to create additional polygons. See Figure 7.24.

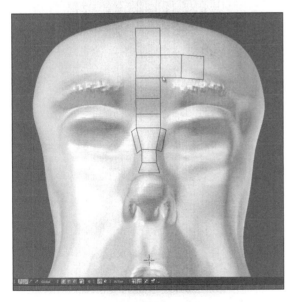

Figure 7.24
Box-model the low-poly mesh.
Source: Blender.

3. After you've positioned the front faces, rotate your view in perspective. You'll see how the faces have conformed to the underlying high-poly mesh, due to surface snapping. (See Figure 7.25.)

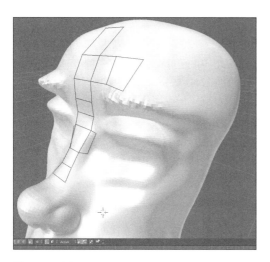

Figure 7.25
Surface snapping helps the low-poly geometry conform to the high-poly mesh with minimal effort.
Source: Blender.

4. Repeat this process until the complete low-poly mesh is generated. (See Figure 7.26.) Be warned: Manual retopology can be time-consuming. Character models can take several hours to retopologize successfully.

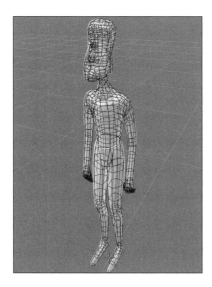

Figure 7.26
Low-poly mesh generated around high-poly original using surface snapping.
Source: Blender.

Note

For more information on mesh snapping, see the Blender online documentation: http://wiki.blender.org/index
.php/Doc:2.6/Manual/3D_interaction/Transform_Control/Snap_to_Mesh.

Retopologizing with Shrinkwrap

There is a second, lesser-used method for retopologizing: using the Shrinkwrap modifier.
This method can be especially effective for quickly retopologizing symmetrical, long, and
cylindrical mesh sections, like legs, arms, and sometimes torsos. It is, however, less effective for asymmetrical and non-linear meshes, such as faces, ears, hands, and hair. It is generally best used in combination with surface snapping. To explore the Shrinkwrap
modifier, let's consider the isolated case of retopologizing high-poly character legs, as
shown in Figure 7.27.

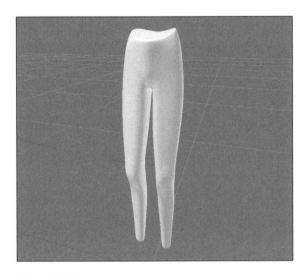

Figure 7.27
The Shrinkwrap modifier is useful for quickly retopologizing long, cylindrical meshes.
Source: Blender.

The character legs could, of course, be retopologized using the surface snapping method
covered in the previous section. But Shrinkwrap can save you time here. To use it, follow
these steps:

1. Approximate a leg using a cylinder mesh. To begin, use the Create panel to
   create a circle. Using both the front and side viewports, position the circle at the
   ankle of the left or right leg of the low-poly mesh. (See Figure 7.28.)

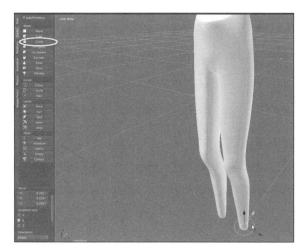

Figure 7.28
Use a circle to approximate the leg volume at the base.
Source: Blender.

2. Enter Edit mode. Then select all edges in the circle and extrude them upward, constraining the extrusion on the Z axis (the up-and-down axis) to create a cylinder that reaches upward to the top of the leg. (See Figure 7.29.)

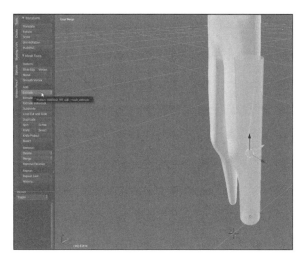

Figure 7.29
Extrude the length of the leg from a circle.
Source: Blender.

3. Insert extra edge loops around the length of the model and position them to approximate the leg shape if required. You don't need to spend a lot of time being overly precise here; as the Shrinkwrap modifier will deform the model. (See Figure 7.30.)

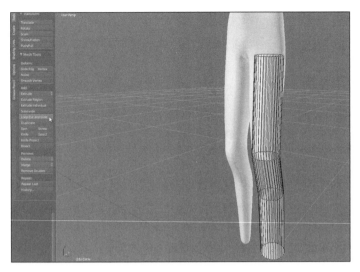

Figure 7.30
Apply some basic shaping to the mesh.
Source: Blender.

4. Insert a final round of edge loops between the main loops you inserted previously to create the tessellation and resolution you need. (See Figure 7.31.)

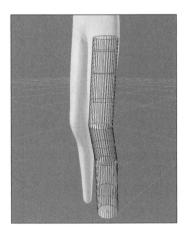

Figure 7.31
Refine the low-poly leg mesh by inserting additional edge loops.
Source: Blender.

5. Now you're ready to apply the Shrinkwrap modifier. Select the low-poly leg and choose the Shrinkwrap modifier from the Modifiers tab in the Properties panel.

6. Specify the high-poly leg mesh in the modifier's Target field. The low-poly leg will automatically conform to the high-poly mesh. Effectively, the Shrinkwrap

modifier surface-snaps all mesh vertices to the nearest surface in the high-poly mesh. (See Figure 7.32.)

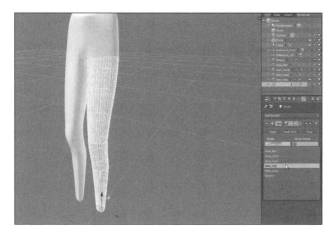

Figure 7.32
Using Shrinkwrap can save lots of time when retopologizing cylindrical meshes.
Source: Blender.

7. When you apply Shrinkwrap, it's likely that some of the vertices will be misaligned or not exactly where you want them to be. Tweak these using the standard surface-snapping technique.

Using Decimate

There's one last quick-and-dirty method for reducing detail in a mesh: the Decimate modifier. Although this modifier is not typically regarded as part of the retopology toolset, it enables artists to achieve the same kind of result, converting a high-poly mesh into a lower-poly version.

The Decimate modifier is procedural and parametric, meaning that it works by you simply typing in numbers. Blender then reduces the mesh detail according to those numbers. I call the Decimate modifier a "quick-and-dirty" method because, while fast, it offers very little control over how the mesh topology is actually reduced. Sometimes it may give you the result you need, and other times not. You simply type in a value and let Blender do its work. Maybe it'll turn out to your liking, and maybe it won't!

To apply Decimate, follow these steps:

1. Select your mesh and apply the Decimate modifier from the Modifiers tab in the Properties panel. (See Figure 7.33.)

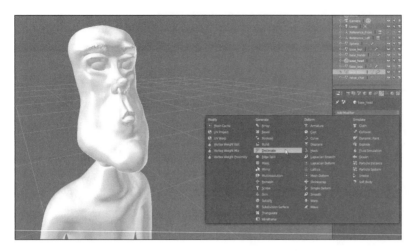

Figure 7.33
Decimate is a fast way to reduce mesh detail. Here, Decimate is applied to the character's head mesh.
Source: Blender.

2. Use the Ratio field to control the degree of decimation for the mesh. A value of 1 leaves the original mesh, with all its resolution, intact and unchanged. A value of 0 decimates the mesh to practically nothing. So typically, the Ratio field will range between 0 and 1, with smaller values resulting in greater detail loss. The idea is to keep the Ratio setting as low as possible while still achieving the look you want. (See Figure 7.34.)

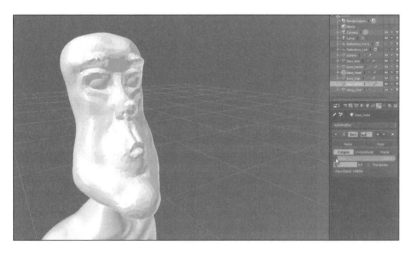

Figure 7.34
Reducing mesh detail with Decimate.
Source: Blender.

Interestingly, Decimate appears to have done a decent job in Figure 7.34, reducing the head polygons from over a million to only several thousand. But if the modifier is applied and the topology examined in Edit mode, a common problem reveals itself. Specifically, Decimate has paid little regard to the mesh topology flow, and has inserted triangles and quads into the mesh in a messy mismatch of geometry. The geometry is so messy that achieving quality animation would be difficult. (See Figure 7.35.)

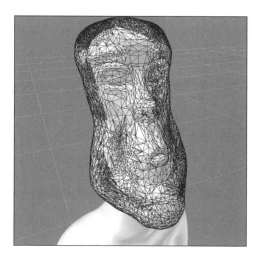

Figure 7.35
Messy geometry typically results from Decimate. Decimate geometry is unlikely to animate with clean deformations.
Source: Blender.

SUMMARY

This chapter focused on retopologizing (sometimes abbreviated as *retopo*). The purpose of this process is simply to translate a high-poly mesh into a lower-poly version—one that will import and perform well in a real-time game engine, like Unity. This is useful because it enables artists to use the high-poly model to bake normal maps, or special textures featuring surface detail. During gameplay, then, the normal maps can be applied to the low-poly mesh to approximate and simulate much of the extra detail found in the high-poly original. Normal maps and baking are discussed in Chapter 9.

In Blender, retopology is achieved through three main methods: surface snapping, the Shrinkwrap modifier, and the Decimate modifier. Typically, the primary and manual method is surface snapping, offering the greatest control and flexibility over the low-poly result. Shrinkwrap can be useful for long, cylindrical objects, like legs. Decimate is generally useful only when retopologizing objects that will never need to animate or deform.

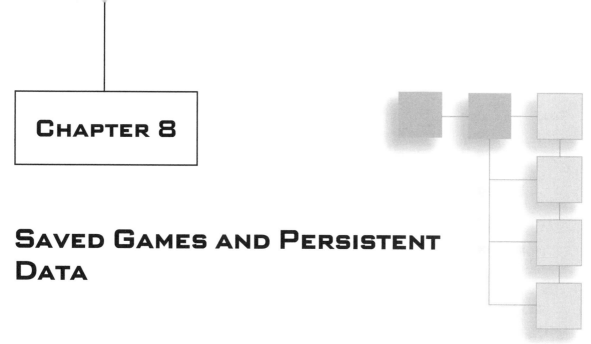

CHAPTER 8

SAVED GAMES AND PERSISTENT DATA

It's difficult to imagine the power that you're going to have when so many different sorts of data are available.

—Tim Berners-Lee

By the end of this chapter, you should:

- Understand what persistent data is
- Understand the PlayerPrefs class
- Appreciate the limitations of PlayerPrefs
- Understand XML and data serialization
- Be able to create load and save game functionality in Unity

One of the most common needs for any game developer is to give the player the ability to save game data to local storage, allowing him or her to resume play at a later time. This kind of data is known as *persistent data* because it persists across time. With persistent data, the user can power off his or her computer and be confident the data will still be there after he or she powers on again. This stands in contrast to volatile kinds of data in RAM, such as the position of the mouse cursor onscreen or the current window being displayed, which is lost at the end of every session. This chapter is concerned with persistent data in Unity—specifically, with how you can create, save, and load game functionality. Unity offers two main methods for this, and both are considered here.

Note

In this chapter, the focus is on Unity, not Blender. It covers the C# scripting workflows for building load and save game functionality.

PERSISTENT DATA

In practically every game, there are two main kinds of persistent data:

■ **Game-specific persistent data.** This is all core asset data that remains unchanged across all play sessions. It includes read-only data such as scenes, audio, movies, animations, meshes, textures, and more. This data is persistent insofar as it remains across play sessions and between power-off and power-on operations, but it's never something the user can change or control. It's just a non-negotiable part of the game.

■ **User-specific persistent data.** This identifies all in-game data that can change throughout a game session and whose state is relevant to gameplay. Notice the two critical ingredients to user-specific data: capacity for change and relevance. User-specific data can change, such as when the player changes his or her world position in the scene, when an enemy character moves from its starting position to search for the player, or when the player opens a door in the environment but never closes it afterward (changing the door from its original closed state to an open state). In all these cases and more, a change occurs: an object is changed from its starting state to a new state. As mentioned, user-specific data also has a degree of relevance. For example, a scene may feature a distant bird object in the sky above, flying along a predetermined path, helping contribute to the game atmosphere of nature and a world in motion. But this object, although it changes, doesn't have a strong enough degree of relevance to in-game events to warrant being considered truly user-specific data. It may be that, when the player saves his or her game, the bird will be in a specific position along its flight path, which will differ from its starting position. But there's no strong reason to record and save the position of the bird because it's not the kind of change that truly matters for gameplay. On restoring a game session, it wouldn't really matter whether the bird resumed flight from a saved position or from its original position.

The only kind of data that needs to be saved for a game is user-specific data. In clarifying this, you can greatly narrow your focus to specific kinds of objects in-game and specific kinds of saving mechanisms. More importantly, keeping this in mind enables you to optimize the design for your games. For this reason, when designing and preparing for game development, always be mindful of the save and load game functionality required further along the line. Take time to identify in advance which objects will need saving and which will not. Don't think of save and load functionality as an afterthought—as something that just comes at the end of development.

Player Preferences

Perhaps the simplest and quickest way to save persistent data in Unity, across all platforms, is to use the `PlayerPrefs` class (short for "player preferences"). As its name implies, the `PlayerPrefs` class is dedicated to saving certain kinds of user-specific data—namely preferences, settings, or option data. Consequently, if you need to save user preferences about game resolution, difficulty, subtitles, brightness, language, control scheme, windowed mode, and more, then `PlayerPrefs` can be your friend.

One of the benefits of working with `PlayerPrefs` is its file system–agnostic nature. `PlayerPrefs` works like a database that you can read from and write to, but it never requires you to specify file names or system paths, enabling you to concentrate only on accessing and writing data. All file handling and interaction is managed internally by Unity.

Let's see this class in action with some code samples. Consider Listing 8.1, for saving the current game resolution to the `PlayerPrefs` database.

Listing 8.1: Saving Game Resolution with `PlayerPrefs`

```
PlayerPrefs.SetInt("ScreenWidth",Screen.width);
PlayerPrefs.SetInt("ScreenHeight",Screen.height);
PlayerPrefs.Save();
```

Note

Unity automatically calls the `Save()` function for `PlayerPrefs` on application exit. However, if your game crashes or exits outside the main game loop, then any unsaved changes will not be committed to disk. For this reason, it's good practice to call the `Save()` method manually whenever you need the data committed to disk immediately.

The `PlayerPrefs` class features a range of methods for saving data, including `SetInt` (for saving integers), `SetFloat` (for saving decimal numbers), and `SetString` (for saving text). In Listing 8.1, `SetInt` is used to save the window dimensions in pixels, both width and height. (Typically, the game window will be full-screen, but not always.)

All the `PlayerPrefs` Set functions take a common form. The first argument specifies a unique name for the value to save. In Listing 8.1, the strings `ScreenWidth` and `ScreenHeight` are used. That means the integer values for screen width and height are saved under the appropriately named entries in the `PlayerPrefs` database. These same values can be retrieved in-game, at any time, using the `PlayerPrefs` class, as shown in Listing 8.2.

Listing 8.2: Loading Game Resolution with `PlayerPrefs`

```
int ScreenWidth = PlayerPrefs.GetInt("ScreenWidth");
int ScreenHeight = PlayerPrefs.GetInt("ScreenHeight");
```

In short, the `PlayerPrefs` class offers a `Get` function for every `Set` function (`GetInt`, `SetInt`, `GetFloat`, `SetFloat`, `GetString`, and `SetString`). Together, these form the basis for retrieving values from and setting values to the database. However, if getting and setting data really is this simple, then some important questions arise:

- ■ Where is this data being stored on the computer?

- ■ What happens if two different Unity games on the same computer both read from and write to keys with the same name? For example, what happens if two games save data to the `ScreenWidth` entry? Will they conflict or overwrite each other?

Let's explore these questions in more depth.

PLAYER PREFERENCES: GOING FURTHER

The `PlayerPrefs` class is intentionally abstract. That is, to be cross-platform and intuitive, it hides much of the lower-lever file-system specifics, which vary from operating system to operating system. This is to offer you (the developer) a single, consistent class and interface for accessing data storage—one that works across all supported platforms using the same code base. The result, however, is that `PlayerPrefs` behaves slightly differently depending on the platform on which you're running your game. That is, it'll store your data in different places and ways, across different operating systems. The details regarding this are explained in the online Unity documentation for `PlayerPrefs`, but let's see what these differences amount to in practice.

Note

More information on the `PlayerPrefs` class can be found in the official Unity documentation: https://docs .unity3d.com/Documentation/ScriptReference/PlayerPrefs.html.

First, before using `PlayerPrefs`, it's good practice to set the company name and product name for your game using the Unity Editor because `PlayerPrefs` uses this data when saving. To set those details, choose Edit > Project Settings > Player (see Figure 8.1) and use the Object Inspector to define a company name and product name for your game. If left at the default values, the company name is "DefaultCompany" and the product name is "source." See Figure 8.1.

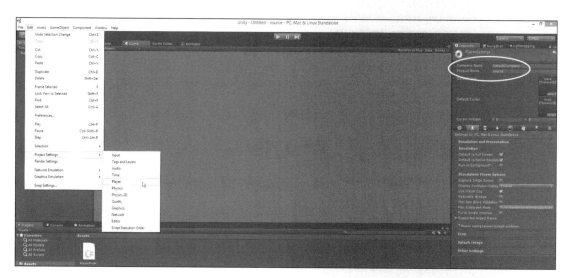

Figure 8.1
Defining your company and product name from the Unity Editor.
Source: Unity Technologies.

The PlayerPrefs database is saved in the following locations, depending on your operating system:

- On Windows platforms, the PlayerPrefs database is stored directly in the Windows Registry, using the key value HKCU\Software\[*companyname*]\[*productname*]. (The values [*companyname*] and [*productname*] will be replaced in the Registry by your company name and product name, as specified in the Unity Editor.) Details on accessing and editing the Registry are beyond the scope of this book. For more information on the Windows Registry, visit http://windows.microsoft.com/en-gb/windows-vista/what-is-the-registry.

- On Mac systems, player preference information can be found in the Library\Preferences folder, in a plist file named unity.[*companyname*].[*productname*].plist. (The values [*companygame*] and [*productname*] will be replaced by your company name and product name.)

- On Linux-based systems, player preferences are stored at /.configunity3d [*companyname*]/[*productname*]. (Again, [*companyname*] and [*productname*] will be replaced by your company name and product name.)

CUSTOMIZING PERSISTENT DATA

PlayerPrefs is a useful and convenient API class for doing exactly what it aims to do: store user preferences. But typically you'll want to save more than user preferences persistently. You'll need to save complete game states: the positions of enemies, the position of the player, player health, enemy health, collected weapons, the open/closed status of doors, drawers, and other props, and more. You could of course adapt your workflow and actually use the PlayerPrefs class to store this data, too, by repeatedly calling the Set and Get methods. But this could result in long and cumbersome configuration files and Registry entries, as well as performance hindrances. In short, the PlayerPrefs solution to storing large quantities of persistent data is not optimal, so an alternative solution is highly recommended. One alternative is to use XML files, and that's the solution detailed throughout subsequent sections.

XML FILES—OR JSON OR BINARY?

C# scripting in Unity relies heavily on the open source Mono framework, which in turn is based on Microsoft's .NET framework. Mono is a free, cross-platform implementation of that framework, offering similarly named classes and functions. This framework offers native support for XML files, which are perhaps the most widely used text-based format for storing persistent user data in video games today. XML files offer a convenient and readable option for saving and reading user data to and from files. There are several classes and methods for working with XML in Mono, but this chapter will focus on a method known as *data serialization*. Listing 8.3 shows a sample save-game XML file.

Listing 8.3: Sample Save Game State in XML File

```
<GameData xmlns:xsi="http://www.w3.org/2001/XMLSchema-instance" xmlns:xsd="http://www
.w3.org/2001/XMLSchema">
  <Enemies>
    <DataEnemy>
      <PosRotScale>
        <X>1.94054472</X>
        <Y>0.019997187</Y>
        <Z>-8.58917</Z>
        <RotX>0</RotX>
        <RotY>129.9697</RotY>
        <RotZ>0</RotZ>
        <ScaleX>1</ScaleX>
        <ScaleY>1</ScaleY>
```

```
            <ScaleZ>1</ScaleZ>
        </PosRotScale>
        <EnemyID>3</EnemyID>
        <Health>100</Health>
      </DataEnemy>
    </Enemies>
    <Player>
      <PosRotScale>
        <X>12.1057281</X>
        <Y>1.05</Y>
        <Z>-17.1096153</Z>
        <RotX>0</RotX>
        <RotY>39.75003</RotY>
        <RotZ>0</RotZ>
        <ScaleX>1</ScaleX>
        <ScaleY>1</ScaleY>
        <ScaleZ>1</ScaleZ>
      </PosRotScale>
      <CollectedCash>200</CollectedCash>
      <CollectedGun>true</CollectedGun>
      <Health>50</Health>
    </Player>
</GameData>
```

Note

You can find more information on the Mono framework at http://www.mono-project.com/Main_Page.

Before you move forward with XML files, however, note that two alternatives to XML could have been used instead here. These are considered next, along with the reasons I've rejected them. These reasons may not apply to your projects, of course. You'll need to decide which format is appropriate for your game.

JSON

Like XML, JavaScript Object Notation (JSON) is text-based. That means anybody who opens a JSON file will be able to read its contents. Unlike XML, however, JSON is a lighter weight and more abbreviated format. In many respects, JSON is an ideal format for producing save-game files for video games. However, Unity does not natively support JSON. In other words, neither the Unity API nor the Mono framework natively support the reading and parsing of JSON files. There are third-party plug-ins and add-ons available that do support the format, but nothing that is an intrinsic part of the Unity main package. For this reason, I've avoided using JSON for creating save-game files in this chapter. The purpose here is to explore save-game support using the native and built-in Unity tools only.

Note

You can find more information on supporting the JSON format in Unity here: http://wiki.unity3d.com/index.php/ SimpleJSON.

Binary

In the context of files, the term *binary* refers generally to any non-text file—the kind of file that looks like nonsense if you open it and read it inside a regular text editor (see Figure 8.2). For video games, binary files are appealing for saving persistent game data. This is because their almost indecipherable appearance makes them difficult for the gamer to edit for the purposes of cheating. The Mono framework offers such a saving mechanism through the `binaryFormatter` class. Here, however, I've stuck with XML because, during development and even beyond, having a text-based save-game file can make debugging and tweaking a lot simpler. Having a human-readable and editable XML file for save-game data enables you to verify the integrity of your save-game data and code, as well as to test out new scenarios, plugging in new values and seeing how they work in-game.

Figure 8.2
A binary file opened for viewing a text editor.

Source: Notepad++.

CLASS SERIALIZATION

The Mono framework offers two main methods for saving persistent data to XML files:

- **Manual.** This method involves node creation and parsing. For the manual method, Mono offers several classes, including `XmlDocument` and `XmlTextReader` (among others). These read from and write to XML files on a node-by-node basis. Using this method for saving data, you would typically create a new node in the XML hierarchy for each value to be saved, just like saving independent nodes using the `PlayerPrefs` class, as shown earlier. This method works, but can be tedious if you're saving lots of data. It can also lead to needlessly lengthy code.

Note

You can find more information on the `XmlDocument` class here: http://msdn.microsoft.com/en-us/library/system.xml.xmldocument%28v=vs.110%29.aspx.

- **Serialization.** Serialization enables you to save or stream a complete object in memory to a file on persistent storage. This file is saved and arranged in such a way that, upon reading it back into memory, you end up rebuilding in memory the class you originally saved. Without serialization, the developer must manually search through classes and objects in the scene, picking out the relevant elements of data to save. In contrast, with serialization, the developer can simply save an entire class to a file. There are limitations to this, however: Only a limited set of data types are natively serializable. Even so, it's possible to save nearly any kind of data you'll need using this method. The next section shows you how.

GETTING STARTED WITH XML SERIALIZATION

To see save-games in practice, let's consider a sample game and data set—specifically, a first-person shooter game, like *Duke Nukem* or *Doom*, that features both a player character and enemies. For this example, let's save the transforms of enemies (position, orientation, and scale) in the scene, as well as some basic player data, including their transform. By recording these values, it's possible to save and restore the positions of all characters in a scene. To achieve this with serialization, the first step is to create some basic classes in C# representing the data you need to save in a non-proprietary way. That is, these classes should use only the most fundamental data types native to C# as a language as opposed to an API or library-specific data type.

For example, in Unity, vectors are expressed as instances of a specific and proprietary `Vector3` class. But more fundamentally, vectors are just three floating-point numbers tied together for X, Y, and Z components. Similarly, object orientation, or rotation, is expressed in Unity as a four-component structure known as a quaternion, but more fundamentally the same data can be expressed using three floating-point numbers representing the amount of rotation to be applied in angles along each of the three 3D axes: X,Y, and Z. In practice, then, a complete object transform could be rewritten in the following class (as shown in Listing 8.4) using only the most fundamental data types.

Listing 8.4: Transform Class Compliant with Serialization

```
public struct DataTransform
{
        public float X;
        public float Y;
        public float Z;
        public float RotX;
        public float RotY;
        public float RotZ;
        public float ScaleX;
        public float ScaleY;
        public float ScaleZ;
}
```

Note

Listing 8.4 uses the `float` data type to serialize the data it needs. You're not restricted to using only this data type, however. Other supported types include `bool`, `int`, `string`, and `list`. You can find more information on data types and classes supporting serialization here: http://msdn.microsoft.com/en-us/library/ms731923%28v=vs.110%29.aspx.

Consider Listing 8.5, which lists a complete C# source file (SaveState.cs) and a set of classes for holding game-related data—specifically, sample player and enemy data. Comments follow.

Listing 8.5: Sample C# Source File for Holding Game-Related Data to Be Saved

```
//Loads and saves game state data to and from XML file
//---------------------------------------------
using UnityEngine;
using System.Collections;
```

```csharp
using System.Collections.Generic;
using System.Xml;
using System.Xml.Serialization;
using System.IO;
//----------------------------------------------
public class SaveState
{
        [XmlRoot("GameData")]
        //----------------------------------------------
        //Transform data for object in scene
        public struct DataTransform
        {
                public float X;
                public float Y;
                public float Z;
                public float RotX;
                public float RotY;
                public float RotZ;
                public float ScaleX;
                public float ScaleY;
                public float ScaleZ;
        }
        //----------------------------------------------
        //Public class for sample enemy character
        public class EnemyData
        {
                //Transform data for enemies
                public DataTransform Transformation;

                //Is enemy armed?
                public bool Armed = false;
        }
        //----------------------------------------------
        //Public class for Player
        public class PlayerData
        {
                //Transform for player
                public DataTransform PlayerTransform;
        }
        //----------------------------------------------
        //Class for holding root data
        public class GameData
```

```
    {
            //Enemy Data
            public List<EnemyData> Enemies = new List<EnemyData>();

            //Main gamer data
            public PlayerData PD = new PlayerData();
    }
    //----------------------------------------------

    //Game data member
    public GameData GD = new GameData();
}
//----------------------------------------------
```

The SaveState class defines a complete collection of classes that hold game-critical data for a save-state session. These classes are brought together into a database in the member GD (an instance of GameData).

The GameData member features one PlayerData member, for holding the player transform, and a list of enemies. The enemies are held in a Mono framework list structure, which can grow and shrink dynamically at run time to accommodate as many elements as you need to store every enemy.

SAVING DATA TO AN XML FILE

The SaveState class coded in the previous section features everything necessary, class-wise, for storing enemy and player positional data in the scene for a save-game session. Specifically, it uses the GameData member to collate all data to be saved. Thus, the GameData member is enough to record and restore the positions of all objects at save and load time. However, the SaveState class so far doesn't actually save the GameData member to a file. It's now time to fix this by adding a Save() function to the SaveState class. This method will accept a complete file path as an argument and serialize the GameData member to an XML file on local storage, storing all game-related data. The implementation details for the Save() function are shown in Listing 8.6.

Listing 8.6: Saving Data to a C# File

```
//Saves game data to XML file
public void Save(string FileName = "GameData.xml")
{
        //Now save game data
        XmlSerializer Serializer = new XmlSerializer(typeof(GameData));
        FileStream Stream = new FileStream(FileName, FileMode.Create);
        Serializer.Serialize(Stream, GD);
        Stream.Close();
}
```

The Save() function accepts a string argument FileName, which expresses a valid and full path on the local file system where an XML file should be saved. The function makes use of the XmlSerializer class to create a FileStream object, where game data can be written. The final two lines complete the operation, converting the GameData class into an XML formatted file. For this function to work successfully, however, it's important to pass it a valid path. A later section demonstrates how you can provide one that works across most platforms.

READ DATA FROM AN XML FILE

Listing 8.6 demonstrates how you can serialize a GameData object to an XML file with the XmlSerializer class. But how do you read the data back into memory after it's been saved? In other words, how do you deserialize the data? To answer this, consider the Load() function in Listing 8.7.

Listing 8.7: Loading Saved Data Back from an XML File

```
//Load game data from XML file
public void Load(string FileName = "GameData.xml")
{
        XmlSerializer Serializer = new XmlSerializer(typeof(GameData));
        FileStream Stream = new FileStream(FileName, FileMode.Open);
        GD = Serializer.Deserialize(Stream) as GameData;
        Stream.Close();
}
```

There's actually very little difference between the Load() and Save() functions given here. The critical difference is in the use of the Serialize() and Deserialize() functions. The Load() function calls on Deserialize() to return a valid instance of GameData, an object initialized on the basis of the XML save data. Listing 8.8 lists the complete SaveState class, with both the Load() and Save() functions added.

Listing 8.8: The Complete SaveState Class

```
//Loads and saves game state data to and from XML file
//-----------------------------------------------
//Be sure to include all relevant mono framework classes for saving games
using UnityEngine;
using System.Collections;
using System.Collections.Generic;
using System.Xml;
```

```
using System.Xml.Serialization;
using System.IO;
//-----------------------------------------------
//SaveState class will handle load and save functionality
public class SaveState
{
        //Save game data
        [XmlRoot("GameData")]
        //-----------------------------------------------
        //Transform data for object in scene
        [System.Serializable]
        public struct DataTransform
        {
                public float X;
                public float Y;
                public float Z;
                public float RotX;
                public float RotY;
                public float RotZ;
                public float ScaleX;
                public float ScaleY;
                public float ScaleZ;
        }
        //-----------------------------------------------
        //Public class for sample enemy character
        //Class to hold all enemy data to be saved to an XML File
        public class EnemyData
        {
                //Transform data for enemies (Position, Rotation and Scale)
                public DataTransform Transformation;

                //Is Enemy armed? (If applicable to your game)
                public bool Armed = false;
        }
        //-----------------------------------------------
        //Public class for player
        public class PlayerData
        {
                //Transform for player
                public DataTransform PlayerTransform;
        }
        //-----------------------------------------------
```

```
        //Class for holding root data
        public class GameData
        {
                //Enemy data
                public List<EnemyData> Enemies = new List<EnemyData>();

                //Main gamer data
                //Instance holding all data related to player (position, rotation,
scale etc.)
                public PlayerData PD = new PlayerData();
        }
        //-------------------------------------------------

        //Game data member
        //Main game data structure holds all data to be saved to an XML file
public GameData GD = new GameData();
        //-------------------------------------------------
        //Saves game data (GameData) to XML file
        public void Save(string FileName = "GameData.xml")
        {
                //Now save game data
                XmlSerializer Serializer = new XmlSerializer(typeof(GameData));
                //Create file on local drive and save GameData to XML File
                FileStream Stream = new FileStream(FileName, FileMode.Create);
                Serializer.Serialize(Stream, GD);
                Stream.Close();
        }
        //-------------------------------------------------
        //Load game data from XML file
        public void Load(string FileName = "GameData.xml")
        {
                XmlSerializer Serializer = new XmlSerializer(typeof(GameData));
                //Open file on local drive and stream to GameData object
                FileStream Stream = new FileStream(FileName, FileMode.Open);
                GD = Serializer.Deserialize(Stream) as GameData;
                Stream.Close();
        }
        //-------------------------------------------------
}
//-------------------------------------------------
```

Note

The complete `SaveState` class is included in the book companion files in the Chapter08 folder.

WORKING WITH THE SaveState CLASS

The `SaveState` class now includes everything needed for saving. When a game creates an instance of this class and populates the `GameData` member with valid game data, the class can be serialized to a file. To save a game, the `Save()` function should be called, and to load a game the `Load()` function should be called. But which path should be used as the save path?

Thankfully, Unity provides an internally constructed string that always points to a valid data location on the local storage. Consider Listing 8.9, which features an `Update()` function. This saves a game state (using the `SaveState` class) whenever the user presses the S key on the keyboard and restores the saved state whenever the L key is pressed. In this sample, the `SaveState` class is represented by the member `SS`.

Listing 8.9: Saving and Loading Game States

```
// Update is called once per frame
void Update()
{
        //If pressing S then save level state
        if(Input.GetKeyDown(KeyCode.S))
        {
                SS.Save(Application.persistentDataPath + "/GameState.xml");
        }
        //If pressing L then load level state
        if(Input.GetKeyDown(KeyCode.L))
        {
                SS.Load(Application.persistentDataPath + "/GameState.xml");
        }
}
}
```

Listing 8.9 uses the `Application.persistentDataPath` member variable to construct a valid save path for game data. This path will vary between computers and operating systems, depending on how the system is configured. But `persistentDataPath` will also reference a location on the local file system where game data can be safely stored.

Congratulations! You've successfully created a load and save system. The Chapter08 folder in the book companion files features a sample project making use of the `SaveState` class to save and load data. I recommend taking a look.

Note

You can find more information on the `persistentDataPath` variable in the online Unity documentation: https://docs.unity3d.com/Documentation/ScriptReference/Application-persistentDataPath.html.

SUMMARY

This chapter detailed how to create load and save game functionality in Unity. It outlined two main methods. First was the `PlayerPrefs` class for saving user preferences and settings, such as game brightness and resolution. Second was serialization using the XML `Serializer` class to translate an object in memory into valid, human-readable XML, and to translate the XML back into the original class. With these two systems, it's possible to save practically any kind of data for your games.

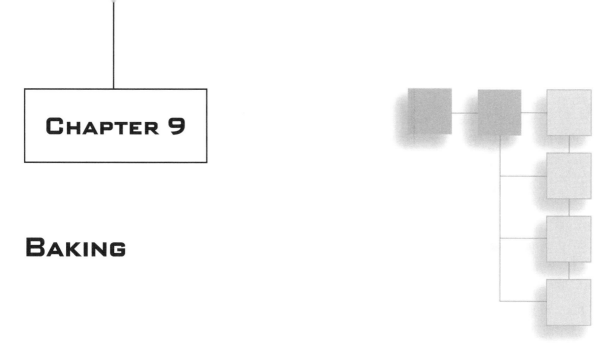

CHAPTER 9

BAKING

Success depends upon previous preparation, and without such preparation there is sure to be failure.

—Confucius

By the end of this chapter, you should:

- Understand what baking is
- Understand texture baking and ambient occlusion in Blender
- Be able to composite baked textures in GIMP
- Understand Unity lightmapping
- Be able to use light probes in Unity

On the one hand, game developers are always striving for new ways to push creative boundaries, add more impressive effects, and make their games more believable and immersive. On the other hand, developers need to be mindful of optimization and performance tweaking. They must be aware of the hardware limitations and the extent to which today's consumer hardware may not be able to match their creative vision. These two antagonistic extremes—pushing boundaries and recognizing limitations—mean that a lot of game development work is about finding the right balance—the point at which you may achieve your vision as far as possible without excluding the majority of users and hardware configurations. One of the ways this balance is achieved is through a common optimization technique known as *baking*. This chapter focuses on many forms of baking, in Blender, Unity, and beyond.

WHAT IS BAKING?

When a game is running, it needs to calculate and process many things on a frame-by-frame basis. These include the positions of enemies and other characters, the effects of lighting, and the volume of sound, depending on where the player is standing. In total, the game must process too many different types of data to list them here comprehensively.

Anytime you can prevent the game from having to do this processing at run time, you improve performance, because it's one less thing the game must worry about. So if you can process data ahead of time and hand it over to the game pre-calculated, then the game won't need to process or calculate it at run time. This kind of pre-calculated data is known as *baked data*; the process of creating baked data is known as *baking*.

This chapter focuses on three main types of baking in Unity and Blender:

- Baked static lighting
- Baked "real-time" lighting
- Baked navigation

Baked Static Lighting

Baked lighting involves pre-calculating lighting effects ahead of time. Baked lighting comes in several forms for video games, and almost all of them make use of textures to encode or store the pre-calculated lighting. The most common light-baking technique is known as *lightmapping*. This method pre-renders all lighting for static (non-moving) objects and saves the result in specialized textures, known as *lightmaps*. These textures usually include both direct and indirect illumination, as well as shadow information. The lightmaps are then used by Unity at run time, where they are blended directly onto static meshes via their UV channel—that is, on top of the mesh's regular textures to make them appear illuminated by scene lights. Figure 9.1 shows a lightmapped scene in Unity.

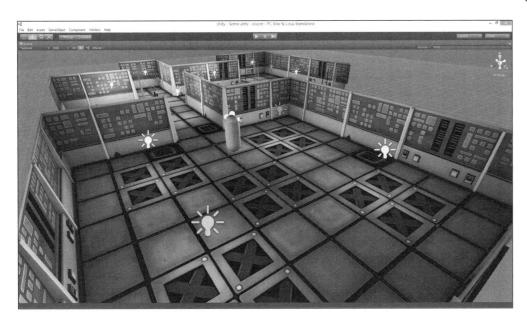

Figure 9.1
A lightmapped scene in Unity. (This scene is included in the book's companion files, in the Chapter09 folder.)
Source: Unity Technologies.

Another technique related to lightmapping is to bake lighting (and ambient occlusion) passes into standard textures using Blender, and to then import the meshes pre-illuminated, bypassing the Unity lightmapping system altogether. You'll learn more about this method later in this chapter.

Baked "Real-Time" Lighting

Lightmapping—and pre-baked, texture-based lighting in general—have an important limitation when it comes to dynamic meshes (that is, meshes that move at run time, such as the player character). The problem is that for changeable and moving meshes, lighting cannot be easily baked or pre-computed because it's not possible to know in advance where a mesh will move and when. The mesh's lighting information will change in a potentially infinite number of ways depending on the orientation of the mesh and the position of the lights. So lightmapping is typically used only for non-moving objects.

To get the most accurate and believable results for dynamic meshes, lighting is often calculated in real time. This completely runs against the purpose of baking, however. So in Unity, there's a more moderate and optimized technique, known as *light probes*. These offer a special kind of semi-baked lighting that works for dynamic meshes. (See Figure 9.2.)

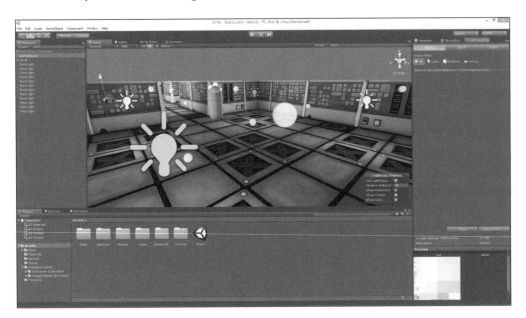

Figure 9.2
Light probes configured to simulate real-time lighting in a scene.
Source: Unity Technologies.

Baked Navigation

Baking is most commonly associated with lighting and textures, but it extends into other areas of game development, too. One area is path-finding and navigation. Characters in a game, such as enemies and other non-player characters (NPCs), need to move around the environment intelligently. They must plan a route from one position to another, and then travel that route to avoid intervening obstacles such as walls, doors, and dangers. Planning and traveling routes can be computationally expensive, however—especially for large and obstacle-ridden environments featuring many characters. One solution for reducing performance overhead is to bake, or pre-generate, an internal mesh that represents the traversable region of the environment. This mesh is commonly known as a *navigation mesh* (or *navmesh*). By using a navmesh (see Figure 9.3), you can greatly optimize navigation calculations so that only the bare minimum must be executed at run time. You'll see navigation meshes in action later in this chapter.

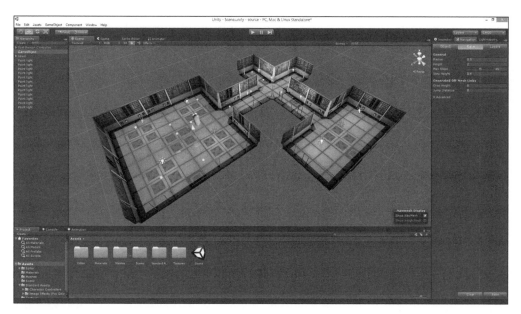

Figure 9.3
Using a navmesh to bake path-finding data for a scene.
Source: Unity Technologies.

PREPARING FOR LIGHTMAPPING IN UNITY

Let's consider the first form of baking in Unity: the lightmapping process, for baking lighting into static environment meshes, making the environment appear illuminated by scene lights in real time. This project assumes you already have an environment assembled and constructed in Unity. If you don't, Chapter 3, "Modular Environments and Static Meshes," details the modular building technique for game environments for making your own. Alternatively, you can open the pre-made environment included in the book's companion files in the Chapter09/LightMapStart folder and use it as a starting point for lightmapping.

Figure 9.4 shows the scene I'm using, from the companion files. The scene begins with lights added but no lightmapping in place. The illumination for the scene is currently calculated in real time by default, which is not optimal—especially because none of the loaded meshes will ever move in-game. Notice also that the scene illumination features no indirect illumination or shadows, and that everything looks slightly darker than you might like. Being darker than needed is generally good practice when starting to lightmap because lightmapping will almost always brighten the scene through indirect illumination.

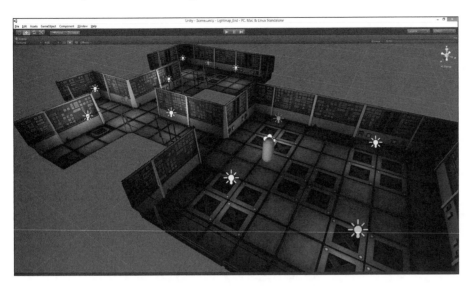

Figure 9.4
Getting ready to lightmap.
Source: Unity Technologies.

Before proceeding, disable ambient light in the scene (if it's not disabled already). By default, every Unity scene features ambient light, which is typically a dull, low-level illumination cast in all directions and with equal intensity throughout the scene. This gives the scene some basic and consistent lighting, allowing objects to be seen even if there are no lights in the scene. Ambient light is useful when you are scene building and before the lighting phase, but once lighting is in place you'll, normally disable ambient light because it results in a general flatness that is undesirable. To disable ambient light, choose Edit > Render Settings and, in the Object Inspector, set the Ambient Light color swatch to black. This disables ambient light because black (darkness) represents an absence of light. See Figure 9.5.

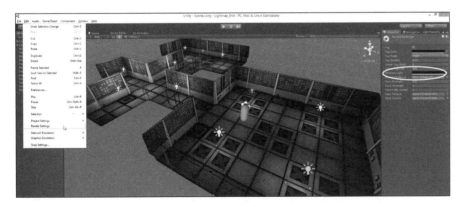

Figure 9.5
Disabling ambient light.
Source: Unity Technologies.

Next, select all static meshes in the scene and mark them as such by selecting the Static checkbox in the Object Inspector (see Figure 9.6). Lightmapping applies only to static (non-moving) meshes, such as walls, doors, floors, and props. Remember, multiple objects can be selected and marked as static in one operation!

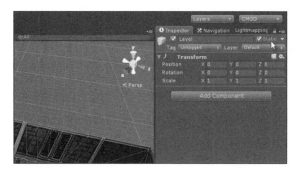

Figure 9.6
Marking objects as static in preparation for lightmapping.
Source: Unity Technologies.

LIGHTMAPPING: LIGHTMAP RESOLUTION

Lightmap resolution controls the detail of the generated lightmap texture. More on this is explained over the following steps. To work with and control lightmap resolution:

1. Choose Window > Lightmapping to open the Lightmapping Editor. The editor typically appears as a free-floating window, but I prefer to dock it in the Object Inspector area, as a separate tab. This enables me to see the lightmap settings and the viewport side by side. (See Figure 9.7.)

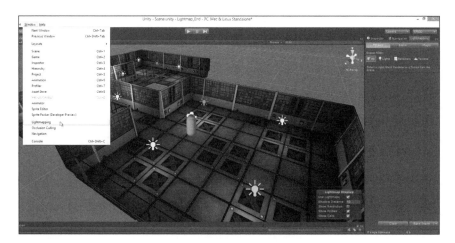

Figure 9.7
Docking the Lightmapping Editor alongside the viewport.
Source: Unity Technologies.

2. Click the Bake tab in the Lightmapping Editor to see the main options for lightmapping the active scene. (See Figure 9.8.) One especially important parameter is the Resolution setting, close to the bottom of the tab. This setting defines how large, in pixels, the generated lightmaps will be.

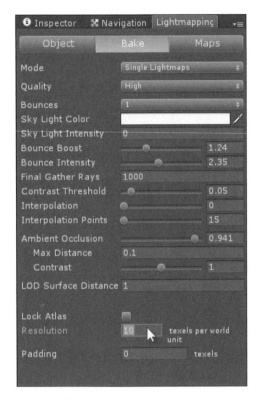

Figure 9.8
Resolution is important for configuring the size of the lightmap texture.
Source: Unity Technologies.

3. The Resolution setting is connected to the Show Resolution checkbox in the Lightmap Display dialog box, shown in the scene viewport whenever the Lightmapping Editor is active. Enable this checkbox, and a checkerboard pattern will be rendered on top of all meshes in the scene (see Figure 9.9). This enables you to preview the pixel density of the lightmap texture that would be generated if you were to bake the lightmap at the current settings. Each square in the pattern represents one pixel in the lightmap texture to be generated. By increasing the Resolution setting in the Lightmapping Editor, you make the checkerboard pattern smaller and denser in the viewport display because you increase the number of pixels

to be allocated across the mesh surfaces. In short, high-resolution values produce larger lightmaps and improved detail, but that comes at a memory and performance expense. Ultimately, the aim is to keep the Resolution setting as low as possible while achieving the best detail and look consistent with your requirements.

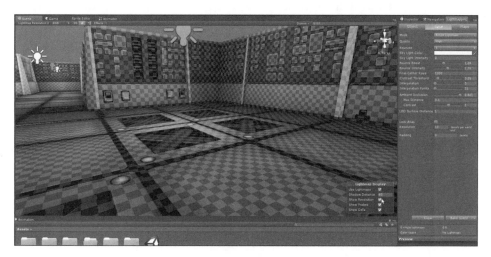

Figure 9.9
Previewing the resolution of lightmaps.
Source: Unity Technologies.

Note

Resolution is not the only factor that determines the size of the generated lightmap. Resolution specifies the ratio between pixels to world units. Thus, the total surface area of all static meshes in the scene, combined with the resolution ratio, will determine the total size of the generated lightmap.

LIGHTMAPPING MODE

Another important lightmapping parameter is the Mode parameter. This parameter controls the balance between real-time and baked lighting for meshes at run time. Specifically, it defines how much lighting will be pre-calculated in texture maps and how much will be left to real-time lighting, creating a blend between the two types.

As shown in Figure 9.10, this parameter can have one of three values:

■ **Single Lightmaps.** In Single Lightmaps mode, all lighting is baked into textures for static meshes, including direct and indirect illumination, ambient occlusion, and shadows. For this example, Single Lightmaps mode will be chosen.

■ **Dual Lightmaps.** In this mode, two variations of the lightmap textures are created. One texture (the far lightmap) contains all lighting information, as with the Single Lightmaps option. This texture is applied to meshes whenever they are seen in the distance at run time. But when the camera moves closer to the meshes, the far lightmap transitions into the near lightmap. The lighting information from the near lightmap replaces the far lightmap. The near lightmap contains all indirect illumination and ambient occlusion data, but not direct illumination, which will be calculated in real time and then blended by Unity with the baked lightmaps to produce a more realistic result. In short, the aim of the Dual Lightmaps option is to produce greater realism, especially for first-person games where the camera distance from meshes varies between near and far.

■ **Directional Lightmaps.** This is an additional specialization of the Dual Lightmaps option, allowing extra information (such as normal mapping) to be baked into lightmaps. The Directional Lightmaps option is beyond the scope of this book.

Figure 9.10
Selecting a lightmapping mode.
Source: Unity Technologies.

Note

For more detailed information on lightmapping, see the online Unity documentation: http://docs.unity3d.com/Documentation/Manual/LightmappingInDepth.html.

Note

Direct illumination refers to lighting created by light rays emitted from a light source, such as a point or directional light, that travel in a straight line, directly hitting a destination, such as a wall, floor, or other mesh. *Indirect illumination* refers to light rays that reach a destination only after previously bouncing from one or more other meshes. Direct illumination generally accounts for the brightest and most prominent light effects, and indirect illumination generally provides secondary or fill lighting.

For this example, we'll set the Mode parameter to Single Lightmaps, which bakes all static lighting into the lightmap textures, as you'll see soon.

INDIRECT ILLUMINATION AND AMBIENT OCCLUSION

If you're using Unity Pro, then you have access to the full range of lightmapping features, including indirect illumination and ambient occlusion baking. If, instead, you're using the free version, then alternatives are available from Blender, considered later in this chapter. Here, I'll assume you have Unity Pro and will consider the built-in baking options available to you for indirect illumination and ambient occlusion.

As shown in Figure 9.11, Unity offers several main settings to control indirect illumination:

- **Bounces.** The Bounces field specifies the maximum number of light ray bounces permitted when generating indirect lighting—that is, the maximum number of times a light ray from a light source may hit another object in the scene and then bounce around to continue illuminating other surfaces. A value of 1 permits one bounce, a value of 2 permits two bounces, etc. A value of 0 disables indirect illumination altogether, prohibiting any bounces. In theory, higher numbers produce more realistic results at the expense of computation time. In practice, a setting of 1 or 2 is usually sufficient.

- **Sky Light Color and Sky Light Intensity.** These fields control the color and strength of an ambient and pervasive lighting created by the sky for outdoor scenes. For indoor scenes, you'll likely want to disable the Sky Light Intensity setting, using a value of 0.

- **Bounce Boost.** This slider enables you to tweak the internal indirect illumination calculations to artificially simulate further light bounces without incurring the same kind of performance cost as increasing the Bounces value. This setting is useful if your scene looks dark and you want to strengthen indirect illumination.

- **Bounce Intensity.** This is a multiplier value, enabling you to uniformly increase or decrease the overall brightness and strength of indirect illumination. A value of 1 leaves indirect illumination at its default brightness. A value of 2 doubles the strength, a value of 0.5 halves the strength, and so on. Like Bounce Boost, this setting is especially useful for moderating or intensifying the contribution of indirect illumination to overall scene lighting.

- **Final Gather Rays.** This setting controls the total number of original light rays cast into the environment to produce scene lighting. The higher this value, the more accurate the lighting. Often, however, this setting can be left at its default.

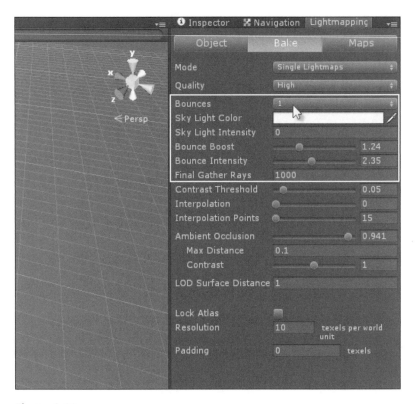

Figure 9.11
Indirect illumination for lightmapping.
Source: Unity Technologies.

Other settings include those for ambient occlusion, a special kind of effect that results from indirect illumination. As light bounces around the environment, it naturally strikes open and more exposed surfaces more than narrow, crevice-like regions such as corners, cracks, perpendiculars, and other meeting points where floors meet walls, etc. In these crevice-like regions, there's a natural darkening, called a contact shadow. *Ambient occlusion* is the process of simulating this effect, as shown in Figure 9.12. The result is a more natural 3D-ness. To achieve this in your lightmaps, you can enable ambient occlusion by moving the Ambient Occlusion slider to any value above 0. The slider is a multiplier, where 1 represents fully on and 0 fully off. See Figure 9.13.

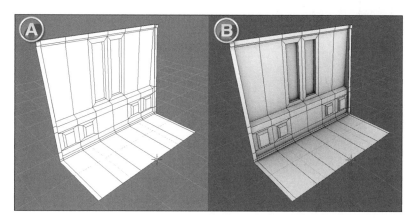

Figure 9.12
Object without ambient occlusion (A), and with ambient occlusion (B). Ambient occlusion adds contact shadows to objects.
Source: Unity Technologies.

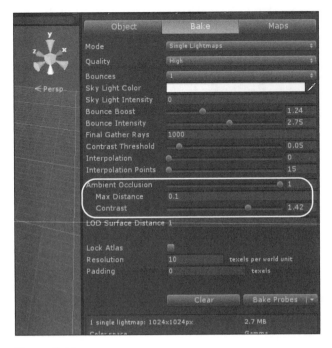

Figure 9.13
Enabling ambient occlusion.
Source: Unity Technologies.

The Ambient Occlusion slider is complemented by a Max Distance slider and a Contrast slider, which enable you to tweak the ambient occlusion effect to your liking. Max Distance influences the total size or spread of the contact shadow produced, and Contrast increases the shadow's intensity, with higher values producing stronger effects.

BAKING LIGHTMAPS

Figure 9.14 shows the settings I've decided on for baking the active scene in Single Lightmaps mode. When you're ready to bake, simply click the Bake Scene button in the Bake tab in the Lightmapping Editor. This initiates the Beast Lightmapper, which calculates direct illumination, indirect illumination, and ambient occlusion, and produces a set of lightmaps. This process can take from minutes to hours, depending on the number of light sources in the scene, the lightmap resolution, the surface area of meshes, the indirect illumination settings, and the power of your hardware, among other variables. When the process is complete, the scene will be lightmapped, as shown in Figure 9.15. To confirm that scene light has been baked into the mesh textures, temporarily disable all scene lights. You shouldn't notice any difference in the scene lighting for static meshes!

Note

"Beast" is the name of the lightmapping engine used internally by Unity to generate lightmap textures for the scene.

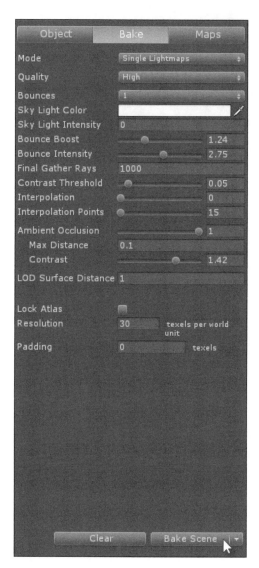

Figure 9.14
Finalizing lightmapping settings.
Source: Unity Technologies.

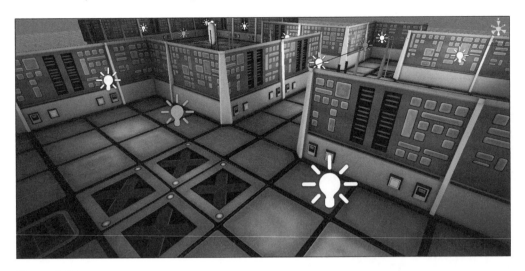

Figure 9.15
The lightmapped scene.
Source: Unity Technologies.

When lightmapping is complete, the baked lightmaps are added as separate texture assets to the project, as shown in Figure 9.16. These maps can be found in an auto-generated folder alongside the saved scene file.

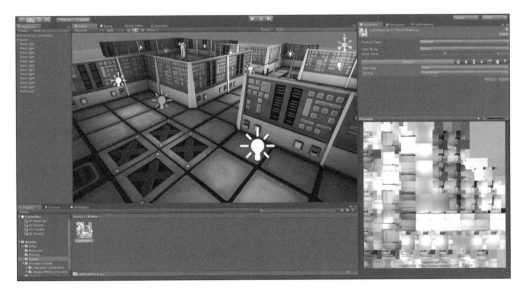

Figure 9.16
Accessing lightmap textures in a project.
Source: Unity Technologies.

Pay close attention to the pixel distribution in your lightmap textures, using the preview panel in the Object Inspector. Make sure they're optimized as far as possible. If your lightmap Resolution setting is too low compared to the mesh surface area in the scene, you'll end up with a lightmap texture filled with many redundant pixels, contributing little to the end result. Lightmap textures will automatically be upsized to the lowest power-2 dimensions needed to accommodate all the pixels required for the lightmap, without scaling or resampling. But sometimes this means the texture will be larger than needed, resulting in wasted space—for example, where a lightmap exceeds a 512×512 map but cannot completely fill a $1{,}024 \times 1{,}024$ map. (See Figure 9.17.) Instead, tweak the lightmap Resolution setting and then rebake to fill as much of the lightmap texture space as possible, getting the most detail from each lightmap.

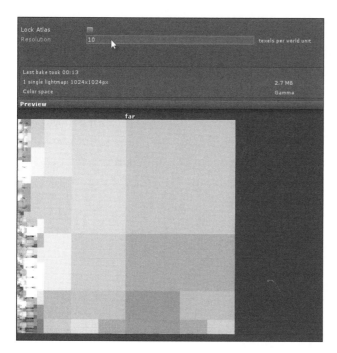

Figure 9.17
A lightmap texture with a Resolution setting of 10. This setting is too low, leading to wasted texture space.
Source: Unity Technologies.

Baking Maps in Blender

Sometimes it's preferable—even essential—to bypass the Unity lightmapping system and textures and generate your own baked textures in Blender. In this case, you'll typically export ambient occlusion maps, base render maps, and other kinds of light passes as separate textures. You'll then composite them into a single diffuse texture using an image editor like GIMP or Photoshop before finally importing them into Unity.

The reason for such an approach is two-fold:

■ Some texture-baking features are simply not present in the Unity free version or are not fully featured there. Specifically, indirect illumination and ambient occlusion baking are not natively supported in the free version. In these cases, the simplest and most obvious method for producing baked lightmaps that include indirect illumination and ambient occlusion—without purchasing the professional version of Unity—is to bake them in Blender to a separate texture, which can be included in the diffuse map.

■ There may be times in Unity Pro when it's preferable to manually bake light textures. This is especially true when using custom shaders and material types or when optimizing run-time performance by reducing the number of separate textures held in memory, cutting out separate lightmaps and using only diffuse textures.

This section considers manual lightmap baking in Blender and GIMP. To follow along, you can open the Blender sci-fi modular environment set, included in the book's companion files in the file Chapter09/ blender_environment/env_final.blend. This set is shown in Figure 9.18. Of course, the baking techniques covered here for this environment set can be used more generally for your own meshes and assets. Here, as elsewhere, be sure to keep in mind how all the tools and practices will work for you.

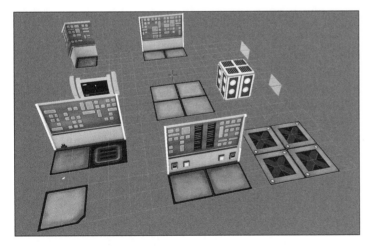

Figure 9.18
Preparing to bake lighting into textures.
Source: Blender.

To bake a texture manually, follow these steps:

1. Ensure that the Blender Internal Renderer is activated as the default render system (as opposed to the Cycles or Freestyle renderer). To do that, open the Render drop-down list on the Info bar and select Blender Render if it's not selected already. See Figure 9.19.

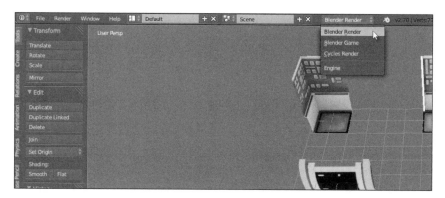

Figure 9.19
Setting the Blender render system.
Source: Blender.

2. Let's bake an ambient occlusion map for the environment set. This will be a separate, grayscale texture representing ambient occlusion data resulting from indirect illumination. To achieve this, create a new and empty texture to receive the ambient occlusion data when rendered. Start by selecting the environment set mesh in the viewport. Then press Ctrl+A to select all faces within the mesh. Next, switch to the UV Editor view and click the Create New Image button in the toolbar (see Figure 9.20).

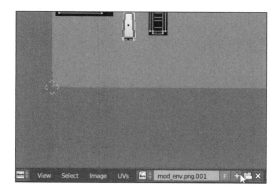

Figure 9.20
Create a new texture to store an ambient occlusion map.
Source: Blender.

3. A settings dialog box opens. Name the image appropriately (I've used the name AO_Map), choose a white background, and deselect the Alpha checkbox. (Alpha transparency will not be required for ambient occlusion textures.) See Figure 9.21. Then click OK. All the mesh faces will turn white to match the newly created texture.

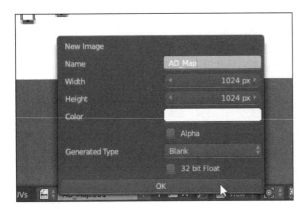

Figure 9.21
Creating an ambient occlusion texture with the UV Editor.
Source: Blender.

4. Click the Render tab in the Properties panel. (Depending on your GUI layout, you'll probably need to switch back to the default GUI view as opposed to the UV Editor view. For more information on configuring the Blender interface, see the section "Configuring the Blender GUI" Chapter 2, "Blender-to-Unity Workflow.") In the Render tab, scroll down to the Bake group, open the Bake Mode drop-down list, and choose Ambient Occlusion (see Figure 9.22). Also select the Normalized checkbox unless you want object materials to affect the rendered result through reflection and refraction. This bakes out the raw texture data for ambient occlusion as opposed to the texture data moderated by the object material.

Figure 9.22
Specifying bake settings from the Render tab on the Properties panel.
Source: Blender.

5. Click the World tab in the Properties panel. From there, enable the Ambient Occlusion, Environment Lighting, and Indirect Lighting groups. This ensures that the full range of indirect illumination effects will factor into the ambient occlusion map. Finally, in the Gather group, enable the Approximate option. (See Figure 9.23.)

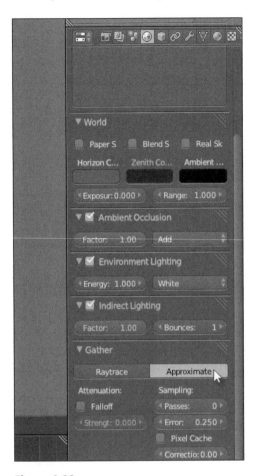

Figure 9.23
Tweaking the World settings for ambient occlusion.
Source: Blender.

6. To initiate the bake process, switch back to the Render tab in the Properties panel and select your mesh in the viewport. Then click the Bake button. Be sure to select your mesh before clicking Bake, as Bake applies to selected objects. Blender will bake an ambient occlusion map for the selected mesh. This can be seen in the UV Editor if you have it open in the GUI. From here, you can save the map to a regular texture file using the Save As Image command from the UV Editor menu (see Figure 9.24).

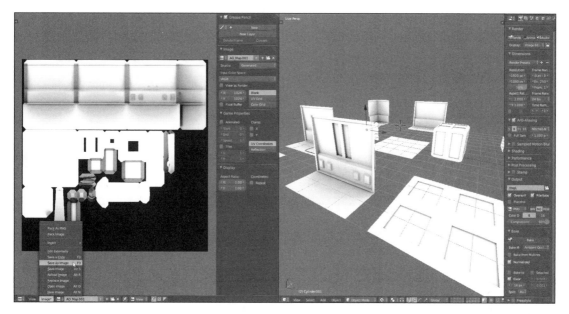

Figure 9.24
Saving the ambient occlusion map to an image file.
Source: Blender.

Of course, you're not restricted to simply baking ambient occlusion maps. You can bake other map types, including specular, normal, shadows, and even a full render, which is a complete consolidation of all other separate render passes into one image. There are, however, significant advantages to be gained by avoiding full render, and by baking out the render passes into separate image files—one file for ambient occlusion, one for specular, one for shadows, and so on. The reason: By baking each pass to a separate file, you can later use image-editing software to composite the files into a single image, giving you complete and independent control over the compositing process. See the next section for more information.

Compositing Render Passes in GIMP

Using Blender's Bake feature, you can save separate render passes into different texture files—passes such as ambient occlusion, specular, shadows, diffuse, and more. Typically, while baking normal or full renders, Blender internally composites the separate passes together, outputting them all to one consolidated image. This makes baking simpler for the artist, as there are fewer images to contend with. But by baking out the separate passes into different files, the artist gains a level of extra control when creating textures. Specifically, all or some of the unique passes can be loaded onto separate layers in an image editor, like GIMP or Photoshop, and composited with blend modes for extra control and fine-tuning. This process is considered in brief for compositing an ambient occlusion map on top of a standard diffuse texture to add lighting effects that would otherwise come from lightmapping in Unity. A Blender-to-Gimp workflow is explored further in the next chapter.

Note

The GIMP software can be downloaded for free, for Windows, Mac and Linux, at the following URL: http://www.gimp.org/. This chapter assumes a basic working knowledge of GIMP. For more information on GIMP, see Chapter 10, "Unity, Blender, and Other Software," and Appendix A, "Game Development Resources."

In Figure 9.25, a diffuse texture created for the environment set has been loaded into GIMP. This file (sized at $1,024 \times 1,024$ pixels) can be found in the book's companion files at Chapter09/GIMP/env_diffuse.png. It represents the default, diffuse texture to be applied to the environment assets, minus indirect illumination and ambient occlusion. In essence, it represents the texture that would be applied to the meshes in Unity, prior to the lightmapping process. This texture has been opened in GIMP as a base background layer.

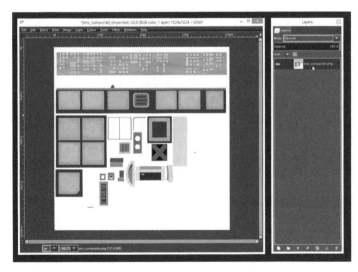

Figure 9.25
Loading a diffuse texture into GIMP, in preparation for compositing.
Source: GNU Project.

The ambient occlusion map (also sized at $1,024 \times 1,024$), created in the previous section, makes use of the environment mesh's UVs when being rendered. That means the ambient occlusion texture can be overlaid as a separate layer on top of the diffuse layer because both textures share the same UVs. You can add the ambient occlusion map to the open diffuse file in GIMP by dragging and dropping from Windows Explorer or Finder into the GIMP software. GIMP will automatically add the dropped image as a new layer in the file. If the ambient occlusion layer is not at the top of layer stack, move it there using the layer-direction arrows. See Figure 9.26.

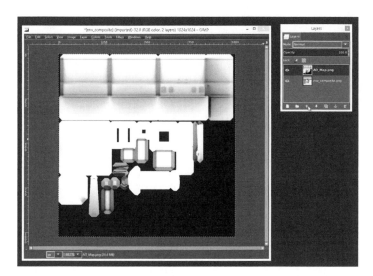

Figure 9.26
Move the ambient occlusion layer to the top of the GIMP stack, ready for blending.
Source: GNU Project.

Because it is at the top of the layer stack, the ambient occlusion layer conceals the diffuse layer below. Rather than being simply stacked, it should be *blended* with the diffuse layer. The ambient occlusion map is rendered in grayscale, which is significant for compositing. Specifically, you can use the Multiply blend mode to blend the ambient occlusion layer with the diffuse layer. (See Figure 9.27.) As a result, the diffuse layer now includes all ambient occlusion detail built-in—data that might otherwise have come through separate lightmaps in Unity. Thus, by compositing in this way, you can save on memory and texture requirements.

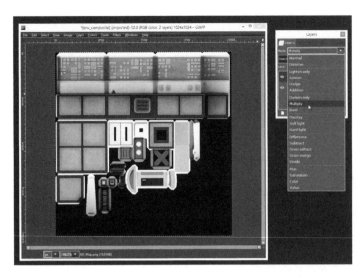

Figure 9.27
Compositing the ambient occlusion map with the diffuse texture.
Source: GNU Project.

BAKING REAL-TIME LIGHTING WITH UNITY LIGHT PROBES

Lightmapping and texture baking usually work best in Unity when applied to static (non-moving) meshes, like scenery and props. Dynamic (moving) meshes present a different kind of problem, however. Because they move around the level during gameplay, their exposure to the surrounding light sources changes over time. That means light should affect them differently depending on where they're positioned.

Unity offers two main, out-of-the-box solutions for working with dynamic meshes in terms of lighting. The first is simply to avoid baking entirely, resorting to full real-time lighting, typically with directional, spot, or point lights. The other solution is to use a network of light probes, which are generated (baked) before gameplay to approximate scene lighting but which work on the mesh, through interpolation, to simulate the appearance of dynamic lighting at run time.

Before you start working with light probes, note that it's assumed you already have a finished scene or level in place, complete with scene lights. For this example, we'll begin from the book's companion Unity project, found at Chapter09/Light_Probes_Start. This scene features an environment set with lightmapping already baked for all static objects, as well as a dynamic character mesh illuminated in real time. This mesh can be moved around the level using standard third-person controls, as shown in Figure 9.28. For this reason, the character lighting will need to use light probes for improved performance.

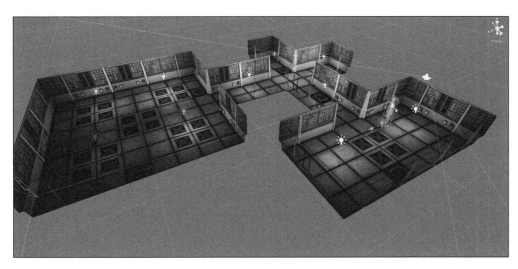

Figure 9.28
Preparing to use light probes.
Source: Unity Technologies.

Note

Light probes are available only in Unity Pro. You can, however, create similar behavior in the free version for illuminating your meshes, either through custom shaders or by creating a class that manually averages light values in the scene and adjusts the mesh's material color to match whatever light the mesh is standing near to.

Developers use light probes to create the appearance of real-time illumination on dynamic meshes by carefully and strategically positioning a set of interconnected nodes (probes) throughout the scene. At design time, through baking, each probe in the network takes a measured light reading from its current position, recording the average direction, intensity, and color from all the surrounding lights. Light probes then work at run time by automatically shading and coloring any dynamic meshes within their range in the scene based on the pre-recorded light-readings, using interpolation to moderate and blend their effect along with the other light probes nearby.

The first step in using light probes involves building the network of probes. Follow these steps:

1. Create a new and empty game object in the scene, positioned at the origin.

2. Add a Light Probe Group component. To do so, choose Component > Rendering > Light Probe Group (see Figure 9.29).

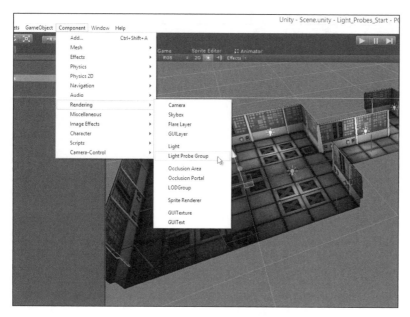

Figure 9.29
Adding a Light Probe Group component to an empty game object to store all probes in the light probe network.
Source: Unity Technologies.

3. Add the first probe in the network. To do so, click the Add Probe button in the Light Probe Group area in the Object Inspector.

4. Select, position, and adjust the probe like you would any regular game object in the scene viewport, using the transformation tools.

5. Repeat steps 3 and 4, adding more probes and positioning them around the level. The probes will automatically connect to each other to accommodate the scene. The idea is to use as few probes as possible, positioning them strategically in areas of light change or transition or wherever a significant light effect is occurring. That means more probes should be used in areas with greater lighting diversity, and less should be used in areas of greater lighting uniformity. Figure 9.30 shows the arrangement I've chosen for the level.

Figure 9.30
Positioning light probes around the level to record the most accurate approximation of scene lighting.
Source: Unity Technologies.

Note

Don't simply position all probes at the same vertical (Y) level. Adjust their vertical position, too, to capture the way light pervades the scene in all three dimensions.

6. Adding light probes to the scene in a connected network isn't enough for light baking to occur. After you create the light probe network, you need to switch to the Lightmapping Editor, click the Bake tab, open the Bake Probes drop-down list, and choose Bake Probes. (See Figure 9.31.) The baking process is often quick—much quicker than lightmapping—but can still take several minutes for larger levels with many probes.

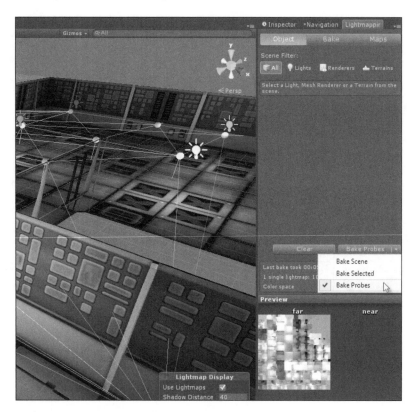

Figure 9.31
Select Bake Probes in the Lightmapping Editor to bake scene lighting.
Source: Unity Technologies.

7. The bake process embeds critical light information into the probes, which is interpolated onto meshes at run time to simulate real-time lighting. However, by default, no meshes in the scene are affected by light probes. For a mesh to interact with light probes, it must be explicitly marked. To do this, select all dynamic meshes to be affected, accessing their Mesh Renderer or Skinned Mesh Renderer component. Then select the Use Light Probes checkbox. (For the character rig in this example, select the character mesh (retop_char) object (see Figure 9.32), which features a Skinned Mesh Renderer component.) Now the character will receive illumination from semi-baked lighting with light probes. Excellent! You can now illuminate dynamic meshes optimally.

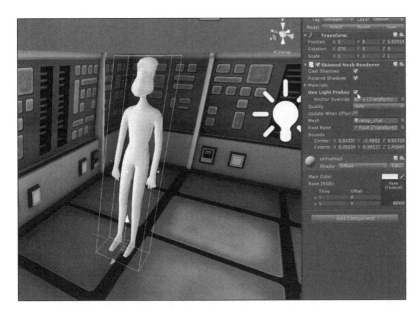

Figure 9.32
Illuminating dynamic meshes with light probes.
Source: Unity Technologies.

BAKING NAVIGATION

The final baking technique considered in this chapter relates to path-finding and navigation. Specifically, enemies and other NPCs must appear smart. They'll need to maneuver about intelligently, avoiding obstacles such as walls, chairs, and doors, and moving as directly as possible to wherever they need to go, taking the shortest and most sensible route. There are many ways to achieve this behavior in Unity. One popular technique, especially in Unity versions prior to 3.5, was to use node-based navigation alongside a custom path-finding algorithm like A* or Dijkstra's algorithm. But since version 3.5, the most common method has been to use Unity's built-in path-finding tools—namely navigation meshes, or navmeshes. Like light probes, navmeshes are semi-baked, because they must naturally work with dynamic meshes. That is, navigation meshes allow the baking of much navigation and path-related data in the scene, but Unity must still use that data to generate paths and routes in real time.

To demonstrate path-finding, let's start with a companion file, Chapter09/Navigation_Start. This scene features a static environment with a character mesh and some box objects. The boxes will act as enemies. They will follow the player around the level, continually tracking their position and avoiding obstacles. To achieve this functionality, navmeshes will be used. See Figure 9.33 for the starting project.

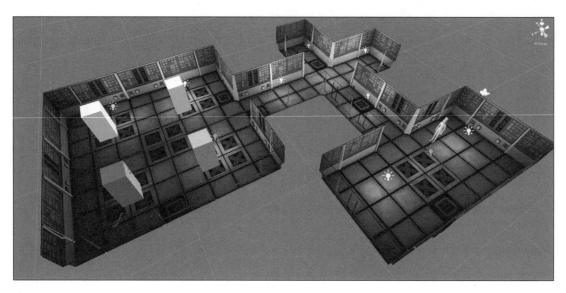

Figure 9.33
Preparing to use navigation meshes. The boxes will need to find and travel to the player, even if the player moves.
Source: Unity Technologies.

To start baking navigation for the level, you must generate a navmesh asset. The navmesh is an internal, low-poly mesh that Unity generates to approximate the walkable region in the scene. This mesh is then used by enemies and other agents at run time to calculate path-finding and navigation operations.

To generate a navigation mesh, follow these steps:

1. Choose Window > Navigation to open the Navigation Editor. Like the Lightmapping Editor, the Navigation Editor can be docked as a tab in the Object Inspector for viewing alongside the scene viewport. See Figure 9.34.

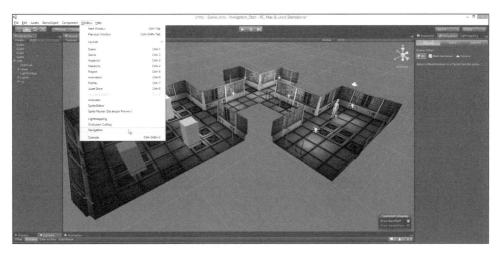

Figure 9.34
Docking the Navigation Editor on the Object Inspector.
Source: Unity Technologies.

2. Click the Bake tab in the Navigation Editor.

3. Make sure the Show NavMesh option is selected in the NavMesh Display window in the bottom-right corner of the viewport.

4. Click the Bake button to generate a navmesh for the scene. The navmesh will appear in the scene, close to floor level, highlighted in blue. This mesh will not be visible at run time; it's for diagnostic viewing only. See Figure 9.35.

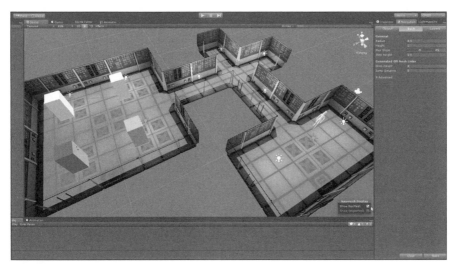

Figure 9.35
Generating an initial navmesh for the scene.
Source: Unity Technologies.

After you generate a navmesh with the default settings, examine the mesh closely. Two main problems may present themselves:

■ The navmesh may appear vertically offset above the true mesh floor, hovering in the air. (See Figure 9.36.)

Figure 9.36
The navmesh appears to be hovering in the air.
Source: Unity Technologies.

■ The navmesh may appear offset away from the walls and, in some thin corridor sections, may even appear broken or disconnected. (See Figure 9.37.)

Figure 9.37
The navmesh appears offset from the wall.
Source: Unity Technologies.

To address the vertical offset problem, lowering the navmesh further to the floor, open the Advanced group in the Navigation Editor and lower the Height Inaccuracy setting. Here, I've changed Height Inaccuracy from 8 to 1. This works well for the current scene. (See Figure 9.38.)

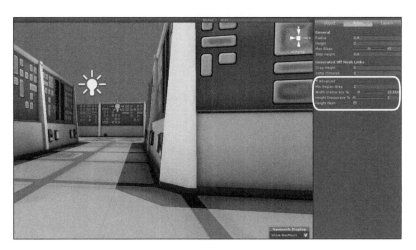

Figure 9.38
Lowering the navmesh closer to the true mesh floor.
Source: Unity Technologies.

Note

After you change settings in the Navigation Editor's Bake tab, you'll need to re-bake the navmesh by clicking the Bake button.

To address the second problem—the space between the navmesh floor and walls—you can use the Radius setting in the Navigation Editor's Bake tab. However, it is important to understand the reason for the gap. By default, space is automatically inserted between the navmesh and walls because the edges of the navmesh represent the furthest position that the center (or pivot) of an NPC may walk when using navigation. The spacing therefore adds a degree of protection, preventing an NPC from partially penetrating walls as it walks. For this reason, it's unlikely that you'll ever want a navmesh to fit tightly and exactly against the walls of the level. You'll almost always want some spacing. The question, then, is simply how much do you need? The answer varies depending on the size of your NPCs, the structure of your walls and environments, and on how you expect everything to behave in-game. In short, you'll need to tweak the Radius setting by trial and error until you arrive at a setting that works best for you. Here, I've changed the Radius setting from 0.5 to 0.4. (See Figure 9.39.)

Figure 9.39
The Radius setting controls navmesh spacing from the wall.
Source: Unity Technologies.

Generating a navmesh is only the first step toward achieving path-finding. The next step involves configuring all NPCs in the scene to integrate and work with the navmesh. Specifically, each NPC that you want to exhibit path-finding and navigation behavior must feature a Nav Mesh Agent Component. In path-finding terms, an *agent* is any entity that can intelligently move from one position to another, avoiding obstacles. To make the four boxes in our scene intelligent, path-finding agents, add a Nav Mesh Agent component to each by choosing Component > Navigation > Nav Mesh Agent. (See Figure 9.40.)

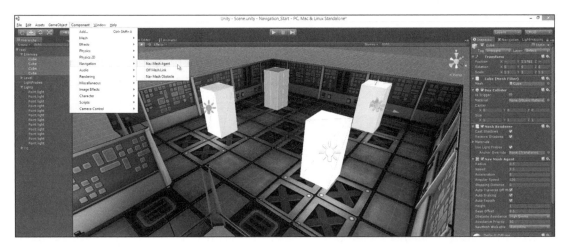

Figure 9.40
Adding a Nav Mesh Agent component to potential enemies.
Source: Unity Technologies.

Next, configure all four box NPCs through their respective Nav Mesh Agent components. For this example, I'll set the agent's Speed setting to 2 (world units per second), and I'll set the Stopping Distance setting to 3. This represents the total distance (in world units) the agent is allowed to come toward its destination before stopping. In short, setting Stopping Distance to 3 will prevent the box enemies from walking through the player if they manage to catch him. Instead, the enemies will reach within 3 units and stop, unless the player moves beyond the distance. (See Figure 9.41.)

Figure 9.41
Tweaking the Nav Mesh Agent component.
Source: Unity Technologies.

If you run the sample project now, you'll see that, although the agent components are configured, nothing prods them into motion to chase or reach the player. Nothing makes them travel a path. To achieve this, you must use a script file and assign it to all NPCs. Consider the code in Listing 9.1, representing the complete file EnemyAI.cs.

Listing 9.1: EnemyAI.cs—AI Follow Functionality

```
using UnityEngine;
using System.Collections;

public class EnemyAI : MonoBehaviour
{
        //Nav Mesh Agent component
        private NavMeshAgent NMAgent = null;
```

```
//Reference to player
private Transform PlayerTransform = null;

// Use this for initialization
 void Start ()
{
        //Get Nav Mesh Agent Component
        NMAgent = GetComponent<NavMeshAgent>();

        //Get player transform
        PlayerTransform = GameObject.FindGameObjectWithTag("Player").transform;
}

// Update is called once per frame
void Update ()
{
        //Set enemy to player
        NMAgent.SetDestination(PlayerTransform.position);
}
}
```

In the Update() function, the code calls on the NMAgent.SetDestination() method to continually update the NPC path destination, specifying the player position as the destination. This code, when assigned to all NPCs, will cause them to always be in motion,
following and chasing the player wherever they move in the level. See Figure 9.42 to see
navigation in action!

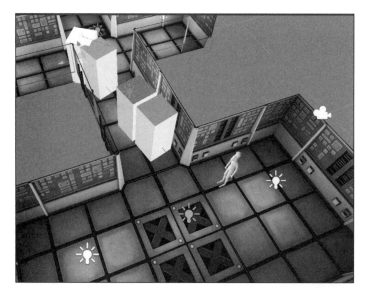

Figure 9.42
Run! NPC agents chase a player.
Source: Unity Technologies.

Note

You can find more information on the Nav Mesh Agent component in the Unity documentation: http://docs .unity3d.com/Documentation/ScriptReference/NavMeshAgent.SetDestination.html.

SUMMARY

This chapter considered the issue of baking in games, using Unity, Blender, and GIMP collaboratively. Baking is about pre-calculating assets, such as lighting and path-finding, for the purpose of improving performance at run time, saving the CPU and GPU from calculating the data manually. Baking is most commonly associated with lightmapping and texture baking, but it doesn't end there. All kinds of other assets can be baked, too, including real-time lighting and path-finding.

Unity offers additional baking tools in the form of occlusion culling, which is beyond the scope of this book. Nevertheless, a range of major baking methods have been included here, and the ways in which you can use Blender and GIMP to help are also significant. Some critical advice that emerges is, when making games, look first to baking as a solution. If data can be baked, then an important performance saving will typically result.

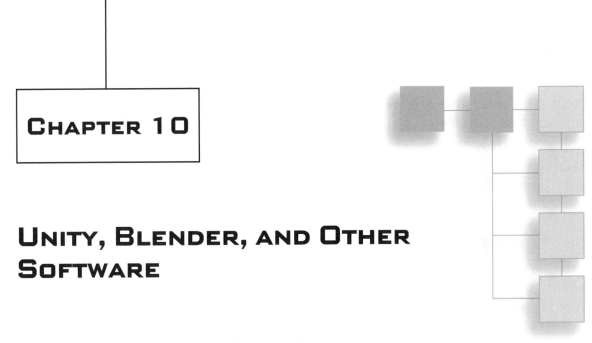

CHAPTER 10

UNITY, BLENDER, AND OTHER SOFTWARE

If you gaze for long into an abyss, the abyss gazes also into you.

—Friedrich Nietzsche

By the end of this chapter, you should:

- Be familiar with additional software available for working with Unity and Blender
- Appreciate the importance other software can have in a Blender-to-Unity workflow
- Be familiar with additional Blender-to-Unity considerations
- Be confident about where to go from here

This chapter brings closure to the book by wrapping things up generally. It considers additional software available that's either free or affordable even to most small developers, and that complements a Blender-to-Unity workflow in a significant way. So let's go!

OTHER SOFTWARE

One of the central aims of this book is to demonstrate just how powerful a combination Unity and Blender can be for game development. Blender offers many professional-grade modeling, rendering, and animation tools for producing game assets that integrate well into Unity. Using either the FBX or DAE format, a lot of data (such as meshes, UV mapping, and rigging and animation data) can be exchanged easily and reliably between the two applications. In addition, Unity supports the native Blender file format (.blend) for those who really want to go that route instead (even though I outline compelling reasons to avoid it in Chapter 2, "Blender-to-Unity Workflow"). But despite the power to be had from these applications working together, there's additional software out there that can further improve the workflow. Subsequent sections consider some of these applications in brief as well as how they can be useful.

It should be noted that, in listing the following applications, I've tried wherever possible to stick with free open source software that works on nearly every desktop platform in use for development today, including Windows, Mac, and Linux. In doing this, my aim is not to promote a political agenda or bias in favor of free software specifically, but to keep with the general indie spirit running through this book. That spirit encourages a deep look at professional-level tools that are accessible to developers everywhere, on almost any budget, on almost any operating system, and for almost any use, both commercial and non-commercial.

MakeHuman

MakeHuman (www.makehuman.org) is free software for procedurally generating character meshes, including low-poly meshes. It's for use primarily in Blender, from which these meshes can be optimized, rigged, mapped, animated, and exported to Unity. In short, MakeHuman offers a quick and simple means for 3D creating template-based characters for games.

There are times when specific looks, character forms, and very custom and unusual types (like three-headed monsters) are not supported natively by MakeHuman. Even in those cases, MakeHuman can be helpful in generating at least a base or starting mesh from which customizations could be made.

With MakeHuman (see Figure 10.1), you can tweak sliders and parameters to refine the features of a character model, controlling head size, facial feature placement, age, gender, weight, height, and more. In addition, MakeHuman exports to a range of industry-supported mesh formats, including DAE and FBX, complete with mapping and even rigging data if required.

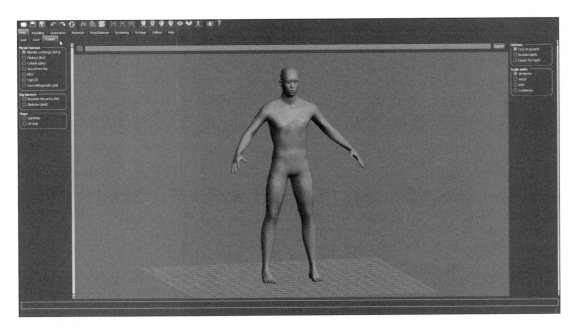

Figure 10.1
Preparing a 3D character model for export.
Source: MakeHuman.

GIMP

GIMP (www.gimp.org) is a powerful, free image-editing application that works in many respects like Adobe Photoshop. It does, of course, have many differences in terms of workflow and style, but its ultimate aim is largely the same. It's especially useful for creating textures, GUI graphics, and marketing materials for games, as well as for other purposes.

The software has some notable and important limitations in its current release—namely, a lack of support for 16-bit depth and CYMK color mode. However, many of these limitations are slated to be addressed in subsequent releases. Besides, for game design, these limitations need not stop you from using GIMP profitably and successfully. For example, most games work with RGB images as opposed to CMYK.

GIMP (see Figure 10.2) supports an impressive and versatile toolset overall, including selection tools, layers, masking, a healing brush, color adjustments, levels and curves, image filters, and lots more.

Figure 10.2
Image editing in GIMP for the video game *Mega Bad Code,* by Wax Lyrical Games.
Source: GNU Project.

Note

I used GIMP as the primary image-editing tool for my own games, *Bounders and Cads* and *Mega Bad Code.*

GIMP works well with both Blender and Unity. Plus, it exports to a wide range of industry-standard formats, including PNG, JPG, BMP, TIFF, TGA, and more. In addition, the Unity Editor can be configured to open all image files automatically with GIMP when they're opened (double-clicked) from the Project panel. To do this from Unity, choose File > Preferences to display the Preferences dialog box. Then, in the External Tools tab, select the GIMP application in the Image Application drop-down list, as shown in Figure 10.3.

Figure 10.3
Setting GIMP as the default image-editing application in Unity.

Source: Unity Technologies.

Note

GIMP also supports a range of third-party add-ons that are especially useful for games, such as the Normal Map plug-in (http://code.google.com/p/gimp-normalmap/). Using this, developers can generate normal maps from grayscale images.

Note

An alternative and popular free image-editing program is Paint.Net. For more information, see www.getpaint .net/.

INKSCAPE

Inkscape (www.inkscape.org) seeks, in many ways, to be a free and open-source alternative to Adobe Illustrator. Its aim is to create vector art, as opposed to raster or pixel-based art, as found in GIMP and Photoshop. Vector art is composed not of pixels, but of mathematically generated shapes and splines with assigned fills and colors. As such, vector art can be upscaled or downscaled to any size without any quality loss. This is because upscaling and downscaling with vector art involves multiplying the underlying numbers that form the shapes rather than image resampling, which works directly on pixel data.

Inkscape (see Figure 10.4) offers a powerful arsenal of vector-drawing features for producing vector graphics in the widely support Scalable Vector Graphic (SVG) format. At first sight, Inkscape may seem a curious choice for a game development tool, as neither Blender nor

Unity support vector graphics directly. But Inkscape can convert vector graphics into standard pixel-based images that are supported, such as PNG and BMP images. This makes Inkscape especially valuable for creating graphics that you may need to resize at a later time.

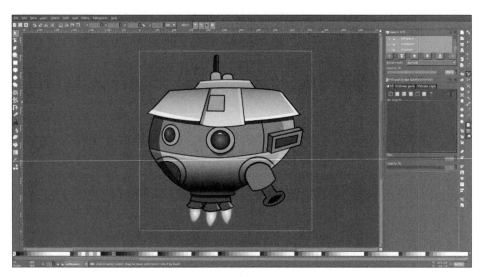

Figure 10.4
Using Inkscape to create a space-station enemy character.
Source: Inkscape.

Note

GIMP supports the import of SVG files from Inkscape. Simply drag and drop your SVG file into GIMP, and GIMP will automatically convert the vector graphic to a pixel-based graphic. See Figure 10.5.

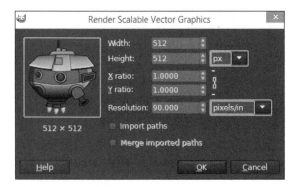

Figure 10.5
Importing an Inkscape SVG file into GIMP.
Source: GNU Project.

MyPaint and Krita

Although many people use GIMP for creating illustrations on the computer, others prefer to use a dedicated painting program, with pre-defined brush tools and other features. Among the free and open source applications for digital painting today, at least two are well known: MyPaint (http://mypaint.intilinux.com; see Figure 10.6) and Krita (http://krita.org; see Figure 10.7). Both these applications offer a wide range of digital painting tools, designed to work well with pen tablets and to simulate the responses of "real-world" media, such as brushes, canvases, sketch pads, and more.

Figure 10.6
Painting a marketing shot using MyPaint.
Source: MyPaint.

Figure 10.7
Painting a marketing shot using Krita.
Source: Krita.

SYNFIG STUDIO

Synfig Studio (www.synfig.org; see Figure 10.8) is a comparatively new entry among the free and open source software for game development. Synfig is a vector graphics solution for creating 2D animation, such as cartoons, presentations, and other animated movies. Synfig uses keyframe animation and interpolation, allowing for 2D animation tweens. Animations can be output to the AVI and Theora movie formats, and also to image sequences such as PNG.

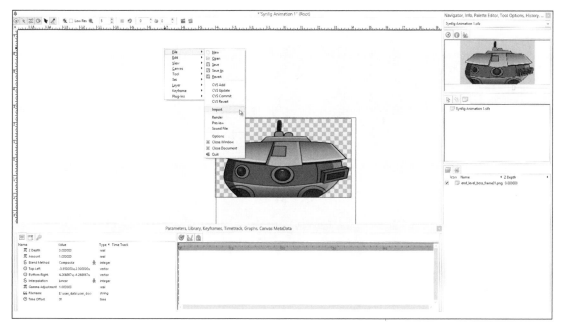

Figure 10.8
Synfig Studio animating an enemy spaceship character.
Source: Synfig Studio.

TILED

The Tiled map editor (www.mapeditor.org) is a free and open source graphical editor for creating engine-independent tile-based levels and maps for your games. Tiled supports various tile arrangements, from top-down (orthographic) maps to isometric maps. Tiled allows you to import custom tile sets in many image formats, such as PNG and JPG, and to arrange them into a map grid to form a complete tile-based level.

Tiled, shown in Figure 10.9, is engine independent in that it's an editor dedicated to producing maps only, which can be saved in an open XML format. These could then be opened and parsed in script by most engines to reconstruct the defined level using their own internal tools and functions. Many engines, such as Unity, already feature scripts and classes available to parse and load Tiled maps.

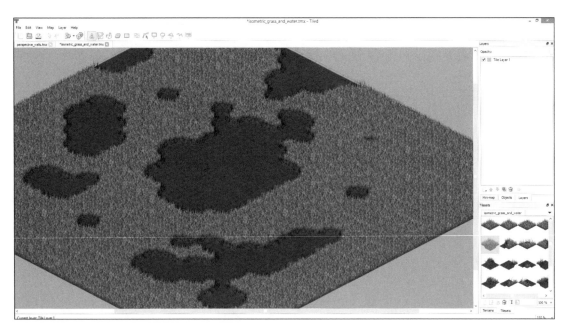

Figure 10.9
Editing a map using Tiled.
Source: Tiled.

Note

There are several third-party libraries and classes available for integrating Tiled maps into Unity. These can be found at the following URLs:

■ http://karnakgames.com/wp/unity-tiled-tilemaps/

■ https://bitbucket.org/PolCPP/unitmx/overview

■ www.wyrmtale.com/products/unity3d-components/orthello-pro

MonoDevelop

Unity ships with MonoDevelop, a third-party IDE that works across most desktop platforms. However, MonoDevelop is useful for more than simply editing script files. It can act as a regular text editor as well as an XML editor. Text editors are especially important in game development and for programming more generally. Many games, as well as other software, make extensive use of configuration and settings files, like XML and JSON data, and text editors are indispensable for viewing and editing such data.

To improve your MonoDevelop workflow for editing XML and other hierarchically struc-tured data, be sure the code folding feature is enabled. This enables the expanding and contracting of nodes to improve the readability of data. To enable code folding in Mono-Develop, choose Tools > Options. Then choose the Text Editor group, choose the General tab, and select the Enable Code Folding checkbox, as shown in Figure 10.10.

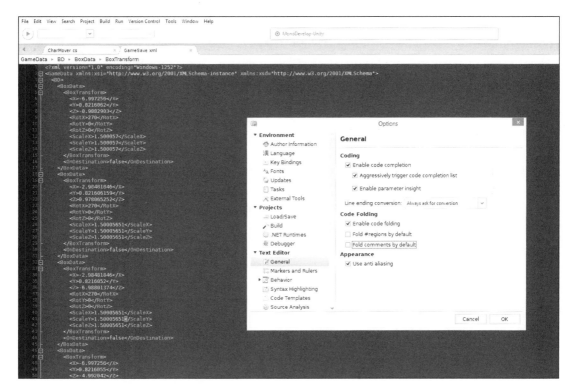

Figure 10.10
Enabling code folding in MonoDevelop.
Source: MonoDevelop.

Note

You can also download MonoDevelop as a separate, standalone application from this URL: http://monodevelop .com/.

Note

An alternative, free text editor with C# syntax highlighting is Notepad++. This software is available only for the Windows platform. You can download it here: http://notepad-plus-plus.org/.

BMFONT

In game development—particularly GUI game development—you need to be able to display text and fonts. Often, the player needs to type his or her name, or to assign a name to save a game. You may also need to display subtitles to make your game more accessible. In these cases, editable and dynamic text needs to be shown at run time.

The primary method for doing this is to render a character set, all alphanumeric characters, onto a pixel based image (like a PNG file), with each character aligned neatly in a fixed sized grid. This allows the engine to convert a string message in memory into a set of UV offsets in the image grid, thereby displaying the correct characters in the correct sequence and at the correct position onscreen.

BMFONT (www.angelcode.com/products/bmfont) is one solution for rendering a complete font set into a single image (see Figure 10.11). However, though free, BMFONT is available only for the Windows platform.

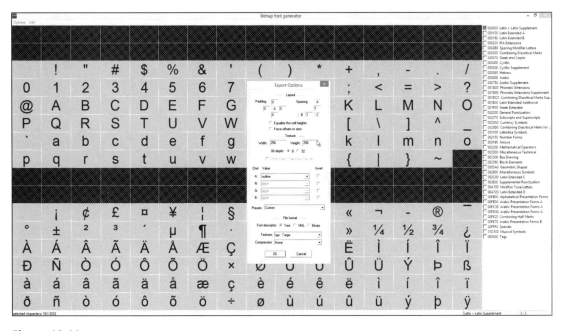

Figure 10.11
Rendering a font set to an image file.
Source: BMFont.

TexturePacker

One of the most common and most effective ways to optimize textures and texture space in Unity is to use atlas textures—that is, textures that consolidate multiple smaller images into one larger image. By referencing specific rectangular regions of space within one texture as opposed to using multiple and independent textures, Unity can optimize scene rendering by reducing draw calls.

You can, of course, create atlas textures manually using GIMP, by copying and pasting specific images into place on a larger canvas. But there are automated utilities available to make the atlas process simpler. One of these tools is TexturePacker (www.codeandweb .com/texturepacker; see Figure 10.12), which is available for most desktop platforms, including Windows, Mac, and Linux.

Figure 10.12
Creating a sprite atlas using TexturePacker.
Source: TexturePacker.

LibreOffice

Design is an important stage of game development. The result of game design is ultimately the game design document. During the design phase, plans must be made, ideas tested, ideas written down, diagrams drawn, scripts formed, and textual localizations considered. To achieve this, some form of office software is usually required, especially a word processor and a spreadsheet application, as well as software for creating diagrams. There are many office applications available, but one free, cross-platform solution is LibreOffice (www.libreoffice.org; see Figure 10.13).

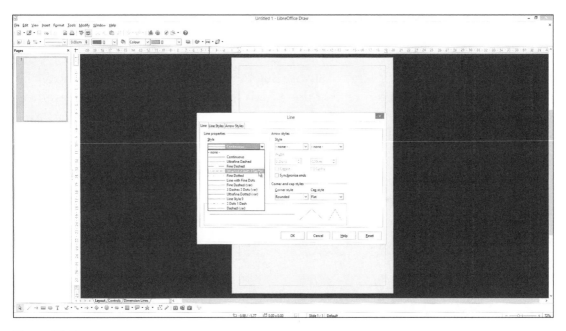

Figure 10.13
Creating a diagram using LibreOffice Draw.
Source: LibreOffice.

LibreOffice offers a range of benefits to game developers, apart from being cross-platform and free. It can open and save to many existing Microsoft Office formats (such as .docx and .xlsx) and can export to read-only formats such as Adobe PDF. Further, it contains diagram drawing software, which is useful for creating UML diagrams and other software development charts.

Anime Studio Pro

One popular commercial solution for creating 2D animation that's affordable to most indie developer budgets is Anime Studio Pro (http://anime.smithmicro.com; see Figure 10.14). This software works similarly to Synfig Studio, mentioned earlier. It offers features such as bones and rigging, as well as inverse kinematics for animating 2D characters and other 2D artwork. It can be used to create cartoons and animated sprites for games, such as player characters and enemies for 2D side-scrolling platform games. In addition, Anime Studio imports from SVG files made in Inkscape and outputs to most accepted video and image formats, including AVI and PNG.

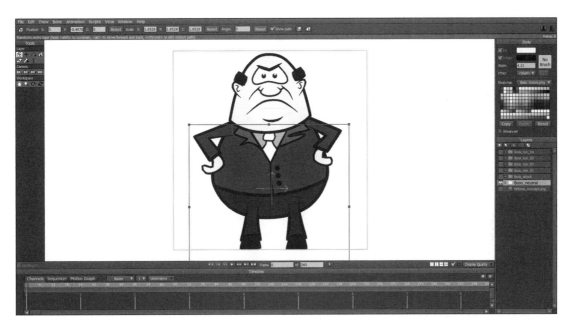

Figure 10.14
Rigging a character in Anime Studio Pro.
Source: Anime Studio Pro.

AUDACITY

Audacity (http://audacity.sourceforge.net; see Figure 10.15) is a famous, well-established, free audio editor that works across a wide range of platforms and has been used on countless game projects. It's often labeled as an "audio editor," but that label is misleading. Audacity can indeed open and edit single audio files, such as WAV files, for tweaking volume, splicing, clipping, and more. But it can also act as a complete multi-track sequencer for composing more intricate music tracks as well as for forming other audio compositions.

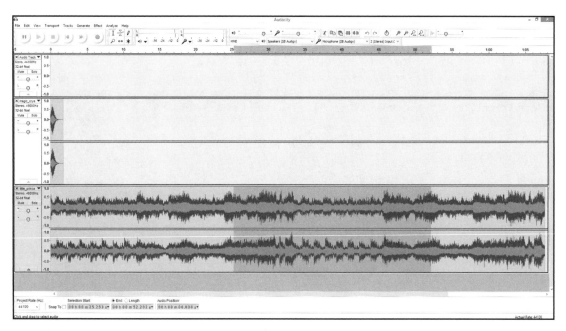

Figure 10.15
Creating a multi-track composition with Audacity.
Source: Audacity.

SFXR

If you develop on the Windows platform and need to quickly generate retro-sounding audio effects for your games—such as for old-school platformers—then SFXR (www .drpetter.se/project_sfxr.html; see Figure 10.16) may come in very useful. SFXR is a procedural sound-effect generator available for free. By tweaking a few sliders and settings, you can quickly preview sound effects for game-critical events such as attack sounds, damage and healing effects, jump sounds, and more. In addition, all sound effects can be exported to the WAV format, allowing them to be imported directly into Unity.

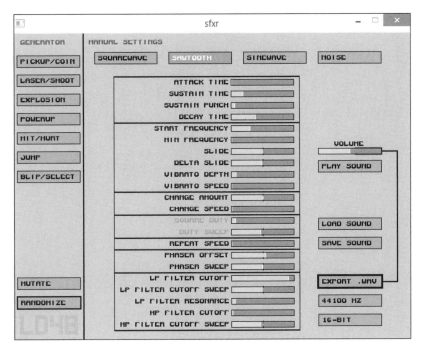

Figure 10.16
Creating game sound effects using SFXR.
Source: SFXR.

SUMMARY

This chapter wrapped up our journey toward practical game development in Unity and Blender. It did so by exploring a range of additional software available for game development—software that integrates seamlessly and easily into a Unity and Blender workflow for developers of almost all budgets working on almost all desktop platforms. By using these tools in combination with Blender and Unity, a developer can apply skill and creativity to produce amazing, professional-grade results that lead to marketable games. Sometimes the tools may take some getting used to; almost all tools do. But with patience, practice, and a willingness to learn, every tool listed here can be applied to create high-quality games. But don't take my word for it. Put them into practice and start making games!

APPENDIX A

GAME DEVELOPMENT RESOURCES

The game development industry is open in many respects, compared to many other industries. To be a doctor or a lawyer or an airline pilot, for example, you need to complete formal institutional training with recognized accreditation to even start working professionally. In many other areas, there are all kinds of formal hoops that must be traversed before you can even pass the starting line. But to be a game developer, you just need a computer, and maybe an Internet connection. *Maybe*. You can make games from an office, a studio, an airport lounge, a café, your garage, and even your bedroom.

Moreover, the current climate of game development puts more software, tools, and power into the hands of more people than ever before. So much so that nearly anybody of any age or background can sit at a computer right now and make games. However, your ability to do that successfully and enjoyably depends very much on know-how—the kind of know-how that you can get from reading books like this, as well as other sources, such as game development courses and the Internet.

However you learn, it's clear that it's not enough just to have the software and tools. It's important also to know how to use them effectively to do what you need to do. You could have the best medicine in the world, but if there's no way to administer it to patients, then it's as good as useless. So in this appendix, I'll list a wide range of resources that can help you learn specific applications and tools, as covered in this book.

Recommended Websites

- **Unity documentation:** http://unity3d.com/learn/documentation
- **Blender documentation:** http://wiki.blender.org/index.php/Doc:2.6/Manual
- **GIMP documentation:** www.gimp.org/docs/
- **Unity articles and tutorials:** http://unitygems.com/
- **Blender tutorials:** www.blender.org/support/tutorials/
- **GIMP tutorials:** www.gimp.org/tutorials/

Recommended Books

- *Unity 4 Fundamentals* by Alan Thorn (ISBN: 978-0415823838)
- *Learn Unity for 2D Game Development* by Alan Thorn (ISBN: 978-1430262299)
- *Pro Unity Game Development with C#* by Alan Thorn (ISBN: 978-1-4302-6746-1)
- *Blender Foundations* by Roland Hess (ISBN: 978-0240814308)
- *Blender Master Class* by Ben Simonds (ISBN: 978-1593274771)
- *The Complete Guide to Blender Graphics: Computer Modeling and Animation* by John M. Blain (ISBN: 978-1466517035)
- *The Book of GIMP* by Olivier Lecarme and Karine Delvare (ISBN: 978-1593273835)
- *GIMP for Absolute Beginners* by Jan Smith and Roman Joost (ISBN: 978-1430231684)

Recommended Videos

- *Complete Beginners Guide to Unity* by Alan Thorn. Available at 3DMotive.com.
- *Materials and Lighting in Unity* by Adam Crespi. Available at Lynda.com.
- *Modular Building in Unity and Blender* by Alan Thorn. Available at 3DMotive.com.
- *Introduction to C# in Unity* by Alan Thorn. Available at 3DMotive.com.
- *Blender Inside Out* by Jonathan Williamson. Available at Blender 3D Shop.

INDEX